Reports and Working Papers 19 1
of the Law Reform Commission of Canada

Reports to Parliament

1. *Evidence** (December 19, 1975)
2. *Guidelines Dispositions and Sentences in the Criminal Process** (February 6, 1976)
3. *Our Criminal Law* (March 25, 1976)
4. *Expropriation** (April 8, 1976)
5. *Mental Disorder in the Criminal Process** (April 13, 1976)
6. *Family Law** (May 4, 1976)
7. *Sunday Observance** (May 19, 1976)
8. *The Exigibility to Attachment of Remuneration Payable by the Crown in Right of Canada** (December 19, 1977)
9. *Criminal Procedure Part I: Miscellaneous Amendments** (February 23, 1978)
10. *Sexual Offences** (November 29, 1978)
11. *The Cheque: Some Modernization** (March 8, 1979)
12. *Theft and Fraud** (March 16, 1979)
13. *Advisory and Investigatory Commissions** (April 18, 1980)
14. *Judicial Review and the Federal Court** (April 25, 1980)
15. *Criteria for the Determination of Death** (April 8, 1981)
16. *The Jury** (July 28, 1982)
17. *Contempt of Court** (August 18, 1982)
18. *Obtaining Reasons before Applying for Judicial Scrutiny — Immigration Appeal Board** (December 16, 1982)
19. *Writs of Assistance and Telewarrants** (July 22, 1983)
20. *Euthanasia, Aiding Suicide and Cessation of Treatment* (October 11, 1983)
21. *Investigative Tests: Alcohol, Drugs and Driving Offences** (November 10, 1983)
22. *Disclosure by the Prosecution** (June 15, 1984)
23. *Questioning Suspects* (November 19, 1984)
24. *Search and Seizure* (March 22, 1985)
25. *Obtaining Forensic Evidence* (June 12, 1985)
26. *Independent Administrative Agencies** (October 23, 1985)
27. *Disposition of Seized Property* (April 24, 1986)
28. *Some Aspects of Medical Treatment and Criminal Law** (June 12, 1986)
29. *Arrest* (November 6, 1986)
30. *Recodifying Criminal Law, Vol. I* (December 3, 1986)
31. *Recodifying Criminal Law — A Revised and Enlarged Edition of Report 30* (May 19, 1988)
32. *Our Criminal Procedure* (June 21, 1988)
33. *Recodifying Criminal Procedure, Volume One, Title I* (February 27, 1991)

Working Papers

1. *The Family Court** (1974)
2. *The Meaning of Guilt: Strict Liability** (1974)

3. *The Principles of Sentencing and Dispositions** (1974)
4. *Discovery** (1974)
5. *Restitution and Compensation** (1974)
6. *Fines** (1974)
7. *Diversion** (1975)
8. *Family Property** (1975)
9. *Expropriation** (1975)
10. *Limits of Criminal Law: Obscenity: A Test Case** (1975)
11. *Imprisonment and Release** (1975)
12. *Maintenance on Divorce** (1975)
13. *Divorce** (1975)
14. *The Criminal Process and Mental Disorder** (1975)
15. *Criminal Procedure: Control of the Process** (1975)
16. *Criminal Responsibility for Group Action** (1976)
17. *Commissions of Inquiry: A New Act** (1977)
18. *Federal Court: Judicial Review** (1977)
19. *Theft and Fraud: Offences** (1977)
20. *Contempt of Court: Offences against the Administration of Justice** (1977)
21. *Payment by Credit Transfer** (1978)
22. *Sexual Offences** (1978)
23. *Criteria for the Determination of Death** (1979)
24. *Sterilization: Implications for Mentally Retarded and Mentally Ill Persons** (1979)
25. *Independent Administrative Agencies** (1980)
26. *Medical Treatment and Criminal Law** (1980)
27. *The Jury in Criminal Trials** (1980)
28. *Euthanasia, Aiding Suicide and Cessation of Treatment* (1982)
29. *The General Part: Liability and Defences* (1982)
30. *Police Powers: Search and Seizure in Criminal Law Enforcement** (1983)
31. *Damage to Property: Vandalism* (1984)
32. *Questioning Suspects** (1984)
33. *Homicide** (1984)
34. *Investigative Tests** (1984)
35. *Defamatory Libel* (1984)
36. *Damage to Property: Arson* (1984)
37. *Extraterritorial Jurisdiction* (1984)
38. *Assault** (1984)
39. *Post-seizure Procedures* (1985)
40. *The Legal Status of the Federal Administration** (1985)
41. *Arrest** (1985)
42. *Bigamy* (1985)
43. *Behaviour Alteration and the Criminal Law* (1985)
44. *Crimes against the Environment* (1985)
45. *Secondary Liability — Participation in Crime and Inchoate Offences* (1985)
46. *Omissions, Negligence and Endangering* (1985)
47. *Electronic Surveillance* (1986)
48. *Criminal Intrusion* (1986)
49. *Crimes against the State* (1986)

---

* Out of print. Available in many libraries.

The Commission has also published over seventy Study Papers on various aspects of law. If you wish a copy of our catalogue of publications, please write to: Law Reform Commission of Canada, 130 Albert Street, Ottawa, Ontario, K1A 0L6, or Suite 310, Place du Canada, Montreal, Quebec, H3B 2N2.

---

*Out of print. Available in many libraries.

REPORT 34

ABORIGINAL PEOPLES

AND CRIMINAL JUSTICE

REPORT

ON

ABORIGINAL PEOPLES

AND CRIMINAL JUSTICE

Equality, Respect and the Search for Justice

As Requested by the Minister of Justice
under Subsection 12(2) of the
Law Reform Commission Act

Canadian Cataloguing in Publication Data

Law Reform Commission of Canada

Aboriginal peoples and criminal justice : equality, respect and the search for justice

(Report ; 34)
Text in English and French with French text on inverted pages.
Title on added t.p.: Les peuples autochtones et la justice pénale : Égalité, respect et justice
à l'horizon.
Includes bibliographical references.
ISBN 0-662-58641-7
DSS cat. no. J31-58/1991

1. Indians of North America — Canada — Criminal justice system. 2. Criminal justice,
Administration of — Canada. 3. Criminal procedure — Canada. I. Title. II. Title:
Rapport, les peuples autochtones et la justice pénale. III. Series: Law Reform Commission
of Canada. Report ; 34.

KE7722.C75L38 1991   345.71'05   C91-098750-5

Available by mail free of charge from:

Law Reform Commission of Canada
130 Albert Street, 7th Floor
Ottawa, Canada
K1A 0L6

or

Suite 310
Place du Canada
Montreal, Quebec
H3B 2N2

©Law Reform Commission of Canada 1991
Catalogue No. J31-58/1991
ISBN 0-662-58641-7

December, 1991

The Honourable A. Kim Campbell, P.C., M.P.,
Minister of Justice
   and Attorney General of Canada,
Ottawa, Canada

Dear Ms. Campbell:

Pursuant to your request under subsection 12(2) of the *Law Reform Commission Act* and in accordance with section 16 of that Act, we have the honour to submit herewith this Report on Aboriginal peoples and criminal justice undertaken by the Law Reform Commission of Canada.

Yours respectfully,

Gilles Létourneau
President

Ellen Picard
Vice-President

John Frecker
Commissioner

Jacques Frémont
Commissioner

Commission

Mr. Gilles Létourneau, President
Madam Justice Ellen Picard, Vice-President*
Mr. John Frecker, Commissioner
Professor Jacques Frémont, Commissioner**

Secretary

François Handfield, B.A., LL.L.

Project Director, Minister's Reference

Stanley A. Cohen, B.A., LL.B., LL.M.

Assistant Project Directors

John E.S. Briggs, B.A., LL.B.
Stephen G. Coughlan, B.A., M.A., LL.B., Ph.D.

Consultants

Jean-Paul Brodeur, M.A. (Phil.), M.A. (Crim.), Ph.D. (Phil.)
Marion Buller, B.A., LL.B.
Paul L.A.H. Chartrand, B.A., LL.B., LL.M.
Glenn A. Gilmour, B.A., LL.B.
Michael Jackson, LL.B., LL.M.
Roger Jones, B.A., LL.B.
H. Archibald Kaiser, B.A., LL.B., LL.M.
Leonard (Tony) Mandamin, B.Sc., LL.B.
Patricia A. Monture-OKanee, B.A., LL.B.
David L. Pomerant, B.A., LL.B.
Rosemary Trehearne
Mary Ellen Turpel, B.A., LL.B., LL.M., S.J.D.
Paul Williams, LL.B., LL.M.
Susan V. Zimmerman, B.A., B.C.L., LL.B.

---

* was not a member of the Commission at the time this Report was approved.

** was appointed to the Commission after the consultations in preparation for this Report were held.

Editor's Note

In keeping with the proposal advanced in *Equality for All: Report of the Parliamentary Committee on Equality Rights,* we have conscientiously endeavoured to draft this Report in gender-neutral language. In doing so, we have adhered to the standards and policies set forth in *Toward Equality: The Response to the Report of the Parliamentary Committee on Equality Rights* pertaining to the drafting of laws, since the Commission's mandate is to make proposals for modernizing Canada's federal laws.

Table of Contents

Acknowledgements

During the course of preparing this Report, we were fortunate enough to have consulted with persons having a wide experience within the Aboriginal community who are committed to preserving and enhancing Aboriginal rights. As well, we benefitted from the opinions and advice of experienced individuals in the fields of policing and law enforcement, law teaching, the practice of law, the judiciary and corrections. Also consulted were various federal and provincial government representatives and members of provincial inquiries into Aboriginal justice. We gratefully acknowledge the significant contribution to our work of all these groups.

Although it is not possible to name everyone consulted with respect to this Report, we especially wish to thank those persons listed in Appendix B.

CHAPTER ONE

Introduction

I. The Nature of the Minister's Reference

In a letter dated June 8, 1990, the Minister of Justice, pursuant to subsection 12(2) of the *Law Reform Commission Act*,[1] asked the Commission to study, as a matter of special priority, the *Criminal Code*[2] and related statutes and to examine the extent to which those laws ensure that Aboriginal persons and persons who are members of cultural or religious minorities have equal access to justice and are treated equitably and with respect. In carrying out its general mandate, the Commission was requested by the Minister to focus on "the development of new approaches to and new concepts of the law in keeping with and responsive to the changing needs of modern Canadian society and of individual members of that society."[3]

The nature of the Minister's request in our view necessitated the division of the work into two components: an Aboriginal justice review, and a cultural or religious minorities justice review. This Report is thus the first of two which we are submitting in response to the Minister's request.

Those who are familiar with the Commission's work and its orientation to the reform of the criminal process may feel that this Report marks a point of departure. Throughout our work we have extolled the virtues of a uniform, consistent and comprehensive approach to law reform. This Reference calls for us to examine, in specific detail, one group of persons and its interaction and unique difficulties with the criminal justice system. It asks us to propose reforms that will offset the sorry results of a history of disadvantage and suffering within the system — reforms that can be proceeded with as a matter of special priority. In fact, many of the proposals in the pages that follow could be implemented throughout the justice system, although they might first be carried out to respond to the particular plight of the Aboriginal peoples. Other proposals in this Report, however, are specific to Aboriginal peoples. While we remain committed to the principles of uniformity and consistency, distinct treatment might be constitutionally justified on the basis of sections 25 and 35 of the *Canadian Charter of Rights and Freedoms*,[4] which put Aboriginal peoples in a unique constitutional position with pre-existing legal rights, or else under the affirmative action clause of the *Charter's* equality provision.

---

1. R.S.C. 1985, c. L-7.
2. R.S.C. 1985, c. C-46.
3. *Law Reform Commission Act, supra*, note 1, s. 11(*d*).
4. Part I of the *Constitution Act, 1982*, being Schedule B of the *Canada Act 1982* (U.K.), 1982, c. 11.

We believe that this Report does no violence to our work in the field of criminal law. Rather, it expresses our basic commitment to the creation of a criminal justice system that pursues the values of humanity, freedom and justice.

In this Report we have consciously employed the designation "Aboriginal" when referring to those persons encompassed by the terms of this Reference. Throughout our consultations, it was emphasized that words such as "natives," "members of first nations" or "Indians" would not reflect the diversity of peoples within Canada who are encompassed by the expression "Aboriginal peoples." Furthermore, labels that incorporate the designation "Indian" are not entirely satisfactory, since many Aboriginal peoples regard that word as pejorative.

Finally, our choice of terminology is consistent with section 35 of the *Constitution Act, 1982*,[5] which refers to the "Indian, Inuit and Métis" peoples as comprising the Aboriginal peoples of Canada.

II. Limitations on This Study

Any undertaking, let alone one to cover a subject as broad and complex as this, must struggle with inherent limitations. Such factors as time, organization and available resources constrain the research and, ultimately, the product. These limitations, for example, had a bearing on the Commission's ability to conduct meaningful consultations: had there been fewer operational constraints, we would have employed a markedly different consultation strategy, including travelling to various Aboriginal communities. Instead, we met in focused sessions with selected Aboriginal representatives in both Eastern and Western Canada.

We see this limited Report as a first step in a much larger enterprise. While it contains much that can be acted upon immediately, our Report also attempts to set out an agenda for the kind of future work necessary if the problems we have identified are to be adequately responded to in the coming years.

III. The Consultation Process

We began our work with a broad general mailing to interested parties, organizations and experts. We sent letters to and established liaison with various government departments and agencies and with all of the currently operating provincial commissions of inquiry.

---

5.   *Canada Act 1982* (U.K.), 1982, c. 11, Sch. B.

From the outset it was apparent to us that, at a minimum, we would have to solicit the views of representatives of the affected communities and recognized experts, as well as government ministries and institutions having direct responsibilities with respect to Aboriginal peoples and the justice system. In all, we convened three consultation sessions with Aboriginal representatives. We sought out the opinions and reactions of individuals who were in a position to provide the Commission with unique Aboriginal perspectives on the operation of the present system. We also commissioned a series of background studies, a list of which appears in Appendix A.

IV. The Law Reform Context

The Aboriginal representatives with whom we consulted voiced strong reservations regarding this Reference. In the Reference's focus on the *Criminal Code* and related statutes, they saw an unacceptable emphasis on "patching up" the current system. In their eyes, no new catalogue of particular deficiencies in the *Criminal Code* or in the practice of the criminal law was required. What they believed was needed was not more study but more action. Also, they conveyed a deep sense of the futility in attempting to change the face of the criminal justice system when broader, more fundamental social change is necessary. *Criminal Code* amendments do not address the socio-economic plight of the Aboriginal peoples and fail to redress long-held grievances concerning the land.

The cold reality, nevertheless, is that the *Criminal Code* and related statutes are defective and do require change. We at the Commission have devoted much of the past twenty years to exploring many of these deficiencies.

Fundamental change of the kind advocated will not be accomplished overnight. Meanwhile, injustice should still be confronted and vanquished in every dark corner where it lurks. The suffering of Aboriginal peoples continues unabated; they tire of being referred to as a "national tragedy" and call for action now. Our laws and practices must be adjusted: we should not be obliged to await the coming of a new age.

We propose two tracks of reform. One track is short-term and ameliorative but, admittedly, may not address the more fundamental issues. The other stakes out a course that ultimately arrives at a destination far removed from the present reality. This parallel-path approach may leave some readers confused, at least initially. Proposed short-term solutions, such as increasing the number of Aboriginal criminal justice personnel, may seem antithetical to the accomplishment of the kind of fundamental change that the proposals for the creation of Aboriginal justice systems entail.

Central to a proper understanding of our approach is the notion of legal pluralism — of multiple systems coexisting within the legal order. We envision Aboriginal communities opting for the creation of a variety of systems of justice, all of which may be described as Aboriginal justice systems. These may be located on a continuum stretching from approximations of the present system through various systems and processes incorporating distinctly Aboriginal features (such as alternative methods of dispute resolution and the use of Elders and peacekeepers) and ultimately on to a profoundly transformed system.

In each of the contemplated reform tracks, we hope to promote conditions of reform that are conducive to the creation of systems that Aboriginal peoples and other Canadians will accept and respect.

CHAPTER TWO

The Aboriginal Perspective on Criminal Justice

Aboriginal communities number in the several hundreds and each has had a distinctive experience of the Canadian criminal justice system. Given this diversity, there is necessarily some oversimplification in the following general description of Aboriginal perceptions and aspirations. Nevertheless, we have been struck by the remarkably uniform picture of the system that has been drawn by Aboriginal speakers and writers.

I.   Aboriginal Perceptions

From the Aboriginal perspective, the criminal justice system is an alien one, imposed by the dominant white society. Wherever they turn or are shuttled throughout the system, Aboriginal offenders, victims or witnesses encounter a sea of white faces. Not surprisingly, they regard the system as deeply insensitive to their traditions and values: many view it as unremittingly racist.

Abuse of power and the distorted exercise of discretion are identified time and again as principal defects of the system. The police are often seen by Aboriginal people as a foreign, military presence descending on communities to wreak havoc and take people away. Far from being a source of stability and security, the force is feared by them even when its services are necessary to restore a modicum of social peace to the community.

For those living in remote and reserve communities, the entire court apparatus, quite literally, appears to descend from the sky — an impression that serves to magnify their feelings of isolation and erects barriers to their attaining an understanding of the system.

The process is in reality incomprehensible to those who speak only Aboriginal languages, especially where little or no effort is made to provide adequate interpretation services. Even the English- or French-speaking inhabitants of these communities find the language of the courts and lawyers difficult to understand. Understanding is more than a problem of mere language. Aboriginal persons contend that virtually all of the primary actors in the process (police, lawyers, judges, correctional personnel) patronize them and consistently fail to explain adequately what the process requires of them or what is going to happen to them. Even those who are prepared to acknowledge certain well-intentioned aspects of the present system nevertheless conclude that the system has utterly failed.

Such efforts as have been made to involve the community in the administration of justice are seen as puny and insignificant, and there is little optimism about the future. Elders see the community's young people as the primary victims of the system — cut adrift by it and removed from the community's support as well as from its spiritual and cultural traditions. They recount experiences of children taken from their communities at an early age who later emerge, hardened from the court and correctional processes and ultimately beyond the reach of even imaginative initiatives designed to promote rehabilitation.

Evident and understandable weariness and frustration attend any discussion of approaches to fixing the system or setting it right. For Aboriginal persons, the system presents an unending course of barriers and obstacles, with no avenues of effective complaint or redress. Their sense of injustice is bottomless. They have little or no confidence in the legal profession or in the judiciary to bring about justice or to effect a just resolution of any particular dispute in which they are involved. If the truth be told, most have given up on the criminal justice system.

II.   Aboriginal Aspirations

Aboriginal people have a vision of a justice system that is sensitive to their customs, traditions and beliefs. This vision is a natural outgrowth of their aspirations to self-government and sovereignty. They desire a criminal justice system that is Aboriginal-designed, -run and -populated, from top to bottom.

Undoubtedly there are many contrasting visions as to what constitutes an Aboriginal justice system, but fundamental is the belief that the system must be faithful to Aboriginal traditions and cultural values, while adapting them to modern society. Hence, a formal Aboriginal justice system would evince appropriate respect for community Elders and leaders, give heed to the requirements of Aboriginal spirituality and pay homage to the relation of humankind to the land and to nature.

The Aboriginal vision of justice gives pre-eminence to the interests of the collectivity, its overall orientation being holistic and integrative. Thus, it is community-based, stressing mediation and conciliation while seeking an acknowledgement of responsibility from those who transgress the norms of their society. While working toward a reconciliation between the offender and the victim, an Aboriginal justice system would pursue the larger objective of reintegrating the offender into the community as a whole.

The Aboriginal vision challenges both common and civil law concepts. Statute law becomes less important. Within an Aboriginal justice system, laws would not be uniform or homogeneous; they would vary from community to community, depending on customary practices. Customary law would be the binding force promoting harmony within the community.

While possessing common general characteristics, an Aboriginal justice system would of necessity be pluralistic. What such a system would actually look like is unclear. This haziness is a source of frustration. Much essential detail is missing, and Aboriginal people are hesitant to provide that detail, not because they are incapable of providing it — some communities have well-developed and well-articulated models — but because, in their view, they should not have to do so. They aspire to local control. Their contention is essentially: "Give us the keys. Let us control the system. We can hardly do worse than you have."

But why is there such a misunderstanding b/w the Abor. and the Con CJS?

CHAPTER THREE

The Meaning of Equal Access to Justice, Equitable Treatment and Respect

---

Highlights

The criminal justice system must provide the same minimum level of service to all people. Further, the criminal justice system must treat Aboriginal persons equitably and with respect. These objectives require that cultural distinctiveness be recognized, respected and, where appropriate, incorporated into the criminal justice system.

One goal of this Reference must be to provide ways to achieve formal equality in respect of access to justice. Mere formal equality is satisfied if Aboriginal persons receive treatment not worse than that received by anyone else. Aboriginal persons must be equally able to obtain legal counsel, or to have the police respond to their complaints. The criminal justice system must not be more likely to arrest, lay charges against, convict or refuse parole to Aboriginal persons. No one would challenge this modest goal.

However, "access to justice" is a broad term. It includes the simple ability to receive adequate services but, more importantly, it speaks of justice. Further, this Reference looks beyond equality, and talks of Aboriginal persons' being treated "equitably and with respect." Criminal law and procedure generally impose the same demands on everyone: in contrast, the concepts of equitable treatment and respect invite a recognition of differences between cultures. "Equitable treatment" raises questions of ultimate fairness. "Respect" requires an acknowledgement that other values can be worthy of protection. In addition, the Reference seeks ways not merely to allow for such differences, but to "ensure" equitable treatment and respect: this wording imposes a high burden.

The traditional perspective of substantive criminal law has been that formal equality is sufficient: as long as everyone is treated identically, then everyone is treated equally. Indeed, this is the meaning of the saying, Justice is blind — differences between people are to be ignored. We believe that the terms of this Reference require a departure from that principle. It is useful first, therefore, to consider the extent to which that principle has shaped criminal law.

The criminal law applies in precisely the same way to everyone. Thus, the differences in values among cultures are not relevant: everyone is held to the same standards, whatever their personal beliefs.[6] This principle applies also to the enforcement of the law by the Attorney General's agents.[7] The same perspective frequently applies in criminal procedure. Trial by jury, for example, is in part intended to allow an accused to be judged by people who are likely to understand the accused's motivations and who perhaps share common attitudes and expectations. However, it is sufficient for the jury panel to be randomly chosen from the community in which the accused is tried. This may result in a jury none of whose members share the accused's race or ethnic association, even though that race or ethnic group is well represented in the community as a whole. Even so, if no deliberate exclusion can be shown, the courts will recognize no cause for complaint.

In sentencing as well, the notion of formal equality has a significant impact. Sentencing judges do take account of the individual circumstances of an accused;[8] at the same time, however, offenders are to be treated "equally," which in the circumstances means that they should be treated more or less identically. Although a fine will be less of a deterrent to a rich person than a poor one, that does not justify jailing the rich person.[9]

While treating everyone identically might seem to imply that external values or considerations would not affect the objective application of rules, we believe that such a view would be mistaken. Any decision enforces some value. When the value enforced is that of the dominant group in society, however, it is easy for members of that dominant group to look upon the decision not as value-based, but as neutral.

Identical treatment does not achieve equality in result. Consider, for example, sentencing: judges apply various factors in "fitting the sentence to the offender." Even when applied even-handedly, however, these factors themselves incorporate certain attitudes and necessarily cause unequal results. Whether the offender might lose a job if imprisoned may legitimately be a consideration in sentencing. The background and prospects of an offender are also relevant — for example, that he or she has been a good student, or is about to embark on a promising career. However, applying these factors means that the poor, the unemployed and those from groups unlikely to maintain stable employment or pursue a university education are likely to be treated more harshly.[10] Similarly, consider sentences that include imprisonment in the event of fine default: the threatened incarceration is only a means of enforcing payment. However, the sentence assumes "that the convicted person has more money than time to spare. This assumption in turn rests upon

---

6. See *Re Church of Scientology and The Queen (No. 6)* (1987), 31 C.C.C. (3d) 449 at 450 (Ont. C.A.): "The criminal law of Canada does operate to limit religious practices even when based upon sincerely or genuinely held religious beliefs."

7. See *R. v. Catagas* (1977), 38 C.C.C. (2d) 296 (Man. C.A.).

8. In order to "fit the sentence to the offender rather than to the crime" — *R. v. Gardiner*, [1982] 2 S.C.R. 368 at 414.

9. See, *e.g.*, *Johnson v. The Queen* (1971), 5 C.C.C. (2d) 541 (N.S.C.A.).

10. The same or similar factors will also be relevant to decisions concerning bail, and concerning absolute or conditional discharges.

the assumption that the individual is an active participant in the cash-economy.''[11] In the case of groups for whom this assumption is not true — many Aboriginal persons, for example — the result is over-representation in prison.

However, despite the historical tenor of criminal law, it has begun to be acknowledged that mere formal equality is not always sufficient. Canadian governments and courts have recognized that the right to counsel, for example, cannot — like the right to a suite at the Ritz — be left available equally to all who can afford it. Rather, steps have been taken to guarantee that the right is genuinely available to everyone, regardless of means. The equality provision in the *Charter* has also had a significant impact: the Supreme Court has held that discrimination can arise from ''a policy or practice which is on its face neutral but which has a disproportionately negative effect on an individual or group.''[12] The court also noted that ''identical treatment may frequently produce serious inequality,'' and that ''the promotion of equality under s. 15 has a much more specific goal than the mere elimination of distinctions.''[13] Accordingly, proposing recognition of a goal beyond mere formal equality is not introducing a completely new concept to the criminal justice system.

In determining whether various groups in society have equal access to justice and whether they are treated equitably and with respect, therefore, we must first ask whether criminal law and procedure provide the same minimum level of service to all members of society. Although that goal may be achieved much of the time, it is also not met in many instances: studies have found racism in the criminal justice system,[14] and even without racism the goal may not be met. The inequities must be addressed.

However, simply to direct our attention to those inequities is not sufficient. Rather, our substantive and procedural law must see to it that relevant differences are not ignored or treated as irrelevant.[15] Instead, our law must recognize that those differences are sometimes crucial and, moreover, that true equality is more than mere formal equality.

The criminal justice system must provide the same minimum level of service to all people. In practice, the system sometimes fails to achieve this goal. The level of service in interaction with police, in access to legal aid and in assisting with comprehension of the court process, among other areas, is not equal among all groups in society, and in particular among Aboriginal people. To the extent that formal equality does not exist, it must be brought about.

---

11. Paul Havemann, Lori Foster, Keith Couse et al., *Law and Order for Canada's Indigenous People* (Regina: Prairie Justice Research, 1985) at 173.

12. *Canadian National Railway Co.* v. *Canada (Canadian Human Rights Commission)*, [1987] 1 S.C.R. 1114 at 1137.

13. *Andrews* v. *Law Society of British Columbia*, [1989] 1 S.C.R. 143 at 171, McIntyre J.

14. See, *e.g.*: Nova Scotia, Royal Commission on the Donald Marshall, Jr., Prosecution, *Findings and Recommendations*, vol. 1 (Halifax: The Commission, 1989) at 162 (Chair: T. A. Hickman) [hereinafter Marshall Inquiry, vol. 1]; Alberta, *Justice on Trial: Report of the Task Force on the Criminal Justice System and Its Impact on the Indian and Métis People of Alberta*, vol. 1 (Edmonton: The Task Force, 1991) at 12-3 (Chair: R. A. Cawsey) [hereinafter *Justice on Trial*].

15. Note the observation of Chief Judge Lilles, quoted in *Justice on Trial, supra*, note 14 at 5-5, that ''[t]he concept of equality in court proceedings is based on the premise that any law is equally applicable to, understood by and concurred in by all those subject to it. It is, in fact, an assumption of cultural homogeneity; it operates to maintain the existing sociological order. In non-legal terms, this assumption is patently false.''

Further, the criminal justice system must treat Aboriginal persons equitably and with respect. These objectives require that cultural distinctiveness be recognized, respected and, where appropriate, incorporated into the criminal justice system. Differences between members of various groups must be considered by police, prosecutors, defence lawyers, judges, legislators and all other participants in the criminal justice system. Indeed, the structure of the criminal justice system itself must be adjusted to allow greater recognition of those differences. Justice can no longer be blind: Justice must open her eyes to the inequities in society and see to it that they are not mirrored in the criminal justice system.

RECOMMENDATION

1. The criminal justice system must provide the same minimum level of service to all people and must treat Aboriginal persons equitably and with respect. To achieve these objectives, the cultural distinctiveness of Aboriginal peoples should be recognized, respected and, where appropriate, incorporated into the criminal justice system.

CHAPTER FOUR

The Desirability of Aboriginal Justice Systems

Highlights

Aboriginal communities that are identified by the legitimate representatives of Aboriginal peoples as being willing and capable should have the authority to establish Aboriginal justice systems. The federal and provincial governments should enter into negotiations to transfer such authority to those Aboriginal communities.

In the course of our consultations on this Reference, one participant, Ovide Mercredi, eloquently expressed a view that was widely shared by others with whom we met:

> One of the problems that I see is the perception that the criminal justice system is near-perfect but can maybe be made a little more perfect by making some changes to it over a period of time to allow for the concerns and the rights of Aboriginal people. The real issue is what some people have called cultural imperialism, where one group of people who are distinct make a decision for all other people.... If you look at it in the context of law, police, court and corrections, and you ask yourself: "Can we improve upon the system?" well, my response is, quite frankly, you can't. Our experiences are such that, if you make it more representative, it's still your law that would apply, it would still be your police forces that would enforce the laws, it would still be your courts that would interpret them, and it would still be your corrections system that houses the people that go through the court system. It would not be our language that is used in the system. It would not be our laws. It would not be our traditions, our customs or our values that decide what happens in the system. That is what I mean by cultural imperialism. So a more representative system, where we have more Indian judges, more Indian lawyers, more Indian clerks of the court, more Indian correctional officers or more Indian managers of the correctional system is not the solution. So what we have to do, in my view, is take off that imperial hat, if that's possible, and find alternatives to the existing system....[16]

New, imaginative solutions offer a brighter promise of enlisting the support and respect of Aboriginal people as well as ensuring equal access and equitable treatment. The time has come to co-operate in the creation of Aboriginal-controlled systems of justice, for which many possible models exist.[17]

---

16. Ovide Mercredi, Remarks (Law Reform Commission of Canada Consultation, Edmonton, Alberta, March 1991).

17. One description of the spectrum of possible court models for Aboriginal persons in Canada is offered in *Justice on Trial, supra,* note 14 at 11-2 to 11-5.

We recognize that the call for completely separate justice systems is part of a political agenda primarily concerned with self-government. We need not enter that debate. Aboriginal-controlled justice systems have merits quite apart from political considerations.

It is often contended that Aboriginal crime arises from the marginalization of Aboriginal societies as a result of colonization.[18] According to that theory, as control of their own destinies has been removed from Aboriginal people, suicide rates have climbed, crime has increased and their societies have broken down. The steps necessary to solve these problems go well beyond criminal justice reform. As LaPrairie has noted: "Deflecting responsibility to the criminal justice system rather than addressing fundamental problems of social and economic disparity as reflected in reserve life, almost assures the continuation of the problems."[19]

Nonetheless, the criminal justice system itself has contributed to the process of marginalization. In traditional Aboriginal societies, "[l]eaders remained leaders only as long as they held the respect of their community."[20] Respect for Elders was "the social glue holding people together in relatively peaceful obedience to commonly accepted rules."[21] However, we are told that "the very presence of our courts has taken away a critical forum in which wisdom can be demonstrated and respect earned."[22] Increasingly, participants in the criminal justice system are questioning whether this cultural hegemony is necessary.

Broadly speaking, we believe that criminal law and procedure should impose the same requirements on all members of society, whatever their private beliefs. However, we also feel that the distinct historical position of Aboriginal persons justifies departing from that general principle. As a general rule, all those coming to or residing in Canada should

---

18. See, *e.g.*, Mary Hyde and Carol LaPrairie, *Amerindian Police Crime Prevention*, Working Paper No. 1987-21 (Ottawa: Solicitor General Canada, 1987), which characterizes Aboriginal crime as a product of social disorganization derived from colonization and dependency. To the same effect, see Michael Jackson, "Locking up Natives in Canada" (1989) 23 U.B.C. L. Rev. 215 at 218-19; Lawrence J. Barkwell, David N. Chartrand, David N. Gray et al., "Devalued People: The Status of the Métis in the Justice System" (1989) 9:1 Can. J. of Native Studies 121; Havemann et al., *supra*, note 11; Nova Scotia, Royal Commission on the Donald Marshall, Jr., Prosecution, *The Mi'kmaq and Criminal Justice in Nova Scotia: A Research Study* by Scott Clark, vol. 3 (Halifax: The Commission, 1989), especially General Finding 2 at 69 (Chair: T. A. Hickman) [hereinafter Marshall Inquiry, vol. 3]; *Northern Frontier, Northern Homeland: The Report of the MacKenzie Valley Pipeline Inquiry*, vol. 1 (Ottawa: Supply and Services Canada, 1977) at 152 (Commissioner: Thomas R. Berger).

19. Carol LaPrairie, *If Tribal Courts Are the Solution, What Is the Problem?* (Consultation Document prepared for the Department of the Attorney General, Province of Nova Scotia, January 1990) at viii [unpublished].

20. Michael Coyle, "Traditional Indian Justice in Ontario: A Role for the Present?" (1986) 24 Osgoode Hall L.J. 605 at 614.

21. Rupert Ross, "Cultural Blindness and the Justice System in Remote Native Communities" (Address to the "Sharing Common Ground" Conference on Aboriginal Policing Services, Edmonton, May 1990) at 13. Our consultants have made similar observations from their own experience.

22. Ross, *ibid.* In Nova Scotia, Royal Commission on the Donald Marshall, Jr., Prosecution, *Consultative Conference on Discrimination against Natives and Blacks in the Criminal Justice System and the Role of the Attorney General*, vol. 7 (Halifax: The Commission, 1989) at 27 (Chair: T. A. Hickman) [hereinafter Marshall Inquiry, vol. 7], Judge Coutu, Co-ordinating Judge for the Itinerant Court of the District of Abitibi, stated: "What is important is not the system we adopt, but that the Native communities regain the social control they have lost because of the changes they have suffered since the coming of Europeans in America."

accept Canadian rules, and the outer limit of allowable behaviour should be set by the criminal law. However, the Aboriginal peoples did not come to Canada. Canada came to them. They have constitutional recognition and treaty rights that set them apart from all other Canadians.

> The Algonquins have lived in the valley of the Ottawa River at least as long as the French have lived in France or the English have lived in England. Before there was a Canada, before Cartier sailed his small ship up the great river, Algonquins lived in, occupied, used, and defended their home in the Ottawa Valley.[23]

To the reality of different constitutional status may be added the feature of cultural difference. Many Aboriginal cultures are essentially non-adversarial. As a result of this different cultural orientation, we are told that they are less likely to be able to use the protections of our justice system, such as the presumption of innocence:

> Amongst the Mohawk, one of the most serious of crimes is lying, which would include not acknowledging those acts of which you were properly accused . . . [I]t is likely that the offence with which they are charged is less serious to them than lying about their involvement in it, precisely what a "not guilty" plea would represent for them.[24]

The effects of cultural difference may be noted at various stages. In the preparation of pre-sentence reports, or in consideration of parole applications, Aboriginal offenders often fare poorly:

> What we may be missing is the fact that the offender behaves as he does because our *techniques* of rehabilitation, of "healing", may not only be very different, but also traditionally improper. His refusal may stem not from indifference or from amorality but from *allegiance* to ethical precepts which we have not seen.[25]

Some Aboriginal communities, we are told, wish to be given the opportunity to rehabilitate offenders and reincorporate them into their societies. They contend that, as constituted, our justice system interferes with that process and our criminal courts cannot serve as a substitute for the community: "Since a person can only be shamed by someone who is respected and looked up to, this cannot be effected by a travelling court."[26] For these

---

23. Chief Greg Sarazin, "220 Years of Broken Promises" in Boyce Richardson, ed., *Drumbeat: Anger and Renewal in Indian Country* (Toronto: Summerhill, 1989) at 169 [hereinafter *Drumbeat*].

24. Rupert Ross, "Leaving Our White Eyes Behind: The Sentencing of Native Accused" [1989] 3 C.N.L.R. 1 at 9. Further, "[t]he traditionally minded Aboriginal personal is predisposed to avoid conflict and argument and will shy away from confrontation. Even if a not guilty plea has been entered, the Aboriginal person may not provide the court *or even his counsel* with evidence unfavourable to the opposing witnesses": Indigenous Bar Association, *The Criminal Code and Aboriginal People* (Paper prepared for the Law Reform Commission of Canada, 1991) at 21 [unpublished] [hereinafter IBA]. Similarly, Aboriginal persons may make bad witnesses, either in their own defence or for the prosecution, because "it is perceived as ethically wrong to say hostile, critical, implicitly angry things about someone *in their presence*": Ross, *ibid.* at 6.

25. Ross, *supra*, note 21 at 10.

26. Submission of the Sandy Lake Band to the Ontario Ministry of the Attorney General, quoted in Ross, *supra*, note 21 at 12.

communities, sending an offender to jail delays the time when reintegration with the community can start. It may also cause an offender to become isolated from the community and more defiant;[27] indeed, imprisonment can allow the offender to avoid more distasteful options.[28]

These Aboriginal desires may be difficult for some observers to square with the squalid reality that exists in the most depressed, demoralized and crime-ridden reserve communities. Such an analysis, however, is ultimately self-defeating. We believe that, where suitable conditions exist, new approaches should be adopted.

Upon examination, we have concluded that the present system fails the Aboriginal peoples and contributes to their difficulties. The problems with the criminal justice system, for the most part, are obvious and long-standing. It is a system that, for Aboriginal people, is plagued with difficulties arising from its remoteness — a term that encompasses not only physical separation but also conceptual and cultural distance. Cultural distance is also manifest in different attitudes to legal control and to the legal environment. Aboriginal peoples continue to believe in the superiority of their traditional methods for resolving disputes and maintaining social order. It is those ancient ways that, ironically, provide the new approaches and concepts of law that the Minister has urged us to explore.

RECOMMENDATION

2. Aboriginal communities identified by the legitimate representatives of Aboriginal peoples as being willing and capable should have the authority to establish Aboriginal justice systems. The federal and provincial governments should enter into negotiations to transfer that authority to those Aboriginal communities.

I.   Implementation

Necessarily, some basic issues need to be resolved to implement this recommendation. Because of the great diversity among Aboriginal communities, the specific arrangements entailed by this proposal would have to be negotiated on a community-by-community basis. The parties themselves, through the negotiation process, would resolve the outstanding issues in a mutually satisfactory manner. Since no one Aboriginal justice system can satisfy the needs and desires of all communities, no single answer exists to the important questions that must be answered. This, again, is a reason for a proposal that is based upon negotiation. Negotiation, after all, is the primary method by which virtually all major Aboriginal issues should be addressed.

---

27. Submission of the Alexander Tribal Government to *Justice on Trial, supra*, note 14 at 6-43.

28. See Michael Jackson, *In Search of the Pathways to Justice: Alternative Dispute Resolution in Aboriginal Communities* (Paper prepared for the Law Reform Commission of Canada, 1991) at 82-83 [unpublished].

Reserves and Inuit villages are clearly identifiable as Aboriginal communities; many, if not most, Métis settlements ought also to be considered Aboriginal communities, even though there may be non-Aboriginal persons living there. But what of Aboriginal people in urban centres? Do they form a community?[29] Is such a community cohesive enough to support control over significant aspects of the justice system? Our proposal is that Aboriginal people themselves should initially make those determinations. Other important questions of this sort remain, to which we now turn.

At first glance, instituting distinct Aboriginal systems of justice might seem a radical suggestion. In fact, Aboriginal peoples in various places throughout Canada already control significant aspects of the justice system and have put in place parallel processes for achieving social peace and harmony within their communities. This proposal, examined in light of those developments, can be looked on as simply a logical extension of advances that have already been made.

The present justice system can also be seen as moving to incorporate Aboriginal innovations. This appears most dramatically where alternative dispute resolution practices are employed.[30] A few examples will illustrate this direction.

The South Island Tribal Council on Vancouver Island has become involved in the local criminal justice system to a remarkable extent. An Elder's Council has been established, the members of which act at various stages in the criminal process. Elders are involved in diversion, bail supervision, preparing pre-sentence reports and speaking to sentence. They also supervise open custody and probation, as well as acting as advisers and healers in correctional facilities.[31] Projects such as these are now essentially integrated parts of the criminal justice system. In each case, Aboriginal persons act in advisory capacities while actual authority rests elsewhere. In other communities, different proposals giving Aboriginal persons a greater measure of actual control have been instituted or proposed.

On the Kahnawake reserve, the community has established a force of "peacekeepers" to perform the police role, although their exact legal status is uncertain.[32] In addition,

---

29. The term "community" has been defined elsewhere as "a group of aboriginal people having a sense of solidarity, a common identity and tradition, forms of organization and a determination to preserve itself as a distinct entity. As such, the term refers to both local and regional groupings": Ontario Native Affairs Directorate, "Guidelines for the Negotiation of Aboriginal Self-Govrnment," tabled in the Ontario Legislature on December 14, 1989.

30. In terms of criminal justice, alternative dispute resolution embraces such concepts as diversion and victim-offender reconciliation. See below, our discussion of sentencing; see especially the discussion in Jackson, *supra*, note 28. See also the Marshall Inquiry, vol. 1, *supra*, note 14, quoting the Minister of Indian Affairs at 167: "The many alternative means of resolving disputes ... are the very methods which are part of customary law."

31. IBA, *supra*, note 24 at 38-39. Another well-known experiment in greater community control is the juvenile justice program on Christian Island in Northern Ontario, which achieved a dramatic drop in delinquencies. See Rick H. Hemmingson, "Jurisdiction of Future Tribal Courts in Canada: Learning from the American Experience" [1988] 2 C.N.L.R. 1 at 50; Jackson, *supra*, note 18; and Coyle, *supra*, note 20.

32. See *R. v. Norton* (27 September 1982), Longueuil 2286-81 (C.S.P.), holding that the peacekeepers are peace officers in accordance with s. 2 of the *Criminal Code*. Their status has not been determined by any higher level at court, or by legislation. An even stronger example of autonomous policing arrangements is evolving with the Cree of James Bay pursuant to the James Bay Agreement. Cree police will have virtually total, legal independence within the next few years.

justices of the peace appointed under the *Indian Act*[33] sit in the community twice a week, hearing and deciding summary conviction matters. This jurisdiction is relatively minor, but does give the community direct control over some aspects of local justice.

Very recently, the Government of Ontario announced the creation of an alternative justice program for adult Aboriginal persons charged with criminal offences. Under this program, candidates selected by Aboriginal courtworkers, the Native Community Council Co-ordinator and the Crown Attorney will be given the option of appearing before the Native Community Council for a traditional form of hearing. The Council, made up of Elders and other respected members of the community, will determine the appropriate disposition.

Similarly, the Marshall Inquiry proposed a "community-controlled Native Criminal Court."[34] The Government of Nova Scotia is also considering various other pilot projects, including a community-based court, a community youth court and community advisory committees.[35]

Initiatives such as these are valuable only when they meet the desires of the community. Some communities will want to control a system that more closely conforms to their notions of justice. The Gitksan and Wet'suwet'en societies suggest, for example, that they cannot accommodate a hierarchical court system or the specialized enforcement powers of the police. Rather, they wish to "explore how the two legal cultures might co-exist with dignity rather than try to thrust large parts of one system onto the other."[36] Our position, in keeping with the Minister's request that new approaches and concepts responsive to the changing needs of Canadian society be explored, is that where Aboriginal communities so desire, the federal and provincial governments should co-operate in establishing Aboriginal justice systems based on traditional models.

We believe that, initially at least, many communities may wish to create alternatives that bear a strong resemblance to our current justice system. Others may advance more distinctive models. It is difficult to describe these latter systems precisely because they may differ from community to community and because traditional Aboriginal methods also differ from community to community.[37] Basic distinctions, such as that between

---

33. R.S.C. 1985, c. I-5.

34. Marshall Inquiry, vol. 1, *supra*, note 14, Rec. 20 at 168. This project would involve an *Indian Act* justice of the peace, diversion and mediation projects, community work projects as alternatives to fines and imprisonment, after-care services on the reserve, community input into sentencing, and courtworkers.

35. LaPrairie, *supra*, note 19. See also *Justice on Trial, supra*, note 14, chap. 11, which at 11-2 sets out seven possible models for alternative justice systems, ranging from models broadly parallel to the present system, to a model which "includes the right of Indians to have their own justice system in whichever way they choose to organize it."

36. *Unlocking Aboriginal Justice*, quoted in Jackson, *supra*, note 28 at 92.

37. "One cannot forcefully demand to know rules when the legal system is not expressed in terms of rules": James W. Zion, "Searching for Indian Common Law" in Bradford W. Morse and Gordon R. Woodman, eds, *Indigenous Law and the State* (Providence: Foris Publications, 1988) 120 at 136. See also Coyle, *supra*, note 20 at 615.

criminal and civil law, might not be recognized.[38] Communities may wish to safeguard rights and secure fairness in different ways than our system does.[39]

It is important not to overstate these differences. As a practical matter, not every community will want to establish its own justice system. Other systems would be roughly parallel to those existing now. Also, even in traditional Aboriginal models, differences may appear to be greater than they really are. The type of behaviour that our criminal justice system seeks to suppress is, by and large, also unwelcome in Aboriginal communities. The overall goals of our justice system (deterrence and rehabilitation, for example) and of any system based on traditional Aboriginal models will be similar.[40] Understood this way, it should be clear that Aboriginal justice systems can be readily accommodated within Canadian society.

Finally, it should be borne in mind that the proposal to provide for the establishment of an Aboriginal justice system is not one that calls for the creation of huge, costly and monolithic structures and institutions. Aboriginal justice systems should not be imagined as being on the same scale as the Canadian criminal justice system. These systems would be scaled to the communities themselves and would reflect their needs and priorities.

II. Objections

Important issues arise with regard to establishing Aboriginal justice systems. None are insoluble.

There are constitutional questions concerning whether the federal government has the authority to allow Aboriginal justice systems to be created. Those issues are pursued at length in a recent study commissioned by us.[41] The clear position of that study is that the purported constitutional impediments are not substantial. This view finds implicit support in the endorsement of Aboriginal-controlled systems by the Ontario and Nova Scotia governments, and is reinforced by the calls for the establishment of such systems in the Marshall, Cawsey and Osnaburgh/Windigo Reports, as well as by the opinion of the Canadian Bar Association.[42] Clearly, the prevailing view of those who have closely examined

---

38. Note the observation in Jackson, *supra*, note 28 at 77, that "in the Coast Salish way a breakdown in family or community harmony requires restoration without attaching labels of criminal or family law to the dispute." See also *Justice on Trial, supra*, note 14, chap. 9, "An Aboriginal Perspective on Justice."

39. In so doing, these communities may develop new laws and procedures which will prove worthy of emulation within the Canadian system. *E.g., The Code of Offenses and Procedures of Justice for the Mohawk Territory at Akwesasne* (a Proposal to the Mohawk Nation Council of Chiefs, Mohawk Council of Akwesasne, Saint Regis Mohawk Tribal Council, August 1989) [unpublished], is an example of an initiative meriting close examination.

40. Coyle, *supra*, note 20 at 627, and IBA, *supra*, note 24 at 7.

41. Patricia A. Monture and Mary Ellen Turpel, eds, *Aboriginal Peoples and Canadian Criminal Law: Rethinking Justice* (Paper prepared for the Law Reform Commission of Canada, 1991) [unpublished].

42. The conclusion of the Canadian Bar Association Native Law Subsection, reproduced by the Cawsey Task Force, is that "there is a sound constitutional basis for the development of parallel native justice systems": *Justice on Trial, supra*, note 14 at 11-5; see also *infra*, note 43.

these questions is that the legal issues, while important, "should not interfere with the practical, social reasons for the development of an autonomous native justice system if that is what the First Nations desire."[43] Having considered these perspectives as well as other literature on the subject, we are of the view that, depending on the specifics of the system that is settled upon, this proposal can largely be accommodated without alteration of the existing Canadian constitutional structure.

One basic difficulty involved in the creation of Aboriginal justice systems arises out of the need to balance the rights and interests of the accused against the rights and interests of the community that chooses to operate under a separate system. In such cases, can and must the rights of the person involved disappear in the face of an assertion of the collective rights of the Aboriginal community? A method must be found to reconcile the legitimate rights of the individual with those collective rights.

Some may see the *Charter* as an obstacle to the establishment of an Aboriginal justice system and those who negotiate these arrangements must remain sensitive to the *Charter's* demands. Certain Aboriginal people, we are told, do not accept that there should be a right to silence or even that a trial is the appropriate method for resolving disputes. One reserve contends that its judicial process has no place for lawyers.[44]

The possibility of differently conceived notions of rights means that any Aboriginal justice system must be carefully constructed and needs widespread community support. Those persons who would be subject to the new system must truly want the change. The challenge is to find a way in which desired departures from the *Charter* can be accommodated. The question of determining to what extent *Charter* rights are negotiable can hardly be avoided. The Government of Canada, as a party to these negotiations, will wish to be sure of its constitutional position, and may even wish to seek a clarification of its position by means of a Reference to the Supreme Court of Canada. Aboriginal representatives seeking to convince federal negotiators of the correctness of their positions may also wish to obtain such a clarification; their access to the courts in this regard should be as generous as the Government's.

Some commentators assert that no special steps need to be taken.[45] Aboriginal rights are protected in section 25 of the *Constitution Act, 1982*, which guarantees that the other rights and freedoms in the *Charter* do not abrogate or derogate from Aboriginal rights, and also in section 35, which recognizes and affirms existing Aboriginal and treaty rights.

---

43. Osnaburgh/Windigo Tribal Council Justice Review Committee, *Tay Bway Win: Truth, Justice and First Nations* (Report prepared for the Ontario Attorney General and Solicitor General, 1990) at 38 [unpublished], [hereinafter Osnaburgh/Windigo Report]. See also that report's treatment of four major, commonly held misconceptions about Aboriginal rights and their status in Canadian society, at 38-41.

44. Although one may bring a lawyer to the court to relate facts, no cross-examination is permitted: Grand Chief Michael Mitchell, "An Unbroken Assertion of Sovereignty" in *Drumbeat, supra*, note 23 at 125, referring to Akwesasne.

45. See, *e.g.*, Monture and Turpel, eds, *supra*, note 41.

Aboriginal rights can be pre-existing rights, not created by any legislative action.[46] These commentators argue that a traditional Aboriginal law system is contemplated under existing Aboriginal rights, and that the legal rights in the *Charter,* to the extent that they become implicated, give way in the face of Aboriginal rights.[47]

Another way in which provision can be made for Aboriginal systems is through use of the override power in *Charter* section 33, although its use can be controversial and politically difficult. Therefore, resort to that section should not be embarked upon lightly.

In addition, it is theoretically possible for each member of the community to waive *Charter* rights. This approach sounds impractical, but if jurisdiction for the Aboriginal system is determined in part by the agreement of the accused, then waiver on a case-by-case basis can be obtained: opting for the Aboriginal system conceivably could be a waiver of *Charter* rights. What is unclear, and may require guidance from the courts, is whether it is possible for a person to make a blanket waiver of all individual rights under the *Charter.*[48]

Conceivably, the negotiations contemplated by the proposal may yield agreement to a certain minimum level of compliance with *Charter* rights. This will depend on the willingness of the parties to make this accommodation, but is unlikely to pose much difficulty for what we believe are the many communities that merely wish to take over greater control of aspects of the criminal justice system, or that choose to institute systems broadly parallel to the present one.

Also, the *Charter* should not be thought of as being inhospitable to Aboriginal justice systems. The right to counsel need not be equated with the right to a lawyer; the right to a fair hearing does not necessarily mean the right to a trial before a robed judge; jury trials are largely optional and, in any event, need not be held for any offence carrying liability to imprisonment for less than five years; and so on.

Some may wonder whether the jurisdictional complexity entailed by this proposal can be readily accommodated. In fact, legal pluralism, in the form of Quebec's control over civil law, and divided jurisdiction are already features of Canadian law. An offence committed by a young person brings into play different rules (the *Young Offenders Act*[49]) than

---

46. *Guerin* v. *The Queen,* [1984] 2 S.C.R. 335. See the further discussion of this point in Monture and Turpel, eds, *supra,* note 41.

47. Further force is given to this argument by the fact that the legal rights in the *Charter,* those in ss 7-15, are subject to s. 33, but Aboriginal rights are immune to that override clause. A different but related question involves s. 96 of the *Constitution Act, 1867* (U.K.), 30 & 31 Vict., c. 3. That question asks whether, short of a constitutional amendment, it is possible to circumvent the requirements of s. 96 in the establishment of an Aboriginal justice system.

48. For discussion of waiver of *Charter* rights generally, see: *Korponay* v. *Attorney General of Canada,* [1982] 1 S.C.R. 41; *Clarkson* v. *The Queen,* [1986] 1 S.C.R. 383; *R.* v. *Turpin,* [1989] 1 S.C.R. 1296; *R.* v. *Askov,* [1990] 2 S.C.R. 1199.

49. R.S.C. 1985, c. Y-1.

does the same offence committed by an adult. Similarly, in military matters, a separate jurisdiction for trying offences is created: the offender is dealt with by a different court system having different rules of procedure. Our military justice system also demonstrates that jurisdiction can be divided by means of the type or seriousness of the offence committed.[50]

Jurisdiction could be based on the offender, the offence or the location of the offence: any of these criteria might be appropriate. An Aboriginal system might automatically acquire jurisdiction where the offender is an Aboriginal person, or jurisdiction might be optional in that case. If optional, there are any number of workable methods for deciding which system will deal with the offender: the decision could be made by a panel of Elders, a Crown prosecutor, the victim, the offender or some combination. Jurisdiction might also be simply divided on the basis that any offence committed on a reserve or designated territory (or perhaps by an Aboriginal person on a reserve) will be dealt with by a local Aboriginal justice system. Thus, although we have not devised precise jurisdictional rules — and it would be inappropriate for us to do so — it is clear to us that a workable formula can be achieved through the process of negotiation that is contemplated by our proposal.[51]

Another difficulty has to do with the relationship between the Aboriginal justice systems and the general criminal justice system. For instance, will prerogative writs be available to accused or condemned persons? Will a convicted person be able to appeal any conviction or sentence, and to whom? Such problems are by no means easy to resolve and will require a serious examination of the issues at stake.

It bears remembering that the calls for these systems come primarily from Aboriginal communities. The doctrine of formal legal equality, of treating everyone identically, has been tried unsuccessfully for many years. Given the problems this approach has created, an insistence on one uniform justice system seems to be an insistence on the appearance of equality at the expense of real, substantial equality.

Our proposal, then, is for the creation of Aboriginal justice systems through a process of negotiation and agreement. While we expect significant variations in approach from community to community, we suggest that participants in these negotiations in many cases may wish to explore the merits of:

(a)   relying on customary law;

(b)   traditional dispute resolution procedures with dispositional alternatives stressing mediation, arbitration and reconciliation;

(c)   the involvement of Elders and Elders' Councils;

(d)   the use of Peacemakers;

---

50. Some offences are unique to the *National Defence Act*, R.S.C. 1985, c. N-5.

51. This is not to minimize the practical difficulties involved in settling questions of jurisdiction. If plural systems evolve, having a variety of bases for asserting jurisdiction could create confusion. *E.g.*, a Cree person coming initially before a court in Toronto might have options different from those of a Mohawk in the same circumstances.

(e)   tribal courts having Aboriginal judges and Aboriginal personnel in other mainstream justice roles;[52]

(f)   autonomous Aboriginal police forces with police commissions and other accountability mechanisms;

(g)   community-based and -controlled correctional facilities, probation and after-care services; and

(h)   an Aboriginal Justice Institute.

We must also face the objections that Aboriginal systems will not be able to cope — in effect, that they will not work. This is clearly a premature judgment. There is no question that the challenge is great. However, let us not establish an unreasonable standard of comparison. It is despair with the way that the present system operates in practice that has led Aboriginal people to call for change. An Aboriginal system could fall well short of perfection and still respond to the needs of Aboriginal persons more effectively than the present justice system. As Donald Marshall, Jr., knows only too well, sometimes the police arrest innocent people, prosecutors pursue them and courts convict them. We do not conclude that our system is unworkable; we strive to improve it. Let us approach Aboriginal justice systems in the same spirit.

---

52.   This option, when defined to mean the specific type of court system in place primarily in the American Southwest, has its share of detractors. The Osnaburgh/Windigo Report, *supra*, note 43 at 37, describes the U.S. tribal courts as "a pale mirror of the U.S. court system" and as something "to be avoided in Canada." Jonathan Rudin and Dan Russell, *Native Alternative Dispute Resolution Systems: The Canadian Future in Light of the American Past* (Toronto: Ontario Native Council on Justice, 1991), concluded, at i, that "simply importing the U.S. Tribal Court system into Canada would not accomplish a great deal" (see especially chap. 5). Also, see generally, the discussion in Jackson, *supra*, note 18 at 225-29.

CHAPTER FIVE

Fostering Understanding and Building Bridges

Highlights

Aboriginal persons should occupy posts in all aspects and at all levels of the criminal justice system, including posts as police, lawyers, judges, probations officers and correctional officials. Aboriginal persons should be recruited, trained and promoted, through affirmative action if necessary.

Cross-cultural training for all participants in the criminal justice system, including police, lawyers, judges, probation officers and correctional officials, should be expanded and improved.

Linguistic and cultural barriers between the criminal justice system and Aboriginal societies must be removed.

Permanent, effective liaison should be established between the police, the prosecutorial, judicial and correctional systems and Aboriginal communities.

The right of Aboriginal peoples to express themselves in their own languages in all court proceedings should be statutorily recognized. Qualified interpreters should be provided to all Aboriginal persons who need assistance in court proceedings or during the pre-trial stage of a police investigation.

Governments should develop clear and public policies concerning the interpretation of Aboriginal and treaty rights.

I. Difficulties in Providing Justice to Aboriginal Communities

We have called for the creation and recognition of Aboriginal justice systems, but we realize that these systems cannot be implemented everywhere immediately. Indeed, some communities may not choose to establish them. Further, even with Aboriginal justice systems in place, there will continue to be circumstances under which Aboriginal persons are involved with the present system. Accordingly, although they would be insufficient on their own in the view of many Aboriginal communities, steps to make the current system more equitable are necessary. This chapter and the next deal with those steps.

We have had the advantage of considering the Reports of several provincial inquiries into the criminal justice system and Aboriginal persons.[53] However, we face one obstacle not faced by those provincial inquiries: our recommendations concern not just local practice, but national laws. Where provincial inquiries have generally only had to concern themselves with the situation of a few communities, our Report is necessarily much more wide-ranging.

This situation creates a pitfall which was brought to our attention by our consultants: once a problem is identified as a way in which the criminal law or the criminal justice system interacts with Aboriginal persons, the problem is seen to be a near universal in Aboriginal communities. Obviously, that assumption must be avoided: Aboriginal persons find themselves in a wide variety of situations. Their experiences and problems, and the appropriate solutions, will vary accordingly.

One can immediately distinguish at least three distinct situations: isolated Aboriginal communities, Aboriginal communities located near non-Aboriginal centres and Aboriginal persons living in non-Aboriginal centres. The problems in each of these circumstances are not the same.[54]

Physical isolation is likely to cause certain problems, among them inadequate police services, limited access to counsel and the release of arrested persons far from the community. Remote communities are also especially likely to suffer from delay. The Cawsey (*Justice on Trial*)[55] and Osnaburgh/Windigo[56] Reports have both noted that courts, particularly itinerant courts, are often cancelled owing to weather. Cases are also delayed because of the non-appearance of accused or witnesses at trials some distance from the community. Equally, the need to find interpreters can cause delay.[57]

---

53. This Report was written and approved, however, before the publication of Manitoba, Public Inquiry into the Administration of Justice and Aboriginal People, *Report of the Aboriginal Justice Inquiry of Manitoba*, vols 1, 2 (Winnipeg: Queen's Printer, 1991) (Commissioners: A. C. Hamilton and C. M. Sinclair).

54. It is desirable to establish a more sophisticated division between types of communities. One study has divided aboriginal communities into four categories, and analysed the types of crime and policing needs in each: see Carol Pitcher LaPrairie, "Community Types, Crime, and Police Services on Canadian Indian Reserves" (1988) 25:4 J. Research in Crime and Delinquency 375.

55. *Supra*, note 14.

56. *Supra*, note 43.

57. To the best of our knowledge, no *Charter* case concerning these issues has been brought, but it seems clear in light of the *Askov* decision, *supra*, note 48, that the lack of adequate resources for conducting trials in or near Aboriginal communities will not justify these delays.

Delay is particularly unfortunate in physically isolated communities. First, holding a trial after a delay might actually interfere in a situation that has been resolved. Equally, the delay could result in the situation's not being adequately resolved in the existing system.[58] As well, the practical difficulty of leaving an offender in the community pending trial can be exacerbated when that community is small and relatively isolated. Already inappropriate bail conditions are more difficult to comply with over a long time, and the offender and the victim are likely to come into contact with each other, with potentially unfortunate results.[59]

At the same time, some solutions to the problems facing isolated communities, such as local supervision of persons on bail or parole or increased cross-cultural training, may be more easily implemented in remote communities. Isolated communities may also be more able to reintegrate offenders into their society.

It has also been suggested to us that, even if not physically isolated, Aboriginal communities can be "culturally remote" from the society around them. Certainly, some communities located very near urban centres have nonetheless been able to retain their distinctiveness. Such communities will also often have greater resources to draw upon in making improvements to the current system or creating their own.

Aboriginal persons in non-Aboriginal communities may also face great difficulties. They have all of the problems associated with not understanding the judicial system, but do not have most of the support that Aboriginal communities are able to offer.

These differences may affect many of our recommendations, and we have tried to bear them in mind throughout. Some of our recommendations are relevant only to isolated communities, some will affect all Aboriginal communities and others should benefit all Aboriginal persons. In each case, we expect that the scope of the recommendation will be clear.

II.   Criminal Justice System Recruitment and Training

Numerous studies and reports have shown a pervasive lack of knowledge about Aboriginal peoples on the part of justice system personnel — a lack that makes the justice system less capable of operating equitably and with respect. There are two major ways to address this problem: hiring more Aboriginal persons as justice system personnel and increased cross-cultural training.

---

58. Ross, *supra*, note 24 at 4, speaks of an Aboriginal teenaged rape victim who refused to testify at a trial over a year after the event: "For her, it was simply too late to put him through it. The past was the past."

59. We are told that, in some areas, accused are routinely ordered to leave the community when released pending trial for certain offences: although this result may be preferable to incarceration, it is not necessarily satisfactory.

A. Increasing System-wide Aboriginal Representation

Hiring more Aboriginal persons might make the system seem less alien to Aboriginal people and create a greater sense of "ownership." Further, the justice system might become more sensitive to Aboriginal culture: Aboriginal officers or judges are less likely to suffer cultural misunderstandings in dealing with Aboriginal persons, and other officials would have exposure to Aboriginal persons among their colleagues.

However, objections have been raised to greater representation. First, Aboriginal persons will not necessarily be more sensitive to Aboriginal culture: "Some very tough attitudes may be engendered in the person who has had to struggle and 'make it the hard way'."[60] Similarly, Aboriginal persons might be "pushed towards the same practices in the exercise of discretion as those now followed in the administration of the criminal law," and therefore might be viewed "as having 'sold out' to the non-Aboriginal ways."[61] Some of our consultants suggested that involving more Aboriginal persons in the present system merely diverts resources, personnel and attention in the wrong direction, away from the creation of Aboriginal justice systems.

We agree that hiring more Aboriginal persons is not a panacea, but neither is it as destructive as some have claimed. On balance, we favour programs to bring more Aboriginal persons into all aspects of the criminal justice system, including as police, lawyers, judges, probations officers and correctional officials. Also, police forces and correctional services[62] should hire Aboriginal persons, through affirmative action if necessary. In addition, an affirmative action policy should be carried over into access to training and promotion decisions. If standards that were recognized as inappropriate for hiring are insisted upon for promotion,[63] Aboriginal persons will not be able to advance and are unlikely to remain.

Aboriginal lawyers are under-represented.[64] Recruitment programs to draw more Aboriginal persons into law schools should be financially supported to a greater extent than they are at present. In addition, Aboriginal persons should be appointed as judges at all levels of the judiciary, based on consultation with Aboriginal communities to identify appropriate candidates. To the best of our knowledge, no Supreme or Superior Court justice is an Aboriginal person, and the number of Aboriginal provincial court judges remains embarrassingly small.

---

60. Peter H. Russell, *The Judiciary in Canada: The Third Branch of Government* (Toronto: McGraw-Hill Ryerson, 1987) at 165.

61. IBA, *supra*, note 24 at 13, 32. The Paper concludes, at 32, that "[d]espite these problems, it is certainly preferable to employ Aboriginal people to serve in Aboriginal communities as police officers."

62. See Barkwell et al., *supra*, note 18 at 139, describing community programs in Manitoba which have involved greater employment of Aboriginal persons.

63. As appears to be the case within the RCMP, for example: see Robert H. D. Head, *Policing for Aboriginal Canadians: The R.C.M.P. Role* (Report prepared for the RCMP, 1989) [unpublished].

64. "Report of the Special Committee on Equity in Legal Education and Practice" (15 February 1991) Law Society of Upper Canada Proceedings of Convocation 16 at 21-22, notes that aboriginal persons make up only 0.8% of lawyers in Ontario, though they represent 1.5% of the adult population.

Aboriginal courtworkers are already a fixture in urban centres and remote communities in many parts of Canada, and can help bridge the gap between Aboriginal offenders and the justice system. They fulfil a wide range of services, including: providing information and explaining procedures to accused persons, justice officials and court personnel; facilitating the use of other agencies; providing out-of-court interpreter and translation assistance; assisting in obtaining lawyers, arranging bail and preparing pre-sentence reports; speaking on behalf of unrepresented Aboriginal persons; and aiding in probation and parole supervision. Ideally, courtworkers should perform more functions[65] and be available in more jurisdictions but, unfortunately, owing to government cutbacks their use is diminishing.[66] In our view, Aboriginal courtworker programs should be expanded, and their functions should include involvement with the Aboriginal accused person at all stages of the investigation and prosecution process, particularly where a lawyer is not immediately and continuously available.

RECOMMENDATIONS

3. (1) Programs should be established to bring more Aboriginal persons into all aspects of the criminal justice system, including as police, lawyers, judges, probation officers and correctional officials. More specifically, the following steps should be taken:

(a) police forces and correctional services should hire Aboriginal persons through affirmative action if necessary, and an affirmative action policy should be carried over into access to training and promotion decisions;

(b) recruitment programs to draw more Aboriginal persons into law schools should be financially supported to a greater extent than is presently the case; and

(c) Aboriginal persons should be appointed as judges at all levels of the judiciary, based on consultation with Aboriginal communities to identify appropriate candidates.

(2) Aboriginal courtworker programs should be expanded, and their functions should include involvement with Aboriginal accused persons at all stages of the investigation and prosecution process, particularly where a lawyer is not immediately and continuously available.

---

65. *E.g.*, the courtworker could be involved in police interrogations, consultations with lawyers, explaining Aboriginal customs to the court and developing strategies and submissions for the court.

66. See Jackson, *supra*, note 18 at 256: programs in four provinces — Prince Edward Island, Nova Scotia, New Brunswick and Saskatchewan — have been discontinued. Following recommendations by the Marshall Inquiry, vol. 1, *supra*, note 14, discussions concerning re-establishing the program in Nova Scotia are taking place.

B. Cross-cultural Training

Greater cross-cultural training was proposed at the 1975 National Conference on Native Peoples and the Criminal Justice System.[67] Despite this, fifteen years later the Cawsey Task Force observed that in general "court personnel know little about the culture of the Aboriginal people of Alberta."[68] Lack of cultural sensitivity operates in a subtle way: we all make assumptions based on our own experience about the way that people behave, and we judge others based on those assumptions. When those other people are from a different culture, however, our assumptions can be mistaken: as one prosecutor has noted: "I had been reading evasiveness and insincerity and possible lies when I should have been reading only respect and sincerity."[69] These mistakes, if made by police, lawyers, judges or correctional officials, can have devastating consequences.

Some cross-cultural training already exists. RCMP officer training includes information about Aboriginal culture,[70] and various judicial educational programs have taken place.[71] Further, cross-cultural training alone may not be sufficient. Although it can provide greater information about Aboriginal customs and behaviour, cross-cultural training is not generally designed to change underlying attitudes. Training aimed directly at those attitudes — generally called racism awareness or "anti-racism" training — should be investigated further (see the discussion of this issue in Chapter 8 under "I. Agenda for Future Action"). Nevertheless, the pace of change is slow and programs need to be adequately entrenched and institutionalized.

RECOMMENDATION

3. (3) Cross-cultural training for all participants in the criminal justice system, including police, lawyers, judges, probations officers and correctional officials, should be expanded and improved. This training should be mandatory and ongoing for those whose regular duties bring them into significant contact with Aboriginal persons. Local Aboriginal groups should be closely involved in the design and implementation of the training.

---

67. *Native Peoples and Justice: Reports on the National Conference and the Federal-Provincial Conference on Native Peoples and the Criminal Justice System*, both held in Edmonton, February 3-5, 1975 (Ottawa: Solicitor General Canada, 1975). The failure to take effective action on these proposals has been the subject of academic criticism and commentary (see Curt T. Griffiths and Simon N. Verdun-Jones, *Canadian Criminal Justice* (Toronto: Butterworths, 1989) at 573, for a selective review of the literature).

68. *Justice on Trial, supra,* note 14 at 5-1. See also Osnaburgh/Windigo Report, *supra,* note 43 at 59.

69. Ross, *supra,* note 24 at 2. Similarly, there is a danger of reading an Aboriginal person's "unwillingness or inability to employ *our* techniques [of rehabilitation] as clear signs of an unwillingness or inability to employ *any* techniques": Ross, *supra,* note 21 at 10.

70. Recommendations for improvement have been made: Head, *supra,* note 63, recommends at 88-89 that more time should be devoted to Aboriginal rights and that cross-cultural training should be given to those responsible for policy development. See also *Justice on Trial, supra,* note 14 at 2-36 to 2-40; and the discussion in Manitoba Métis Federation, *Submission to the Aboriginal Justice Inquiry* (1989) at 28 [unpublished].

71. See, *e.g.,* Papers of the Western Workshop, Alberta, co-sponsored by the Western Judicial Education Centre and the Canadian Association of Provincial Court Judges in conjunction with the Canadian Judicial Centre, at Lake Louise, Alberta, May 12-18, 1990 [unpublished]. See also remarks of Associate Chief Provincial Judge Diebolt to a conference sponsored by the Affiliation of Multi-cultural Societies and Service Agencies of British Columbia (Vancouver, June 3-5, 1991) describing cross-cultural training and sensitization courses for British Columbia provincial court judges.

The programs will need to be offered by a variety of bodies — judicial education centres, provincial bar associations, correctional institutions, and so on. Information concerning Aboriginal culture should be incorporated into law school programs. Steps toward this end have been taken in some, although not all, law schools.[72] Similarly, legal aid services should make arrangements to allow some lawyers to specialize in representing Aboriginal persons. Lawyers who deal regularly with Aboriginal persons will be familiar with the unusual legal issues that may arise.[73]

RECOMMENDATIONS

3. (4) Information concerning Aboriginal culture should be incorporated into law school programs.

(5) Legal aid services should make arrangements to allow some lawyers to specialize in representing Aboriginal persons.

III. Overcoming Language Difficulties and Cultural Barriers

In principle, problems with translation for Aboriginal persons ought not to exist, even under the current law. Section 14 of the *Charter* guarantees an interpreter to anyone who does not understand the language of proceedings, a guarantee that existed at common law in any event.[74] As in many areas, the problem here is ensuring that Aboriginal persons actually receive the rights to which they are entitled.

Language-related problems for Aboriginal persons that have been remarked upon to us include suggestions that: judges tend to deny requests for an interpreter if the accused can speak some English; interpreters are often not neutral, in the sense that they are familiar with the accused; interpreters are not adequately trained; many legal concepts have no equivalent words in Aboriginal languages;[75] and, even where assistance is available, it is not sought, nor is the need for it appreciated by counsel and other personnel.[76]

---

72. "Report of the Special Committee on Equity in Legal Education and Practices," *supra*, note 64 at 21, notes that "[t]here were also concerns expressed about the lack of sensitivity shown by law schools and the Law Society in course curricula." It was suggested to us that information about Aboriginal culture and history ought to be introduced into school curricula generally, a suggestion which seems sensible, although outside the terms of this Reference.

73. See a similar recommendation (Rec. 26) in the Marshall Inquiry, vol. 1, *supra*, note 14.

74. See *Société des Acadiens* v. *Association of Parents*, [1986] 1 S.C.R. 549.

75. A variety of problems in translating the fundamental word "guilty" have been reported, including translating the request for a plea as "Did you do it?" and "Are you being blamed?": see Marshall Inquiry, vol. 3, *supra*, note 18 at 47-48, *R.* v. *Koonungnak* (1963), 45 W.W.R. (N.S.) 282 (N.W.T. Terr. Ct), or Ross, *supra*, note 24 at 9-10.

76. On these problems generally, see *Justice on Trial*, *supra*, note 14 at 4-14 to 4-18; Marshall Inquiry, vol. 1, *supra*, note 14 at 171-73; Monture and Turpel, eds, *supra*, note 41 at 11-12; John Bayly, "Unilingual Aboriginal Jurors in a Euro-Canadian Criminal Justice System: Some Preliminary Views of the Northwest Territories Experience" in Commission on Folk Law and Legal Pluralism, *Proceedings of the VIth International Symposium, Ottawa, August 14-18, 1990*, vol. 1 (Ottawa: The Commission, 1990) at 305 (President: Harald W. Finkler).

Even Aboriginal persons with a command of English or French can be at a disadvantage. The Marshall Inquiry, for example, noted that Donald Marshall, Jr., appeared more comfortable when testifying in Mi'kmaq than in English, a language in which he is fluent.[77] Matters of nuance can make the difference between giving an inculpatory or exculpatory statement to the police, between being believed or disbelieved, between being convicted or acquitted and between receiving a harsh or lenient sentence.

Making adequate provision for those who speak other languages is a major way in which the justice system can show respect for Aboriginal persons: "It is little wonder that the First Nations find the legal system alien when the system does so little to foster an understanding of its processes, practices and procedures in the language of the majority of the residents."[78] Solutions proposed elsewhere, such as greater cross-cultural training and greater recruitment of Aboriginal persons as justice system personnel, could help alleviate these problems. However, specific recommendations regarding language are also required.

RECOMMENDATION

4. (1) The right of Aboriginal peoples to express themselves in their own Aboriginal languages in all court proceedings should be statutorily recognized. Qualified interpreters should be provided at public expense to all Aboriginal persons who need assistance in court proceedings.

The right to an interpreter under *Charter* section 14 is available only to a "party or witness" — that is, at the trial stage. There is an argument that a similar right exists at the investigative stage,[79] but the matter is not entirely clear. We suggest that legislation should provide that interpreters are required to be available during the pre-trial stage of a police-conducted investigation, including questioning, to any suspect who needs assistance. Any investigation carried out through an interpreter should ideally be recorded, so that no questions about the adequacy of translation could arise later.

In addition, the Cawsey Report heard complaints that accused persons had been required to pay for the cost of an interpreter. Such an order could "effectively undermine the right guaranteed by the *Charter*,"[80] and we expect that the order is unusual. Nonetheless, if there is any doubt on the issue, the *Criminal Code* and the *Canada Evidence Act* should provide that the costs of interpreter services rendered to accused persons at any stage of the criminal process must be borne by the state.

Further, the *Charter* does not specifically require that accused or witnesses be informed of their rights under section 14. However, persons who do not speak English or French are especially unlikely to be aware of the *Charter* right, while some accused, particularly

---

77. Marshall Inquiry, vol. 1, *supra*, note 14 at 171-72.

78. Osnaburgh/Windigo Report, *supra*, note 43 at 58-59.

79. See *Charter* s. 10(*a*) and (*b*), and *R. v. Evans* (18 April 1991), File No. 21375 (S.C.C.).

80. André Morel, "Certain Guarantees of Criminal Procedure" in Gérald-A. Beaudoin and Edward Ratushny, eds, *The Canadian Charter of Rights and Freedoms*, 2d ed. (Toronto: Carswell, 1989) 497 at 536 n. 177; see also *Justice on Trial, supra*, note 14.

those with some command of the language, may be reluctant to raise the issue. As well, the contact between the accused and the court — or even with defence counsel in some cases — may be too limited to reveal that the accused's command of the language is less than sufficient.

RECOMMENDATIONS

4. (2) Legislation should provide that interpreters be provided during the pre-trial stage of a police-conducted investigation, including questioning, to any suspect who needs assistance.

(3) The *Criminal Code* and the *Canada Evidence Act* should provide that the costs of interpreter services rendered to accused persons at any stage of the criminal process must be borne by the state.

(4) Notices should be prominently posted, in languages frequently used in the community, in each court house or preferably outside of each courtroom, explaining the section 14 *Charter* right to an interpreter. These notices should set out:

(a) the requirements for obtaining an interpreter;

(b) that an accused or witness who speaks some English or French may still be entitled to an interpreter; and

(c) that, if an interpreter is ordered, the accused or witness will not be required to pay for it.

(5) Duty counsel should be instructed to pay particular attention to the language abilities of Aboriginal accused.

If necessary, counsel should use interpreters to conduct their own interviews with the accused and make applications to the court for interpreters to assist the accused during proceedings. This may require that legal aid plans establish mechanisms for quickly providing interpreters to be present at interviews when needed, and for postponing the calling of cases until an interpreter-assisted interview has taken place.

RECOMMENDATION

4. (6) Unless advised by counsel that it is unnecessary, judges should satisfy themselves on first appearance that Aboriginal accused or witnesses speak and understand the language in which the proceedings are to be conducted.

The needs of the accused or witness on the issue of language should be noted in court documents so that once ordered, an interpreter will be present for subsequent appearances.

One should also consider the situation of members of the community who are neither accused nor witnesses but who are present in court. Court hearings are intended publicly to reinforce values and condemn misbehaviour, but members of Aboriginal communities "are often left in ignorance of what is transpiring since the proceedings are neither conducted nor translated in a language known to the majority of them."[81]

---

81. Osnaburgh/Windigo Report, *supra*, note 43 at 58.

RECOMMENDATION

4. (7) The need for, the feasibility and the cost of providing simultaneous translation services to members of the Aboriginal public attending court hearings on or near reserves should be examined.

The final problem relates to the qualifications of interpreters: the evidence suggests that the quality of translation is generally not high. The difficulty of translating some legal concepts into Aboriginal languages makes it important that interpreters have special training: in fact, interpreters "are often called upon, in an *ad hoc* fashion from those available in court, irrespective of their understanding of local dialects."[82] Our consultants tell us that anyone available, even persons related to the accused, may be asked to interpret, without having had any training. The need for more trained interpreters has also been noted elsewhere.[83]

Case law requires that interpreters should be competent and impartial,[84] but there is good reason to doubt that this standard is met routinely in cases involving Aboriginal persons.

RECOMMENDATION

4. (8) A system should be established to train independent, competent professional interpreters for criminal cases. As a general rule, only such interpreters should qualify to assist in criminal cases.

IV. Increasing Community Involvement with the Justice System

Understanding, respect and a sense of control can be engendered only if the Aboriginal community is involved at all key points of interaction with the system:

> Court officials must know what each community considers serious, how it should be dealt with, and the kind of sentence the community expects. Court officials do not act in a void: their acts, deliberations, and results affect not only the offender but the victims and communities as well. Judges and prosecutors must know the people and communities on whose behalf they are acting. They too must be accountable to the people.[85]

In most instances, the community will have the best understanding of its own problems and how those problems should be handled.

---

82. *Ibid.*

83. See Bayly, *supra*, note 76 at 305, reporting the lack of trained interpreters in the Northwest Territories.

84. *Unterreiner* v. *The Queen* (1980), 51 C.C.C. (2d) 373 (Ont. Co. Ct).

85. Gift Lake Council, Joint Submission to the Task Force on the Criminal Justice System and Its Impact on the Indian and Métis People of Alberta, quoted in *Justice on Trial, supra*, note 14 at 5-2.

Community involvement in the criminal justice system is crucial to effective reform. We see this participation as taking a variety of forms — advising on general policy, having greater input into particular cases, even serving as an alternative to the criminal justice system in some cases. The potential benefits include decreasing the number of Aboriginal accused persons, increasing the likelihood that decisions will have community support and decreasing the extent to which the community sees the court as imposing an alien system upon it. Of course, community involvement at any stage will only be possible when the community has the human resources to make a contribution and chooses to do so.

One way to gain community acceptance of the system is to facilitate the use of customary practices in resolving disputes.

RECOMMENDATION

5. (1) Consideration should be given to making "Peacemakers" a formal aspect of the justice system to mediate disputes.

The Peacemakers,[86] who function in a customary informal mediation process, draw their members from the family, Elders and elected community leaders. The Peacemaker role includes teaching and enforcing values and traditions, counselling, placing children in foster homes and resolving disputes.[87] The Dakota Ojibway Tribal Council has proposed using Peacemakers in a self-governing Native justice system to:

(a) determine whether they will deal with a particular situation or refer it to a Crown attorney;

(b) appoint persons within the community to deal with specific situations, offences or problems;

(c) appoint persons to exercise protective functions within the community to maintain social order;

(d) call for ceremonies, celebrations or other events to keep relationships within the community healthy; and

(e) settle disputes between persons or families, or provide assistance to persons experiencing problems. Peacemakers might also speak at community functions to remind members of their obligations, standards and values and to call for necessary discipline.[88]

---

86. "Peacemakers" should not be confused with the peacekeepers at Kahnawake, who act essentially as a police force.

87. *Reflecting Indian Concerns and Values in the Justice System: Joint Canada-Saskatchewan-FSIN Justice Studies of Certain Aspects of the Justice System as They Relate to Indians in Saskatchewan,* vol. 6 (1985) at 29 [unpublished].

88. Dakota Ojibway Tribal Council, *Submission to the Commission of Inquiry on the Administration of Justice for Aboriginal Peoples* (Paper presented at a public meeting in Brandon, Manitoba, April 27, 1989) at 8-9 [unpublished].

There is great scope, we believe, for involving the community in specific aspects of the current justice system. For example, formally incorporating Peacemakers into a recognized diversion program would move the system much closer to the conciliation and mediation traditions of Aboriginal communities and away from the adversarial methods of courts.[89]

RECOMMENDATION

5. (2) Permanent liaison mechanisms should be established between local Crown prosecutors and Aboriginal communities and leaders.

These meetings would provide an opportunity for Crown attorneys and community leaders to discuss criteria for laying charges, the suitability of cases for diversion, the adequacy of community resources and other criminal justice issues of concern to the community. Regular reports should be submitted to the Attorney General, the Deputy Attorney General and the concerned Aboriginal communities.

For example, section 518 of the *Code* sets out the evidence that may be heard at a bail hearing. In Australia, courts have taken traditional Aboriginal punishments into account in determining bail.[90] However, the *Code* contains no express procedure allowing a community to make submissions in this regard. We suggest that representatives of the accused's community should be allowed to give evidence, at bail hearings, of available alternatives to custody pending trial. One must, of course, ascertain accurately who speaks for the community, but we see no reason that a representative group should not be able to offer evidence.[91] By the same token, lay assessors (Elders or other respected members of the community) ought to be permitted by express statutory provision to sit with a judge to advise on appropriate sentences. They should be present during the trial or recitation of facts upon which a guilty plea is made. Their duties would include consulting those involved and recommending an appropriate disposition to the judge. Similar programs already exist[92] or are being created[93] in some communities. The advisers' recommendations may

---

89. See also: Brad Morse and Linda Lock, *Native Offenders' Perceptions of the Criminal Justice System* (Ottawa: Dept. of Justice, 1988); Australian Law Reform Commission, *The Recognition of Aboriginal Customary Laws: Summary Report*, Report No. 31 (Canberra: Australian Government Publishing Service, 1986); and Jackson, *supra*, note 18 at 242-55.

90. In *R. v. Jungarai* (1981), 9 N.T.R. 30 (N.T. Supreme Ct), an accused charged with murder was released on bail, on condition that he suffer a traditional form of corporal punishment. Part of the purpose served by this unusual order was to prevent the accused's family from being attacked by the members of the victim's family. For a brief summary of this case, see Jackson, *supra*, note 18 at 270-71.

91. We recognize that this proposal will not always benefit the accused personally, but it will benefit Aboriginal communities as a whole.

92. The South Island Tribal Council (B.C.) has such a program, as does the community on Christian Island (Ont.): see Hemmingson, *supra*, note 31 at 50 and Coyle, *supra*, note 20. Similar programs exist in Australia: see Australian Law Reform Commission, *supra*, note 89, para. 142 at 68.

93. The Ontario government has initiated Elders programs in two Northern Aboriginal communities, to participate in provincial court sentencing, to "provide paraprobationary services and be involved in the administration of traditional justice measures, counselling, legal education and cross-cultural training for non-Natives" ("Natives Get $200,000 to Study Justice System" *Law Times* (23-29 April 1990) 3).

differ from the range of sentences established by case law, or may be contrary to general court of appeal jurisprudence. We see no real difficulty in this: indeed, it is because such guidelines are on occasion inappropriate to Aboriginal communities that we make this recommendation.

We also suggest that a process of ongoing consultation between Aboriginal service providers and officials of the Correctional Service of Canada and the National Parole Board should be established. This consultation should occur with a body representative of Aboriginal groups generally rather than with individual communities. More frequent meetings would facilitate the exchange of information, more effective development and delivery of programming and greater uniformity and consistency in the application of correctional programs for Aboriginal offenders. In this regard, Aboriginal communities should be involved in the preparation of release plans for Aboriginal offenders and the supervision of those persons in their communities following release. Aboriginal communities have a stake in the release plans and supervision of offenders returned to their communities. The appropriateness of returning a particular offender to the community, or the adequacy of parole supervision and its impact on community resources, are questions that the communities concerned are best able to answer.

RECOMMENDATIONS

5. (3) Representatives of the accused's community should be allowed to give evidence, at bail hearings, of available alternatives to custody pending trial.

(4) Lay assessors (Elders or other respected members of the community) should be permitted by express statutory provision to sit with a judge to advise on appropriate sentences.

(5) A process of ongoing consultation between Aboriginal service providers and officials of the Correctional Service of Canada and the National Parole Board should be established.

(6) Aboriginal communities should be involved in the preparation of release plans for Aboriginal offenders and the supervision of those persons in their communities following release.

However, concerns regarding all of these proposals must be raised. Human resources are scarce. Ideally, Elders would fill the advisory and decision-making roles we propose, since their decisions are most likely to give legitimacy to the process. Yet in many communities, there will not be enough people available to fill these roles,[94] and in others, the community may simply not be interested in this type of involvement. Also, while we hope to give legitimacy to the present system by virtue of the involvement of Elders, it is possible that those Elders who become closely involved in this kind of process

---

94. We have been advised that even administering a fine option program can strain the resources of a community (see IBA, *supra*, note 24 at 48-49), and that the number of Elders available for friendship centres or to offer counselling in prisons is insufficient.

will be seen as having been co-opted, and will lose their own legitimacy. Having considered this, we nevertheless suggest that these options should be available to any Aboriginal community. Some communities may be unable to take advantage of them all, while others may reject them as counter-productive. Nonetheless, each community should have the option of greater involvement at every stage of the process.

V. Applying Customary Law and Practices

For many years, it was felt that Aboriginal persons should be assimilated rather than encouraged to retain their own culture. Owing to assimilation efforts, some knowledge of "traditional" ways has been lost or is in danger of being lost. Given the interest in more traditional ways in some communities, the need for information about the past has become important.

Customary law can be just as effective a mechanism of social control as statutory law:

> It is unfortunate that the term "custom" implies something that is somehow less or of lower degree than "law." There are connotations that a "custom" is somehow outside the "law" of government, which is powerful and binding. This is an ethnocentric view....[95]

Sentencing decisions might be affected by customary law. Courts have been inconsistent in reconciling Aboriginal custom with the criminal law. In *R. v. Fireman*,[96] for example, the Ontario Court of Appeal considered the appropriate sentence for an accused from an isolated Aboriginal community. The community at first ostracized Fireman but, by the end of the preliminary inquiry, it was once again prepared to accept him. The court of appeal concluded that it was not the length of the sentence but the fact of condemnation and the separation from his community that would deter this accused. Indeed, the court acknowledged that too long a sentence could interfere with the reintegration of Fireman into his community, which would diminish the effectiveness of deterrence.

In contrast, the Northwest Territories Court of Appeal in *R. v. Naqitarvik* gave very little emphasis to traditional Aboriginal methods of dealing with social problems. The court held that counselling received by the accused from the Inumarit Committee of Arctic Bay, a community on the northern coast of Baffin Island, was not from a "traditional governing and counselling body of early time ... [or] a remnant of ancient culture" but was "the usual ... counselling service"[97] that exists within the criminal justice system. Seemingly, Arctic Bay was not sufficiently linked to past customs and practices to justify a modification of ordinary sentencing practices: the presence of electricity, telephones and

---

95. Zion, *supra*, note 37 at 123-24.

96. (1971) 4 C.C.C. (2d) 82.

97. *R. v. Naqitarvik* (1986), 26 C.C.C. (3d) 193 at 196.

record players militated against the use of custom. *Naqitarvik* appears to demand that Aboriginal cultural institutions remain frozen in time, and that cultures and their customs cannot evolve.

We believe that modern practices can be reflections of traditional methods. Judges must be better sensitized to the customary practices of Aboriginal communities.

Information about Aboriginal customary law could affect many procedural decisions within the current criminal justice system. Such information might influence a trier of fact's decision about the behaviour of a "reasonable person," which would be relevant to many decisions about criminal intent, including questions of recklessness, criminal negligence and provocation. Aboriginal customary law might also affect various defences allowed under the *Criminal Code*,[98] such as whether one acted with legal justification or excuse (subsection 429(2)) under colour of right (section 322 and subsection 429(2)) or in obedience to *de facto* law (section 15). Before specific proposals can be made in this area, more information is necessary.[99]

RECOMMENDATION

6. The federal government should provide funding for research into Aboriginal customary law.[100]

VI. Asserting Treaty Rights in Criminal Courts

As the ability to control their own destiny has been removed from Aboriginal peoples, their societies have broken down. The introduction of our British-inspired justice system into Aboriginal communities undermined their traditional, informal methods of social control. But our justice system has been an unsuccessful substitute. As a result, over time many Aboriginal communities have been left largely without real methods of discouraging anti-social behaviour.[101]

The conflict between Aboriginal values and the values expressed in the present justice system does not, to any significant extent, relate to deciding what behaviour is objectionable. It has been suggested that "for the most part 'our' crimes are crimes to them as

---

98. The Australian Law Reform Commission, *supra*, note 89 at 43, has proposed legislating a partial customary law defence. Such a defence would not exonerate an accused but would, like the defence of provocation, reduce the level of liability.

99. Some work is being done — see, *e.g.*, E. Jane Dickson-Gilmore, "Resurrecting the Peace: Traditionalist Approaches to Separate Justice in the Kahnawake Mohawk Nation" in Commission on Folk Law and Legal Pluralism, *supra*, note 76 at 259.

100. Further to this recommendation, see our Rec. 15(2) to create an Aboriginal Justice Institute, below at 89. Moreover, although Aboriginal justice systems would not simply involve a readoption of methods used hundreds of years ago, information about customary law is necessary if Aboriginal justice systems are to be established.

101. This situation is often described as the product of colonization: see the discussion above in chap. 4 at 14 and below in chap. 6 at 67, under "VI. Sentencing."

well.''[102] Rather, the conflict arises in determining the appropriate response to objectionable behaviour.

That being said, one specific area of conflict is worth special consideration: the assertion of treaty rights in criminal courts. Some of our consultants expressed dissatisfaction that the criminal courts are the primary forum in which Aboriginal persons are called upon to assert their treaty rights. This procedure, they feel, is demeaning. Treaty rights define the relationship of Aboriginal persons to the rest of Canada. However, the primary circumstance in which these rights are given meaning is when they are raised in court as a defence to a criminal charge. The effect, Aboriginal people contend, is that they become ''contingent persons,'' having no rights save those declared by criminal courts. Further, there is the practical difficulty that such a defence may be raised by any Aboriginal individual, no matter how ill-prepared, thereby binding all others party to the same treaty. While others who litigate their rights must also do so in the criminal courts (for example, free expression may be determined in criminal cases involving obscenity), the Supreme Court of Canada offers support to the Aboriginal claim, noting that ''the trial for a violation of a penal prohibition may not be the most appropriate setting in which to determine the existence of an aboriginal right.''[103]

In our view, a criminal court is not necessarily the most appropriate forum for determining Aboriginal and treaty rights. Indeed, the courts generally are not the best setting for giving substance to treaty rights, which ought really to be determined through negotiation where possible, and through litigation only where necessary. This approach shows greater respect for Aboriginal sensitivities in this area.

RECOMMENDATION

7. Governments should develop clear and public policies concerning the preferred methods for determining Aboriginal and treaty rights. These policies should encourage identifying areas of conflict through discussion with Aboriginal communities, for the purpose of negotiating agreements about those issues with the affected parties. Where litigation is necessary, declaratory relief or court references should be preferred to the laying of charges, but if prosecutions are commenced, multiple proceedings should be vigorously discouraged and only a single test case pursued.[104]

---

102. Ross, *supra*, note 24 at 13. IBA, *supra*, note 24 at 41, notes that most Aboriginal concerns ''address questions relating to criminal justice processes rather than the substantive offences prescribed by the Criminal Code and related statutes.''

103. *R.* v. *Sparrow*, [1990] 1 S.C.R. 1075 at 1095.

104. This approach was adopted in Ontario and Quebec during the currency of the constitutional challenges to the *Criminal Code's* abortion provisions arising out of the prosecution of Dr. Henry Morgentaler.

Under this proposal, many issues now decided on a case-by-case basis could be determined on a broader scale. For example, although the *Indian Act* gives treaty rights priority over provincial laws,[105] Aboriginal persons are still sometimes convicted of provincial offences.[106] Negotiation could resolve important general issues far more readily, and save much needless litigation.

---

105. See *supra*, note 33, s. 88.

106. Various decisions have disagreed, *e.g.*, over whether an Aboriginal person using a night light to hunt is guilty of an offence (compare *Prince* v. *The Queen*, [1964] S.C.R. 81, and *Myran* v. *The Queen*, [1976] 2 S.C.R. 137) or whether it is an offence for Aboriginal persons to have loaded weapons in a vehicle (compare *R.* v. *Anderson and Beardy*, [1983] 2 C.N.L.R. 117 (Man. Cty. Ct) and *R.* v. *Polchies*, [1982] 4 C.N.L.R. 132 (N.B. Prov. Ct)).

CHAPTER SIX

Changing Roles and Reforming the Process

Highlights

The police must be more involved in and accountable to the communities they serve. This objective should be promoted through the use of community-based policing in Aboriginal communities that desire external police services. Also, the federal and provincial governments should facilitate autonomous Aboriginal police forces wherever local communities desire them.

Although police officers should retain the discretion to decide when to lay charges, they should routinely seek advice from Crown prosecutors, including advice about whether it is appropriate to lay charges at all. Prosecutors should be clearly instructed, by directives and through the training they receive, that they are to exercise their discretion independent of police influence or pressure and that their advice to the police must remain dispassionate and impartial.

Special interrogation rules governing the taking of statements from Aboriginal persons should be created, including rules concerning the presence of counsel during questioning.

Provincial bar associations and legal aid societies should make public legal education materials, especially information about how to obtain legal aid, readily available to Aboriginal persons.

Wherever possible and desired by the community, court sittings should be held in or near the Aboriginal community where the offence was committed.

Criminal procedures, such as those concerning swearing an oath, bail or requiring the attendance in court of Aboriginal persons, should be adapted in ways that are sensitive to Aboriginal needs, culture and traditions.

Alternatives to imprisonment should be used whenever possible. Such alternatives should be given first consideration at sentencing.

A list of factors should be enunciated which, in conjunction with other circumstances, would mitigate sentence where the offender is an Aboriginal person.

Incarceration for non-payment of fines should only occur upon a refusal or wilful default to pay a fine, not upon an inability to pay.

A review of the design and cultural relevancy of all programs that are used as part of diversion, probation or parole should be undertaken in co-operation with Aboriginal persons and organizations. There must be appropriate education of the judiciary, Crown prosecutors and defence counsel concerning the purposes and availability of these programs.

The criteria governing eligibility for probation should be formulated and probation reports should be prepared so as to have proper regard for cultural differences and to meet the needs of Aboriginal offenders and communities.

Aboriginal spirituality should, by legislation, be given the same recognition as other religions, and Aboriginal Elders should be given the same status and freedom as prison chaplains.

The National Parole Board and the Correctional Service of Canada should develop a national policy and guidelines concerning waiver of parole and review hearings. Information concerning waiver should be made available to correctional staff and inmates.

Smaller, local correctional facilities under community control should be created.

I.   The Police

The police are charged with enforcing the law. However, their actual responsibilities extend much further. The police are also a residual social service. "When [the police] are called, unless they can recommend a more appropriate agency, they are expected to respond. The police do not say, 'Sorry, that's not our job'."[107] This broad level of service accounts for the largely good reputation of the police with the general public.

Unfortunately, the same observation cannot be safely made about police relations with Aboriginal persons.[108] Although the situation must vary from community to community, the complaint is frequently made and was certainly heard by us during our consultations

---

107. Lloyd L. Weinreb, *Denial of Justice* (New York: Free Press, 1977) at 15. See also André Normandeau and Barry Leighton, *A Vision of the Future of Policing in Canada: Police-Challenge 2000*, Background Document (Ottawa: Solicitor General Canada, 1990) at 43 [hereinafter *Police-Challenge 2000*].

108. See Douglas Skoog, Lance W. Roberts and Edward D. Boldt, "Native Attitudes toward the Police" (1980) 22 Can. J. Crim. 354, where favourable White attitudes towards the police in Manitoba are contrasted with "ambivalent" Native attitudes.

that the police are only seen in Aboriginal communities when they come to make an arrest. In terms of mere reactive policing, Aboriginal communities may not be underserviced: indeed, one reasonable interpretation of the higher charge rate on reserves is that, in some respects, those communities are overpoliced. However, to the extent that Aboriginal communities do not receive the same type of service from the police as does the majority of society, Aboriginal persons do not enjoy equal access to the law and are not treated equitably and with respect.

Further, even with respect to the reactive enforcement function of the police, a large gap exists between the values and culture of members of the police force and of Aboriginal people. Suspicions arise based on simple misunderstanding owing to culture but, even worse, the cultural gap can engender intolerance and overt racism.

A.   Structural Changes Regarding Police Forces

RECOMMENDATION

8. (1) The police must be more involved in and accountable to the communities they serve.

This goal can be accomplished in two main ways: arrangements concerning existing police forces can be changed; alternatively, existing police forces can be replaced by Aboriginal police forces, directly answerable to, run by and created in consultation with the community.

B.   Community-based Policing

" 'Community' policing is the most appropriate response by policing to the challenges and problems of the next decade."[109] Although community-based policing is not a complete solution for Aboriginal communities, it is a step in the right direction.[110] It decreases the emphasis on reaction to complaints, seeking rather "a police-community partnership in dealing with crime and related problems."[111] Greater emphasis is given to identifying problems through consultation with the community and addressing their underlying causes. Accountability to the community is created through both informal public consultation and legal means such as review bodies. This approach allows for Aboriginal community priorities to be more accurately determined.

---

109. *Police-Challenge 2000, supra*, note 107 at 41.

110. *Policing in Relation to the Blood Tribe: Report of a Public Inquiry, Commissioner's Report: Findings and Recommendations*, vol. 1 (Edmonton: Alberta Solicitor General, February 1991) (Commissioner: C. H. Rolf) at 189 [hereinafter *Policing in Relation to the Blood Tribe*], where community policing is endorsed as "appropriate to meet the cultural needs of the Bloods."

111. *Police-Challenge 2000, supra*, note 107 at 43.

At present, assessments of detachment needs, and ultimately budget allowances, are based on statistics that reflect reactive policing of crime.[112] Equally, the established criteria for measuring the performance of individual officers emphasize the reactive model of policing. Community-based policing, however, entails new evaluative techniques, including new criteria by which to evaluate an officer's performance.[113]

RECOMMENDATION

8. (2) Community-based policing should be facilitated to the fullest extent in Aboriginal communities that wish to continue to have external police services.[114]

Increased community involvement by police, and greater advice by the community concerning the behaviour of the police, should decrease the perception that the police are mere outsiders enforcing an externally imposed law.

However, advising on priorities and having some role in review of behaviour do not amount to control. Also, community-based policing will sometimes be difficult to implement, especially in isolated Aboriginal communities.[115] Certain communities may wish to establish autonomous, rather than external, community-based police forces. Clearly, approaches other than community-based policing are thought necessary by at least some Aboriginal communities.[116]

C.   Aboriginal Police Forces

At present, policing on reserves is governed by a wide variety of arrangements.[117] Although one might initially think it desirable to bring about greater uniformity in police

---

112. *Justice on Trial, supra*, note 14 at 2-17. This creates a dilemma: less reactive policing means a smaller complement, making community involvement more difficult. As less time is spent on community involvement, more is spent on reactive policing, leading to an increase in the complement, and commencement of the cycle again. See also *Policing in Relation to the Blood Tribe, supra*, note 110 at 151.

113. See *Police-Challenge 2000, supra*, note 107 at 48.

114. According to Solicitor General Canada, *1988-1989 Annual Report* (Ottawa: Solicitor General Canada, 1989) at 25, community-based policing has been successfully introduced on eight of a possible 355 reserves with additional detachments planned.

115. According to the Department of Indian Affairs and Northern Development, *Indian Policing Policy Review: Task Force Report* (Ottawa: DIAND, 1990) at 4 [hereinafter *Indian Policing Policy Review*], there are 599 Indian bands, of which approximately 135 are in remote or isolated areas.

116. See also the discussion in Manitoba Métis Federation, *supra*, note 70 at 27-33.

117. *Indian Policing Policy Review, supra*, note 115, describes 12 different Aboriginal-specific policing programs. At least 14 funding arrangements exist, in which funding is provided either exclusively by federal, provincial and tribal governments, or shared between them: Head, *supra*, note 63 at 150. Most reserves are served by the RCMP (for detailed descriptions of these programs see Head, *supra*, note 63 or *Indian Policing Policy Review, supra*, note 115). Some have autonomous police forces, with constables generally deriving their authority from provincial Police Acts, and often reporting to police commissions with federal and provincial, as well as tribal, representatives. One exceptional arrangement is the Kahnawake peacekeepers, who are not appointed as peace officers under any federal or provincial Act, and report to a police committee appointed by the tribal council.

services, in these circumstances we see no problem with diversity *per se*. Different communities have different requirements, aspirations and needs.

RECOMMENDATION

8. (3) The federal and provincial governments should facilitate autonomous Aboriginal police forces wherever local communities desire them. No single structure or role for that police force should be demanded. If the force is to be autonomous, then its structure and its role must be determined by the community.

Many possible structures could fall within the scope of this recommendation, including agencies parallel to those currently available, but with community control. However, the functions an Aboriginal community will wish to see the police perform are not necessarily the same as those in other communities.[118] The most appropriate response to social problems on a reserve, and the response most in keeping with traditional Aboriginal justice systems, may not be a body operating as what we think of as a police force, but something that performs a much broader social service function — counselling, advising, conciliating and resolving disputes. Although there are no legal impediments preventing any community from proceeding to establish such an agency immediately, there are practical ones, especially financial obstacles. Governments should bear in mind that these agencies can, to some extent, serve as an alternative to policing services.

RECOMMENDATION

8. (4) Funding for autonomous police services should not be limited to programs that are directly analogous to existing agencies.

D. Overcharging

As we noted previously, Aboriginal communities, whether remote or urban, are often the subject of intense police scrutiny. One result can be the laying of unjustified charges or too many charges where merely the formal requirements for a charge exist. Discretion, in such cases, is poorly exercised or not exercised at all. This condition is sometimes termed overcharging.

RECOMMENDATION

8. (5) Although police officers should retain the discretion to decide when to lay charges, they should routinely seek advice from Crown prosecutors, including advice as to whether it is appropriate to lay charges at all.[119]

---

118. Robert Depew, *Native Policing in Canada: A Review of Current Issues*, Working Paper No. 1986-46 (Ottawa: Solicitor General Canada, 1986) at 125.

119. See Law Reform Commission of Canada [hereinafter LRC], *Controlling Criminal Prosecutions: The Attorney General and the Crown Prosecutor*, Working Paper 62 (Ottawa: The Commission, 1990) Rec. 19 at 73.

Such supervision, where properly practised, would provide a valuable second look and should have salutary effects on the exercise of official discretion.

To supplement this proposal, we recommended at page 36 that Crown prosecutors should seek general policy advice from Aboriginal communities about charging policy. In addition, we proposed at pages 35 and 36 that Peacemakers, Elders or other community members should be consulted concerning the diversion of some offenders away from the criminal justice system. The combined effect of these recommendations, we believe, will be to offset in some measure any tendency to overcharge Aboriginal persons.

E. Appearance Notices

Aboriginal persons, particularly in remote areas, often do not understand the significance of the appearance notice given to them by an arresting officer securing their release. They may not understand that they are required to appear in court, or appreciate the consequences of failing to do so. This problem is compounded by the appearance dates themselves, which are set in a routine manner and may conflict with times when Aboriginal persons must be hunting or trapping in order to support themselves. The resulting non-appearances simply multiply the problems faced by Aboriginal persons, who then find additional charges laid against them.

This situation is not unique to Aboriginal persons, but their needs and difficulties are especially troublesome. Provided there is some good reason, police or prosecutors are able to postpone initial court appearances to a more convenient time: no one benefits from wasted court time or the issuance of unnecessary arrest warrants. However, postponement will only be granted on request. Aboriginal persons, especially those in remote communities who have difficulty gaining access to counsel, are not likely to make that request.

To alleviate the problem of non-appearance, therefore, and to place Aboriginal persons in effectively the same position as everyone else, we suggest the following.

RECOMMENDATIONS

8. (6) The police should take special care, when presenting an Aboriginal person with an appearance notice, to confirm that that person understands the significance of failing to appear in court and is clearly made aware of the appearance date; in particular, the officer should inquire whether there is any reason the person will be unavailable and make reasonable accommodations concerning the date. Instruction manuals and training courses should be altered so as to give effect to this recommendation. It should be emphasized, however, that no accused should be unnecessarily detained simply to comply with this recommendation.

(7) Police forces should be encouraged to use forms translated into the language of the relevant community where possible and where the nature and extent of police contact with the community justifies the practice.

II.   Prosecutors

A.   The Attorney General and the Crown Prosecutor

The Attorney General is the Minister responsible for the proper administration of criminal justice. The Attorney General (both informally and through guidelines and directives) establishes the general tenor of the relationship between the Crown Prosecution Service and Aboriginal communities. The Service, over which the Attorney General has general direction and control, is personified in the office of the local Crown prosecutor.[120]

The prosecutor acts as the agent of the Attorney General and, for all practical purposes, exercises nearly all of the Attorney General's enormous discretionary prosecutorial powers. The Crown prosecutor occupies a unique position in our legal tradition. The prosecutor's role, sometimes characterized as "quasi-judicial," "excludes any notion of winning or losing; his function is a matter of public duty than which in civil life there can be none charged with greater personal responsibility."[121] In Canada, the prosecutor is distinct from and independent of the police. This separation is crucial and must be zealously guarded against encroachment lest the utility of the office be compromised and its importance undermined.[122]

Elsewhere in this Report we discuss issues intimately bearing on the prosecutor's role and responsibilities. We have advocated increased community liaison between the Crown Prosecution Service and Aboriginal communities. Also, we have noted the need for more Aboriginal prosecutors as well as for cross-cultural training and sensitization of Crown attorneys. We will explain that a more open process for the exercise of important discretionary powers in areas such as plea bargaining is necessary to modify the unfortunate legacy of distrust and misunderstanding. Other important prosecutorial issues remain to which we now turn.

---

120. The classic work in this field remains John Ll. J. Edwards, *The Law Officers of the Crown* (London: Sweet & Maxwell, 1964). See also LRC, Working Paper 62, *supra*, note 119.

121. *Boucher* v. *The Queen*, [1955] S.C.R. 16 at 24, Rand J.

122. Unfortunately, one judge has concluded that such compromise occurs in the Canadian North: "Surprisingly, [federal Crown attorneys in the Yukon and Northwest Territories] appear to be reluctant to exercise any significant prosecutorial discretion, as evidenced by the aggressive prosecution of relatively minor charges and the reluctance to withdraw or stay charges during a proceeding where it is apparent that the main Crown witness simply has not produced the evidence anticipated. . . . [I]t is likely that as career Crowns, they are less willing to over-rule or disagree with the police . . . [for reasons of] promotion and advancement. In the result, Crown prosecutors may be more amenable to taking directions from the police, and to exercising prosecutorial discretion in only rare instances, in the clearest of cases." Heino Lilles, "Some Problems in the Administration of Justice in Remote and Isolated Communities" (1990) 15 Queen's L.J. 327 at 340.

B. Police Prosecutors

Because remote communities are underserviced, public functions often collapse and settle on a single individual (for example, a mayor may also be a justice of the peace). Sometimes this practical compromise is not harmonious and the results, where the justice system is implicated, may be unfortunate. This happens when peace officers serve as prosecutors in supposedly minor cases.[123] While the practice has been upheld as constitutional,[124] in cases prosecuted by the police the professional detachment and impartiality of a true public prosecutor is absent and the appearance of justice suffers. We therefore repeat the recommendation made in our Working Paper 62, *Controlling Criminal Prosecutions*, that all criminal prosecutions should be conducted by a lawyer responsible to and under the supervision of the Attorney General.[125] With regard to the particular circumstances of Aboriginal people, we further propose that no person other than a lawyer responsible to and under the supervision of the Attorney General should be entitled to conduct prosecutions of hunting, trapping and fishing offences.

RECOMMENDATIONS

9. (1) All public criminal prosecutions should be conducted by a lawyer responsible to and under the supervision of the Attorney General.

(2) No person other than a lawyer responsible to and under the supervision of the Attorney General should be entitled to conduct prosecutions of hunting, trapping and fishing offences.

C. Prosecutorial Discretion

The Crown has enormous discretionary power in deciding whether to pursue or halt a prosecution once charges have been laid. In some jurisdictions, these decisions are made in the absence of clearly stated and publicly accessible criteria. We believe it important to maintaining confidence in the administration of justice that those factors that should be taken into consideration in exercising this discretion are known to the public at large. Much of Aboriginal criminality involves the laying and prosecution of relatively minor (and often alcohol-related) charges. In many individual cases the prosecutions can be justified, but equally clearly, in many others discretion could be better exercised.

As we have noted elsewhere: "The decision to prosecute is a discretionary one lying at the heart of the system."[126] There is a pressing need, we believe, for explicit and publicly known guidelines for the exercise of the prosecutor's discretion.

---

123. As we note elsewhere, no case can be regarded as truly minor for Aboriginal persons since incarceration as a result of fine default is a recurrent reality.

124. See *Re R. and Hart* (1986), 26 C.C.C. (3d) 438 (Nfld C.A.) and *R. v. White* (1988), 41 C.C.C. (3d) 236 (Nfld C.A.).

125. *Supra*, note 119, Rec. 15 at 62.

126. *Ibid.* at 80.

RECOMMENDATIONS

9. (3) Prosecutors should be clearly instructed, by directive and through training, that they are to exercise their discretion independent of police influence or pressure and that their advice to the police must remain dispassionate and impartial.

(4) A clearly stated policy should be published and implemented concerning the public interest factors that should and should not be taken into consideration in decisions on whether to commence or stop a prosecution.[127]

With respect to the prosecution of alleged offences occurring in Aboriginal communities or involving Aboriginal offenders, the following factors merit consideration in decisions about whether to initiate or terminate proceedings:

(a) the likely effect of a prosecution on peace, harmony and security within Aboriginal communities;

(b) the availability or efficacy of any alternatives to prosecution (including traditional Aboriginal alternatives) in the light of the purposes of the criminal sanction;

(c) the views and concerns of affected Aboriginal communities, as well as their ability to effect reconciliation or otherwise address criminal justice problems, whether by traditional means or means other than a prosecution;

(d) whether the consequences of any resulting conviction would be inordinately harsh or oppressive;

(e) the necessity of maintaining the confidence of Aboriginal communities in legislature, courts and the administration of justice;

(f) the prevalence of the alleged offence and any related need for deterrence within Aboriginal communities; and

(g) the relevance of Aboriginal treaty rights such as hunting and fishing.

---

127. In *ibid.*, Rec. 23 at 79, we have noted that the factors should include: whether the public prosecutor believes there is evidence whereby a reasonable jury, properly instructed, could convict a suspect and, if so, whether the prosecution would have a reasonable chance of resulting in a conviction; whether considerations of public policy make a prosecution desirable despite a low likelihood of conviction; whether considerations of humanity or public policy stand in the way of proceeding despite a reasonable chance of conviction; and whether the resources exist to justify bringing a charge.

D. Disclosure

The Crown prosecutor plays a crucial role in ensuring that the criminal justice system operates in a scrupulously fair and just manner. The prosecutor's responsibility for ensuring the fairness of an accused person's trial is reflected in the Crown's obligation to disclose fully its case to the accused. The Donald Marshall, Jr., case stands as a sad reminder of the tragic consequences of a "critical failure of the Crown to disclose its case."[128]

An accused's right to make full answer and defence is clearly dependent on having complete and timely disclosure of the Crown's case. The continuation of a system that appears to be largely dependent on the *ad hoc* vagaries of local and regional practices obviously impairs the system's ability to provide equal access to justice and equitable treatment.

RECOMMENDATION

9. (5) The *Criminal Code* should be amended to provide for a statutory duty of complete and timely disclosure in all prosecutions.[129]

E. Charge Screening

The practice of plea bargaining and the particular problems for Aboriginal peoples which are associated with that practice are discussed elsewhere in this Report. A potential danger inherent in the plea-bargaining process resides in the police practice of overcharging. Faced with an array of charges, an unsophisticated accused may accept an essentially bad bargain rather than risk the potential jeopardy of a trial. Early post-charge screening and the close scrutiny of multiple charges by prosecutors could greatly modify this practice.

RECOMMENDATION

9. (6) Federal and provincial attorneys general should adopt a policy of early post-charge screening of charges by Crown prosecutors.

III. Defence Counsel

Aboriginal persons face unique difficulties in the criminal justice system: cultural misunderstanding may lead a police officer or a prosecutor to lay or continue charges; conditions of bail that are otherwise routine may be unusually arduous for an Aboriginal accused; an Aboriginal person may have unusual difficulties in understanding the trial process; legal defences unique to an Aboriginal accused may be appropriate; an understanding of Aboriginal culture may be necessary for the trier of fact to assess credibility; a sentence may

---

128. Marshall Inquiry, vol. 1, *supra*, note 14 at 238.

129. See LRC, *Disclosure by the Prosecution*, Report 22 (Ottawa: Supply and Services Canada, 1984).

have unusually harsh effects on an Aboriginal accused. In each of these cases, sensitivity on the part of police, prosecutors, judges, juries and probation officers is required, and a failure by any one group can have unintended adverse consequences. In all of these situations, defence counsel can do much to compensate for the shortcomings.

An Aboriginal accused person's lawyer, owing to the protective nature of counsel's role, is the one most intimately engaged in ensuring that his or her client is treated not only equally, but in an equitable manner and with respect. Lawyers acting on behalf of Aboriginal persons must therefore be aware of Aboriginal justice issues and able to raise them in a meaningful way.

A.   Access to Counsel

In principle, Aboriginal persons may obtain a lawyer in the same way as any other accused: those unable to afford counsel may seek legal aid. In practice, there seem to be obstacles. Aboriginal persons in isolated communities may have no lawyer nearby. Even when a community is not isolated, access to legal aid can be difficult. In particular, lack of awareness may lead to less use of legal aid by Aboriginal persons, particularly young offenders.[130]

While some legal aid offices produce pamphlets in Aboriginal languages to make Aboriginal persons more aware of available services, deficiencies in the availability and accessibility of such information have been noted.[131] To underscore the importance of ensuring that awareness, we recommend the following.

RECOMMENDATION

10. (1) Provincial bar associations and legal aid societies should make public legal education materials — in particular, information about how to obtain legal aid — readily available to Aboriginal persons. Where necessary, video technology should be used or materials should be produced in Aboriginal languages.

---

130. This possibility may help explain the finding in a 1985 study in Labrador that although young offenders were informed at the time of arrest of their right to counsel "more often than not, a guilty plea is entered before access to counsel." The Report called for public education on the *Young Offenders Act, supra,* note 49: RES Policy Research Inc., *Needs of Native Young Offenders in Labrador in View of the Young Offenders Act: Final Report* (Ottawa: Dept. of Justice, 1985) at 43-44.

131. The Marshall Inquiry, vol. 1, *supra,* note 14 at 158, noted that Aboriginal persons "have little access to information about the law," and recommended that public legal education materials and services specifically aimed at Aboriginal and Black communities should be provided: see Rec. 16 at 158. See also Alberta, *The Report of the Task Force on Legal Aid* (Edmonton: The Task Force, 1989) and *Justice on Trial, supra,* note 14 at 3-4, to the same effect.

In addition, Aboriginal persons can face inequities in legal aid eligibility guidelines. Hunting and fishing offences are often not covered by legal aid.[132] Similarly, in the Yukon Territory, an accused person will only be provided with a lawyer when facing imprisonment as a sentence. This rule, although applied equally to all, has an unequal and inequitable effect on Aboriginal persons since a high percentage of Aboriginal persons are imprisoned for default on fines resulting from minor infractions not covered by legal aid.[133]

RECOMMENDATION

10. (2) Legal aid eligibility guidelines should be reviewed to ensure that they do not have an unequal impact on Aboriginal persons. The governments concerned should ensure that funding is available to provide necessary legal services to all Aboriginal persons who require assistance.

We have also heard complaints from Aboriginal persons about the quality of legal services they receive, whether from private or legal-aid-funded counsel:[134] that counsel are unfamiliar with Aboriginal issues or culture, take (or fail to take) matters to trial improperly, spend too little time with clients and do not explain things clearly enough. These problems would be remedied to some extent by recommendations made elsewhere about cross-cultural training, but clearly more than that is needed. Whether more steps should be taken through provincial bar associations or legal aid societies, or perhaps through the creation of national standards for providing legal aid, is a matter that we suggest requires further research.

B.   Interrogation and the Role of Counsel

Specific problems have been noted for Aboriginal persons at the police interrogation stage. *Justice on Trial* remarked that some Aboriginal persons are especially deferential to authority, which causes them not only to answer any questions posed, but also to offer the answer they believe the questioner wants to hear.[135] The prejudice this could cause is obvious, particularly when coupled with the reluctance Aboriginal persons feel to criticize someone else in his or her presence.[136] There is good ground to question whether such statements would be reliable, although under the current law they seem to be considered voluntary and hence admissible.

---

132. IBA, *supra*, note 24 at 44.

133. *Justice on Trial*, *supra*, note 14 at 3-16, notes a similar problem in Alberta.

134. See also *ibid.*, chap. 3.

135. The Australian Law Reform Commission, *supra*, note 89, has made a similar observation.

136. A tendency also noted in Ross, *supra*, note 21.

In Australia, rules governing the admissibility of statements from Aborigines have been created by the courts, primarily in the case of *R. v. Anunga*.[137] Consistent with this, the Australian Law Reform Commission has recommended that "[t]here should be a requirement that a 'prisoner's friend' be present in cases where an Aboriginal suspect is in custody or (though not in custody) is being questioned in respect of a serious offence"[138] and that any statement obtained in breach of the rules should be deemed inadmissible, unless certain conditions are met.[139]

We believe that a similar approach is called for in Canada.

RECOMMENDATION

10. (3) Special interrogation rules governing the taking of statements from Aboriginal persons should be created, including rules concerning the presence of counsel or some other person during questioning.

Rules such as those contained in the *Young Offenders Act*[140] or the Australian rules[141] are appropriate models for consideration. Such rules may be appropriate for other disadvantaged groups as well.

Important details need to be worked out before this proposal can be implemented. Acting as a "prisoner's friend," to explain rights during interrogation, may be a duty which could be assigned to Aboriginal courtworkers. However, a courtworker's effectiveness might be jeopardized by too great an involvement in police investigations. Further, because the police may not always be aware that they are interrogating an Aboriginal person, questions of when to apply the rules arise. Questions also arise regarding the nature of the rules themselves — whether legislation or guidelines — and the consequences flowing from any breach of the rules.

IV. The Courts

Most Canadians find the arcane procedures and formal setting of the criminal court intimidating and confusing. It is no wonder, then, that the process is foreign and frightening to many Aboriginal persons. Courts are almost invariably located outside, often far distant from, Aboriginal communities. The judges, prosecutors, defence lawyers and court staff are almost all non-Aboriginal. In many remote areas the court is on circuit and flies

---

137. (1976) 11 A.L.R. 412 (N.T.S.C.), described in *Justice on Trial, supra*, note 14 at 2-57.

138. *Supra*, note 89, para. 115 at 56.

139. Including that "the answers were not given merely out of the suspect's suggestibility or deference to authority": *ibid.* at 57. The *Anunga* rules stress that questions should be formulated to avoid suggesting in any way the expected answer.

140. See, *e.g.*, ss 11 and 56, *supra*, note 49, which confer enhanced rights to counsel and to explanations as to the significance of proceedings and the importance of counsel.

141. See *Anunga, supra*, note 137, and the discussion in *Justice on Trial, supra*, note 14 at 2-56 to 2-59.

into Aboriginal communities. The judge, prosecutor and defence lawyer often arrive on the same plane, contributing to the belief that all of those officials are on the same side and have already decided the outcome of upcoming cases, and that the criminal court process is designed solely for the convenience of judges and lawyers. To give expression to the principles of equal access to justice and respectful and equitable treatment, we must make the system more accessible to Aboriginal persons.

A.   The Courtroom Atmosphere

Most accused probably find courtrooms intimidating; in a certain sense, that is part of the purpose of a criminal hearing — to impress the accused with the seriousness of the situation. Since Aboriginal persons view the system itself as alien, the effect increases:

> Many Aboriginal people find these rooms frightening and intimidating, with an atmosphere made worse by the Judge looking down on them from a raised platform. They would like to see some articles representative of their culture displayed in the courtrooms that they are required to attend, and have the rooms arranged in a more culturally sensitive manner.[142]

If courtrooms were less intimidating to and more respectful of Aboriginal culture and sensitivities, we believe that they would be better able to command the respect of Aboriginal persons.

RECOMMENDATION

11. (1) Courtrooms serving Aboriginal communities should be physically set up in a way that is sensitive to Aboriginal culture and tradition.

B.   Aboriginal Justices of the Peace

The process might also be made less intimidating by the appointment of more Aboriginal justices of the peace to preside in Aboriginal communities.[143] Justices of the peace play a "crucial role"[144] for Aboriginal communities, dealing with arrest warrants, bail and trials for minor offences. However, justices of the peace are generally appointed provincially, although a little-used federal appointment power, limited to a few minor *Code* offences, is found in section 107 of the *Indian Act*. We see little value in the federal limitation.

---

142. *Justice on Trial, supra*, note 14 at 4-46.

143. Note Rec. 3(1)(c), above at 29, our proposal to appoint Aboriginal persons to *all* levels of the judiciary.

144. Ontario Native Council on Justice, *The Native Justice of the Peace: An Under-employed Natural Resource for the Criminal Justice System* (Toronto: The Council, 1982) at 10.

RECOMMENDATION

11. (2) Federal legislation should give federally appointed justices of the peace jurisdiction to deal with all matters conferred on justices of the peace under both the *Criminal Code* and the *Indian Act*. Greater use should be made of this federal appointment power so as to appoint more Aboriginal justices of the peace.

C.   Swearing an Oath

At present, witnesses usually testify in criminal trials after swearing on oath on the Bible to tell the truth. Aboriginal persons would prefer to swear an oath in a way that reflects their own culture.[145] Placing their faiths on the same footing as those of Judeo-Christian Canadians gives both tangible and symbolic expression to the principle of treating Aboriginal persons with respect.

RECOMMENDATION

11. (3) The right of Aboriginal persons to swear an oath in a traditional way when giving evidence in court should be recognized.

D.   The Location of Court Sittings

The criminal process often requires numerous courtroom appearances to take pleas, hear bail applications and hold trials. The physical isolation of many communities presents Aboriginal persons with problems not experienced by most Canadians, who have relatively easy access to courts. Many isolated communities face enormous transportation problems, including a complete lack of transportation, exorbitant cost and harsh weather and road conditions. This physical inaccessibility of courts and the need to hunt and trap in order to subsist often give rise to "failure to appear" charges and, indeed, even to unwarranted guilty pleas.[146] Also, Aboriginal persons from remote communities are sometimes arrested and then released on bail into non-Aboriginal communities, with no means to return home.[147]

Several solutions could help alleviate these problems.

---

145. *Justice on Trial, supra,* note 14 at 4-46. Note also the litigation surrounding Aboriginal oath taking in trials of charges arising out of the Oka incident.

146. See, *e.g.*, the submission of the Métis Association of Alberta to the Cawsey Task Force in *Justice on Trial, supra,* note 14 at 4-26.

147. See the Osnaburgh/Windigo Report, *supra,* note 43 at 58.

RECOMMENDATION

11. (4) Court dates for Aboriginal accused persons should be scheduled to avoid, where possible, hunting and trapping seasons. Chief justices of the affected courts should develop scheduling policies in conjunction with and on the advice of community representatives.

To provide such flexibility is merely to extend to Aboriginal persons the same treatment given others, who could more readily arrange a postponement of awkward court dates. Also, the court process could be streamlined to eliminate unnecessary appearances. Many routine court appearances do not really require the physical presence of the accused. To this end, greater use of modern telecommunications systems should be explored; even bail applications might be handled electronically.

RECOMMENDATION

11. (5) Statutory authority should allow for appearances to be made through electronic means.

We suggest, however, that these alternative means should only be used after a policy has been developed by chief justices involving, among other things, the consent of an accused.

Further, transportation problems should be addressed directly.

RECOMMENDATIONS

11. (6) An accused who is released by a court some distance from the place where the arrest was made should, in the discretion of the court, be returned home or to such other place as is reasonably designated by the accused. The *Criminal Code* should contain a statutory direction requiring the judge to inquire into this issue. The cost of transportation should be borne by the state.

(7) The *Code* should provide that a detainee who is released "unconditionally" (that is, without charges being laid) should automatically be returned to the place of arrest or to such other place as is reasonably designated by the detainee.[148]

---

148. A similar recommendation is made by the New South Wales Law Reform Commission, *Police Powers of Arrest and Detention*, Discussion Paper 16 (Sydney: The Commission, 1987) Proposal 50 at 130.

(8) Where court hearings are not held in or near an Aboriginal community, accused persons and witnesses under subpoena should be provided with transportation to and from court hearings or sufficient conduct money to cover the cost of transportation.[149]

Also important is the location at which courts will be held. The Cawsey Task Force concluded that the reasonable solution is to take the court to the people. Aboriginal communities should have greater access to court services than is now generally the case, although we do not suggest imposing this solution against the wishes of the people.[150]

RECOMMENDATION

11. (9) Wherever possible and desired by the community, the court sitting should occur in or near the Aboriginal community in which the offence was committed.

This does not mean that we favour the idea of itinerant courts. On the whole, we prefer to see these mobile courts eliminated where possible. However, we recognize that, in some cases, court sittings in Aboriginal communities are only possible through the unfortunate device of fly-in courts. Where they are retained, improvements to these itinerant courts are needed.[151]

---

149. Some administrative details need to be worked out — one might not want the accused and the Crown witnesses travelling together, for example. Some jurisdictions are grappling with these difficulties, though not effectively. The Osnaburgh/Windigo Report, *supra*, note 43 at 55, states:

> Because of the distance to court, the Ontario Provincial Police send a bus to the reserve. However, we were told, that only accused who are on a list provided to the driver are entitled to travel on the bus, even if they have documents showing that they have a case in court that day. No witnesses are allowed on the bus and, accordingly, unless special arrangements are made, they have to fend for themselves. We were told that numerous cases are withdrawn or dismissed because of the non-appearance of witnesses.

150. In *ibid.* it is noted, at 55, that "the Osnaburgh community does not desire the presence, on its territory, of a court which dispenses a law which they perceive to be irrelevant to their needs, operating in a language which many of its members do not understand and using procedures which are, to them, incomprehensible."

151. Note the remarks of Judge Coutu, Co-ordinating Judge for the Itinerant Court of the District of Abitibi, in the Marshall Inquiry, vol. 7, *supra*, note 22 at 25:

> Generally speaking, the Native population is not satisfied with the way we are administering justice in their community, and more and more I am not; and the judges are not satisfied with the work they are doing in the north because they feel there is no consequence to the work they are doing.

. . . Judges, lawyers, and courtworkers rush in and out of the communities on circuit, always conscious of their drive or flight back to their home bases. As a consequence, people are rushed through the process or their cases are continually delayed for reasons that are only apparent to the court parties who visit them. Weather conditions are often the cause of a postponement of proceedings. In some communities, this means that monthly sittings become bi-monthly sittings as the missed date is not generally re-scheduled. Dockets build up, which simply results in more delays. Meanwhile, the Aboriginal concept of healing and forgiveness has already been applied and makes the delayed court appearance redundant.[152]

Establishing legal service centres in all major Northern communities[153] addresses part of the problem, but is of no real help to isolated communities. To treat Aboriginal persons in remote communities equally, we would need to simulate the situation that exists in communities that have regular access to counsel and courts. Defence counsel should be available not merely a day or two in advance of a hearing, but at regular intervals; witnesses should be consulted while their evidence is still fresh. This goal might be accomplished by having lawyers (for both the defence and the Crown) or paralegals travel regularly within the area. The public interest requires that all parties be adequately prepared. In addition, to avoid rushed schedules at the actual hearings, it would presumably be necessary to appoint more judges. Greater resources would also be required to deal with the problems of hearing dates cancelled owing to bad weather.

RECOMMENDATION

11. (10) Because fly-in courts do not provide remote communities with legal services equal to those available elsewhere, they should be phased out where possible. Where fly-in courts are used, steps should be taken to guarantee that

(a) defence counsel is available to all accused persons on a date meaningfully in advance of the court hearing;

(b) Crown prosecutors consult with the affected communities enough in advance of court hearings to ensure that the public interest is protected; and

(c) sufficient resources, including additional judicial appointments, if necessary, are provided to ensure that court hearings need not be rushed and can be held within a reasonable time after the offence.

---

152. *Justice on Trial*, *supra*, note 14 at 4-19 to 4-20. Our consultants suggested that plea bargains are reached on the aircraft, before counsel has consulted with any clients; that the time available for consultation and preparation is unrealistically brief, with inevitable results for the quality of the defence; and that the arrival of the judge and the lawyers together would be grounds for challenging the fairness of the trial anywhere else, but in the North it is routine. In some areas, Crown and defence lawyers have begun to arrive a day earlier than the judge, in order to consult with the parties: Osnaburgh/Windigo Report, *supra*, note 43 at 56-57. This step is an improvement, although it will not ensure that adequate preparation time is provided, nor will it necessarily diminish concerns about plea bargains.

153. As proposed in *Native Peoples and Justice*, *supra*, note 67 at 31.

V. Bail

"Bail" refers to the power to release or detain an arrested person pending trial. What little empirical evidence there is suggests that Aboriginal persons do not fare well under our present bail laws. Some projections indicate that twice as many Aboriginal persons are detained without bail as are other arrested persons.[154] In the ensuing discussion, we propose changes to eliminate some of the inequities in this situation.

A. The Police Power to Release Persons after Arrest

Section 499 of the *Code* permits a peace officer, after executing an arrest warrant, to release the arrested person by way of a promise to appear or a recognizance only if the issuing justice has endorsed the warrant to that effect. But the justice can endorse the warrant only in the case of "minor" crimes, and sometimes the justice has simply not considered endorsing the warrant to allow a peace officer to release the accused. As a result, some Aboriginal persons have been detained pending trial even though the police considered those persons to be no real threat to the community. This detention is particularly disruptive for those in remote communities, since arrested persons must be transported a great distance in order to be detained.

RECOMMENDATION

12. (1) An endorsement permitting a peace officer to release an arrested person on an appearance notice should be available for all crimes. Legislation should expressly require a justice to consider making an endorsement when issuing an arrest warrant.[155]

These policies could reduce the number of persons transported from the North to Southern holding facilities, reduce detention costs, reduce delays in court appearances by having the accused available in the community and reduce the trauma and dislocation suffered by young offenders who are transported and held in the South for extended periods on rather minor charges.[156]

A similar issue arises under present *Code* section 498. The arresting officer has no power to release persons accused of certain crimes: only the more senior officer in charge may do so, and only on certain conditions or with certain guarantees (such as the provision of sureties and the deposit of money or other valuable security) or both.

---

154. See Ontario Native Council on Justice, *supra*, note 144 at 9-10, or A. C. Birkenmayer and S. Jolly, *The Native Inmate in Ontario* (Toronto: Ontario Ministry of Correctional Services, 1981).

155. As we have previously recommended in LRC, *Compelling Appearance, Interim Release and Pre-trial Detention*, Working Paper 57 (Ottawa: The Commission, 1988) Rec. 16(2)(c) at 56.

156. See Thérèse Lajeunesse, *Administration of Justice in Northern and Isolated Communities* (Discussion Paper prepared for the Manitoba Department of Justice, October 8, 1986) at 9 [unpublished].

In Working Paper 57, we recommended that any peace officer should have the discretion to release a person arrested for any crime, by means of an expanded appearance notice which could include conditions that, at present, only the officer in charge can impose.[157] We also proposed that a peace officer should be required to release the person unless specific grounds of detention are satisfied.[158] We see potential benefits for Aboriginal suspects in these proposals.

Allowing the peace officer to release for any crime could assist in preventing needless detention where the arrested person must be taken before an officer in charge located some distance away. This proposal's ultimate success depends on the officer in the field using this discretion in a manner consistent with favouring release rather than detention.

RECOMMENDATION

12. (2) Any peace officer should have the discretion to release a person arrested for any crime, by means of an expanded appearance notice which could include conditions that, at present, only the officer in charge can impose. A peace officer should be required to release the person unless specific grounds of detention are satisfied.

B.   Conditions of Release

Section 515 of the *Code* allows a justice to release an accused person in a variety of ways: on an undertaking; on a recognizance without sureties and without deposit of money; on a recognizance with sureties but without deposit of money; and on a recognizance without sureties but with deposit of money (cash bail deposits). Each of these situations raises issues for reform.

(1) Undertakings

When an accused is released on an undertaking, conditions are usually imposed. These conditions may be applied to anyone, but some have a particular impact on Aboriginal persons. It has been suggested to us that judges impose many conditions routinely, with no real consideration of whether they are necessary or appropriate.

In urban settings, we are told, judges often order accused persons to stay away from particular areas of the city which, in many cases, are also the areas in which most Aboriginal persons live or congregate; the result is an unintended banishment of the accused from his or her community. Similarly, a condition requiring abstention from alcohol is difficult for an accused who is alcohol-dependent, as many Aboriginal accused are, to comply with. Our consultants also point out that orders not to associate with particular persons can present difficulties: in small Aboriginal communities it may, practically speaking, be impossible to avoid contact with specific individuals, or to avoid associating with anyone having a

---

157. *Supra*, note 155, Recs 1 to 3 at 43-44.

158. *Ibid.*, Rec. 7(1) at 48.

criminal record. Further, an Aboriginal person making a living by hunting and trapping will be more inconvenienced than most members of society by a restriction on the use of firearms[159] or a requirement to report regularly to a probation officer.

We do not suggest that Aboriginal persons should never be subject to any of these conditions. At the same time, courts must recognize the different impact these types of conditions can have: conditions must not be imposed routinely, but rather only when they are appropriate and relevant to the offender and the offence. Paragraph 515(4)(*f*) refers to "reasonable conditions." If a condition is clearly one with which the accused cannot comply, then it is not a reasonable condition. However, it may be useful for the *Code* to provide a clearer standard to guide the imposition of reasonable conditions.

RECOMMENDATIONS

12. (3) Bail legislation should specifically provide that, in assessing the reasonableness of any condition of release, the justice must consider:

(a) an accused's occupation, place of residence and cultural background;

(b) the geographical location and size of the community to which the accused belongs; and

(c) the special requirements of traditional Aboriginal pursuits.

(4) A condition requiring an accused to refrain from the use of alcohol should only be attached if the use of alcohol contributed to the offence with which the accused is charged.[160]

(2) Recognizances

A recognizance is a promise to pay a sum of money in the event of failure to appear for trial or to comply with certain non-monetary conditions. A person breaching a recognizance (or indeed the conditions in an undertaking) may be guilty of the crime of breach of a condition of release without reasonable excuse. This result poses a dilemma for the system. On the one hand, imposing conditions may be the most effective way to ensure the protection of the public or to prevent the commission of another crime. On the other hand, the result can be a type of double punishment: the accused suffers revocation of bail and is also subject to a new criminal charge, both for the same conduct. This problem of double punishment applies to anyone released on bail but, once again, is particularly acute for Aboriginal persons because of the unequal impact of many conditions.

---

159. Courts have found that a prohibition on the possession of firearms is cruel and unusual punishment for Aboriginal persons: *R.* v. *Chief* (1989), 51 C.C.C. (3d) 265 (Y. Terr. C.A.); *R.* v. *McGillivary* (1991), 12 W.C.B. (2d) 192 (Sask. C.A.). *Contra*, see *infra*, note 208.

160. A condition requiring the accused to enrol in an alcohol treatment program should not be imposed without the consent of the accused. In some areas, we are told, the limited spaces in treatment programs are taken up by accused who are present only by court order, and who therefore receive little real benefit.

In our view, as a general rule of criminal procedure applicable in all cases, there should be no criminal liability for breaching non-monetary conditions of release. Misconduct that is itself a crime is separately chargeable, and we would continue the offence of failing to attend court. Otherwise, the revocation of bail is a sufficient punishment if the accused breaches a condition. The imposition of both penalties opens the way to double punishment.[161]

RECOMMENDATION

12. (5) There should be no criminal liability for breaching non-monetary conditions of release.

(3) Sureties

Under the present law, an accused person who is released may be required to obtain sureties. A surety is one who essentially guarantees the performance of the accused's obligations and agrees to forfeit an amount of money if the accused fails to perform those obligations.

For Aboriginal persons two issues arise. First, from the point of view of an accused, is the power to impose sureties too broad? Second, from the point of view of a prospective surety, is the present law too harsh in its treatment of the surety? Our consultants have suggested, for example, that it is very difficult for Aboriginal persons to find sureties. In part, this problem results from economic status, but it is compounded by the fact that, because Aboriginal persons on reserves cannot individually own their land, they cannot post houses, for example, as collateral.

The New Zealand Criminal Law Reform Committee proposed several practical reforms in this area.[162] First, it recommended making the requirement of sureties formally subject to the general provision that no condition should be imposed unless it appears to the court to be necessary for the purpose of preventing absconding, offending or the obstruction of the course of justice. Also, all relevant matters, such as character, criminal record and financial resources, should be taken into account in an assessment of the need for and suitability of a surety. Finally, the New Zealand Committee suggested that a surety should not be disqualified simply because he or she does not at present possess sufficient means to meet the obligation of the bond, since this would disqualify persons of limited means. "Financial resources" should merely be a relevant factor to be taken into account in assessing the suitability of a surety. The focus should rest primarily on the surety's character and reliability.

---

161. See a similar recommendation in the New Zealand Criminal Law Reform Committee, *Report on Bail* (Wellington: The Committee, 1982) para. 140 at 48.

162. The option of abolishing sureties was considered but rejected by the New Zealand Criminal Law Reform Committee, which concluded that abolition would actually increase the number of persons detained. They believed that the courts would more often consider the risks in releasing an accused too high unless other people had a stake in the accused's conduct. We agree. See *ibid.* at 52.

These proposals are equally appropriate to Canada. A flexible approach to assessing the adequacy of a surety may lessen the need to require property as collateral in the first place. If the surety is related or closely tied to the accused and is of good character, these factors could affect the surety's acceptability and the amount for which he or she might be responsible.

RECOMMENDATIONS

12. (6) Bail legislation should be amended to provide that, in considering the suitability of an intended surety, a justice shall consider:

(a) the financial resources the intended surety has or may reasonably be expected to have;

(b) his or her character and the nature of any previous convictions;

(c) his or her proximity (whether in kinship, place of residence or otherwise) to the accused; and

(d) any other relevant matter.

(7) A justice should only be allowed to require a surety to deposit cash or other security if the justice is satisfied that exceptional circumstances related to the surety require such an order — for example, where the intended surety resides in another jurisdiction.

The New Zealand Criminal Law Reform Committee also recommended that a surety's liability should be limited, and we agree. In our view, although the surety should formally undertake to supervise the conduct of the accused, misconduct by the accused should not result in forfeiture of the surety's bond. We see merit in imposing by law this kind of moral obligation, even though it is not reinforced by an accompanying legal sanction.

RECOMMENDATION

12. (8) A surety should be under a duty to take all reasonable steps to ensure the attendance of the accused in court. The surety should not be liable to forfeiture for the accused's breach of other bail conditions.

A related problem, not unique to Aboriginal persons, is that an accused may be granted bail, only to remain in custody because of an inability to find an acceptable surety. Requiring bail to be reassessed where conditions have not been met within a short time may prevent persons from being detained merely because they are poor and cannot meet what at first appeared to be reasonable release conditions. We suggest the following, as has the New Zealand Committee.

RECOMMENDATION

12. (9) If a justice orders a person to obtain a surety and that condition is not met within twenty-four hours, the imposition of that condition should be reconsidered.

(4) Cash Bail Deposits

For the same economic reasons that make providing sureties difficult, providing cash bail can be a special obstacle for Aboriginal persons.

The English Home Office Working Party Report rejected the concept of cash bail and called for its abolition for two primary reasons: discrimination against the less well off, and difficulty or hardship in raising money.[163] The New Zealand Criminal Law Reform Committee recommended that a limited power to require a cash deposit be preserved — that the court should have the power to require a cash deposit or other security only if there are reasonable grounds for believing that, in the absence of the deposit, the defendant would leave the country.[164] The Hong Kong Law Reform Commission recommended that cash bail be retained as an option for the bail authority but that its use be de-emphasized. The proposed Hong Kong code would make it clear that a cash deposit should be demanded only where it is necessary to ensure the appearance of the defendant.[165]

The present law regarding cash bail as it applies to Aboriginal persons raises the spectre of unequal treatment.

RECOMMENDATION

12. (10) The requirement of a cash deposit by the accused should either be abolished or be subject to greater restriction, such as requiring a cash deposit only where the justice believes on reasonable grounds that the deposit is necessary to prevent the accused from leaving the country.

VI. Sentencing

The impact of the justice system on Aboriginal persons is most apparent at the sentencing stage. Many studies over many years have noted the high rate of incarceration of Aboriginal offenders. In the Western provinces and in the North, the statistical picture

---

163. Great Britain, Home Office Working Party, *Bail Procedures in Magistrates' Courts* (London: HMSO, 1974) at 32-33.

164. New Zealand Criminal Law Reform Committee, *supra*, note 161 at 46.

165. Law Reform Commission of Hong Kong, *Report on Bail in Criminal Proceedings*, Topic 16 (Hong Kong: Govt. Printer, 1989) at 83.

is particularly stark.[166] Even more disturbing is that Aboriginal representation in prison has moved upwards over time — a situation which is completely unacceptable in a society that prides itself on being free and democratic.

Many explanations have been offered. The most general and far-reaching of these is that of colonization.[167] It has also been suggested that there is discrimination on the part of justice system personnel. Other explanations point to the frequency of imprisonment for fine default, or the criminalization of alcohol consumption.[168] Obviously, the explanations for Aboriginal over-representation, like its solutions, are complex and defy easy categorization.

A. Alternatives to Incarceration

One prevalent focus within the literature on solutions to the problem of over-representation has been on what are called "alternatives to incarceration." While even the most recent of analyses continue to support the creative use of well-designed and adequately funded alternatives to incarceration or community sanctions, we recognize that many experiments with these alternatives in recent years have been severely criticized.[169]

Theoretically, several alternatives to imprisonment exist at the sentencing stage, such as conditional discharges, suspended sentences, community service orders, compensation, restitution and fine option programs.[170] In addition, options such as diversion, victim-offender reconciliation programs and mediation are also alternatives to imprisonment in

---

166. Nearly one in three inmates in prairie penitentiaries is of Aboriginal ancestry. Aboriginal people make up almost 10% of the federal inmate population, though they make up less than 2% of the Canadian population as a whole. Aboriginal women constitute over 70% of the inmate population in the Northwest Territories, Manitoba and Saskatchewan. The young offender crime rate for Aboriginal youths is three times higher than their percentage of the national population: Jackson, *supra*, note 18. See also, *Correctional Issues Affecting Native Peoples*, Working Paper No. 7 (Ottawa: Solicitor General Canada, 1988).

167. This analysis of the causes of over-representation tends to merge with theories of crime causation. Hence in Jackson, *supra*, note 18, the assertion is found, at 217-18, that "their over-representation in the criminal justice system is a particular example of the well-known correlation between economic deprivation and criminality." Jackson's views on this are complex. He goes on, at 218, to indicate that "attributing the problem to poverty itself is not a sufficient explanation" and focuses on a "process of dispossession and marginalization" otherwise referred to as "colonization." This colonization theory is also accepted in the Osnaburgh/Windigo Report, *supra*, note 43 (see especially at 4-9) and forms the basis for the analysis in Havemann et al., *supra*, note 11. It also has implicit acceptance in the Marshall Inquiry.

168. These explanations are summarized in John Hagan, "Locking Up the Indians: A Case for Law Reform" (1976) 55 Canadian Forum 16. See also Carol P. LaPrairie, who, in "The Role of Sentencing in the Over-representation of Aboriginal People in Correctional Institutions" (1990) 32 Can. J. Crim. 429, in a careful, contextually based discussion, offers three possible explanations: (1) Aboriginal people and non-Aboriginal people are not treated the same way in policing, charging, prosecution, sentencing and parole decisions; (2) Aboriginal people commit more crime owing to non-racial factors such as poverty or alcohol use; and (3) Aboriginal people commit crimes that are more detectable than those committed by non-Aboriginal people.

169. See, *e.g.*, Norval Morris and Michael Tonry, *Between Prison and Probation: Intermediate Punishments in a Rational Sentencing System* (New York: Oxford University Press, 1990).

170. One should bear in mind in this section of our Report the important distinction between alternatives to incarceration and intermediate forms of punishment (bush camps, intensive surveillance probation, shock incarceration, house arrest under electronic monitoring) with which they are sometimes confused.

the sense that they do not entail resort to the ordinary process of trial and sentencing. Our Commission has long supported these alternatives, but they are underused.[171]

RECOMMENDATION

13. (1) Alternatives to imprisonment should be used whenever possible. The *Criminal Code* provisions creating such alternatives should ensure that those alternatives are given first consideration at sentencing. A judge imprisoning an Aboriginal person for an offence amenable to the use of alternative dispositions should be required to set forth the reasons for using imprisonment rather than a non-custodial option.

The case for the use of creative Aboriginal methods of dispute resolution is cogently argued and described by Jackson in our commissioned study entitled *In Search of the Pathways to Justice*.[172] In our view, special alternative programs for Aboriginal persons are important for several reasons. First, they possess the potential to reduce the number of Aboriginal persons in prisons. Further, they could with very little adjustment incorporate customary law, thus increasing their acceptability to the affected population. Finally, they are organized around the concept of community involvement and thus can promote social peace and a sense of community control. Alternative programs are consistent with Aboriginal values in that they seek reconciliation between an offender and the community as a whole, and pursue the goal of restoring harmony.[173]

Two recurring concerns in the material that follows are the commitment and adequacy of resources.

RECOMMENDATION

13. (2) Programs providing alternatives to incarceration should, to the extent possible, be universally available. To pursue this goal, adequate financial and human resources must be made available and comprehensive cost-feasibility studies should be undertaken immediately.

Enabling legislation must be in place, but the mere presence of that legislation is of little significance in the absence of adequate resources and planning. To be successful, programs should be informed by research and individually tailored to particular communities.

---

171. "One reason why Native inmates are disproportionately represented in the prison population is that too many of them are being unnecessarily sentenced to terms of imprisonment": *Taking Responsibility: Report of the Standing Committee on Justice and the Solicitor General on Its Review of Sentencing, Conditional Release and Related Aspects of Corrections* (Ottawa: Supply and Services Canada, 1988) at 211-12 (Chair: David Daubney) [hereinafter *Taking Responsibility*].

172. *Supra*, note 28.

173. The Osnaburgh/Windigo Report, *supra*, note 43 at 37, notes that the use of alternatives such as alternative dispute resolution systems, "can be seen as part of the general trend towards developing [such] systems in society at large."

RECOMMENDATION

13. (3) Research must be accompanied by monitoring of the programs, together with policy analyses, to allow for structural readjustment as experience is gathered.

Moreover, we believe that much of this research could be assigned to and developed by an Aboriginal body (such as an Aboriginal Justice Institute which, elsewhere in this Report, we propose be created).

One group of reforms, not strictly speaking part of the sentencing process, that is nevertheless regarded as an alternative to imprisonment is victim-offender reconciliation.

(1) Victim-Offender Reconciliation

Victim-offender reconciliation programs may involve diverting offenders away from the criminal process entirely.[174] Such diversion could serve as an ideal mechanism for involving communities in the disposition of some cases (especially minor ones where alcohol may have played a role). Other reconciliation programs occur later in the process, before sentence, with the aim of facilitating mediation and restitution[175] between the offender and the victim. Such programs help restore peace within the community through a reconciliation of the parties. They exist in some Canadian jurisdictions, but are not found in Newfoundland, Prince Edward Island, Nova Scotia, New Brunswick and Alberta.[176]

RECOMMENDATION

13. (4) Victim-offender reconciliation programs should be expanded and ought to be evaluated more thoroughly than has been done to date. Federal and provincial governments should provide the necessary financial support to ensure that community programs are made more generally available and to encourage their greater use.

Additional resources must be made available to communities to ensure that these programs are effective.

---

174. Diversion is not limited to the early pre-trial stages of the process. It may occur at various stages of the process, from relatively early (pre-charge) and involve police discretion, to relatively late (pre-sentence) where prosecutorial and judicial discretion may come into play. There is no provision in the *Code* or elsewhere for pre-charge diversion, or for victim-offender reconciliation programs. By contrast, post-charge diversion is recognized under the *Young Offenders Act, supra*, note 49, as an "alternative measure."

175. Restitution is an important part of many Aboriginal dispute resolution processes: See Jackson, *supra*, note 28. It is closely allied to the concept of victim-offender reconciliation and may take many forms — the return of stolen property, an apology, voluntary payment or victim or community service. See LRC, *Restitution and Compensation*, Working Paper 5 (Ottawa: Information Canada, 1974). Recent amendments to the *Criminal Code* have expanded the law concerning restitution, in large part in line with recommendations in LRC, *Guidelines: Disposition and Sentences in the Criminal Process*, Report 2 (Ottawa: Information Canada, 1976).

176. Canadian Sentencing Commission, *Sentencing Reform: A Canadian Approach* (Ottawa: Supply and Services Canada, 1986) at 352.

RECOMMENDATION

13. (5) The *Criminal Code* should contain a counterpart to the "alternative measures" provisions in the *Young Offenders Act*, for disposing of and diverting cases against adult Aboriginal offenders.

Indeed, in our view such alternative measures should be available in all criminal cases.

Measures of this nature are more consistent with the Aboriginal perspective on how criminal justice ought to be administered. They are consistent with Aboriginal values and, indeed, can be a useful means of moving toward greater Aboriginal control over the justice system. One study prepared for us notes that imprisoning Aboriginal offenders can be counter-productive: because of exposure to prison life "[t]hey may return ... a greater threat to the peace and order of their community than when they left."[177] Rehabilitation and reconciliation are important considerations for the Aboriginal community.

(2) Fines

Generally speaking, a fine is an appropriate disposition only if the offender is a meaningful participant in a cash economy. That assumption cannot be made of Aboriginal persons who become entangled in the criminal justice system. Fines command little or no respect in their communities, and cease to act as a deterrent when it is generally recognized that they cannot be paid. A substantial proportion of Aboriginal persons in prison are there simply because of an inability to pay fines. The imposition of a fine thus often serves only to postpone incarceration. Three proposals can help alleviate this problem: fine option programs, a "day-fine" system and reform of the law regarding imprisonment for default.

(a) *Fine Option Programs*

Fine option programs have recently been provided for in the *Criminal Code*.[178] These programs allow offenders to work off their fines at a given rate per hour by performing work in the community. They are designed as an alternative to imprisonment for fine default. Unfortunately, such programs are not universally available and, where they exist, are not of uniform quality.[179] Aboriginal women, in some places, are restricted in their access to such programs because of travel difficulties and inadequate child care in their communities.[180] Further:

> Sometimes Fine Option programs pose dilemmas for Aboriginal community administrators because they are not linked to genuine projects that lead to a sense of accomplishment and self-worth. The Fine Option programs require effort to set up and ingenuity to make relevant for Aboriginal communities. In Aboriginal communities where there is usually scant administrative resources to spare this diversion of energy is not always a priority.[181]

---

177. IBA, *supra*, note 24 at 25.

178. See s. 718.1.

179. See *Justice on Trial*, *supra*, note 14 at 6-40 and 6-41, for a description of some particular defects of these programs in Alberta Aboriginal communities.

180. *Ibid.* at 6-41.

181. IBA, *supra*, note 24 at 49.

RECOMMENDATION

13. (6) Fine option programs should be created in communities that wish to institute them. The programs should be provided with resources adequate to allow the community to mount projects that will promote a sense of accomplishment and self-worth. Special measures should be taken to make these programs accessible to Aboriginal women.

(b) Day Fines

In our 1974 Working Paper on *Fines*,[182] we examined the Swedish "day-fine" system, whereby a fine is calculated as a fraction of the yearly gross income of the offender. The Canadian Sentencing Commission recently suggested that further investigation into transplanting a day-fine system to Canada is needed because of our different system of income reporting and taxation.[183] The Sentencing Commission concluded, and we agree, that the provinces should be encouraged to institute pilot projects on the use of day-fine systems. In our view, Aboriginal communities ought to be among the first beneficiaries of such projects.

RECOMMENDATION

13. (7) The provinces should be encouraged to institute pilot projects on the use of day-fine systems, and Aboriginal communities ought to be among the first beneficiaries of such projects.

(c) Imprisonment for Default

The imposition of a "semi-automatic" prison term for fine default has been the subject of relentless criticism in the sentencing literature. There is statistical evidence to support the conclusion that the imprisonment of fine defaulters without reference to their ability to pay discriminates against impoverished offenders. One highly visible example of this phenomenon is the over-representation of native persons in provincial institutions.[184]

Various models for avoiding imprisonment for fine default have been proposed, all of which have certain common features.[185]

---

182. LRC, *Fines*, Working Paper 6 (Ottawa: Information Canada, 1974).

183. See Canadian Sentencing Commission, *supra*, note 176, discussion at 378.

184. *Ibid.* at 380.

185. We advanced one in our Working Paper 5, *supra*, note 175. Another enforcement scheme was set out in Bill C-19, *An Act to amend the Criminal Code* . . . , 2d Sess., 32d Parl., 1983-84 (first reading 7 February 1984), and the Canadian Sentencing Commission put forward a proposal in *supra*, note 176.

RECOMMENDATION

13. (8) Incarceration for non-payment of fines should only occur upon a refusal or wilful default to pay a fine, not upon an inability to pay. An offender should not be imprisoned unless the following alternatives have been tried:

(a) show-cause hearings over why the offender has not paid the fine;

(b) attachment of wages, salaries and other moneys;

(c) seizure of the offender's property;

(d) community service equal to the fine; and

(e) alternative community sanctions.[186]

(3)   Community Service Orders

Like fine option programs, community service order (CSO) programs have the potential to do good but, if improperly structured, they can become a burden to the community and fail to live up to their promise.[187]

Typically, a CSO requires an offender to perform, without pay, a number of hours of work for the community.[188] The CSO can help achieve a reconciliation between the community and the offender by repairing the harm done, and by applying a positive form of censure to an offence.[189] The general (as contrasted with the Aboriginal) experience with such orders has been positive.[190]

A study of the fine option/CSO program in Manitoba concluded that it "seems to serve the Treaty Indian/Métis/Non-Status Indian community quite well. High use is made of the program by Aboriginal people, their completion rate is better than average, and the jail admissions for default are not out of line with default admissions from the non-Aboriginal community."[191] However, a study in Ontario describing the results of two programs specifically designed for Aboriginal persons in London and Kenora reported very mixed results with CSOs.[192] Clearly, firm conclusions cannot be drawn from the

---

186. Consideration should also be given to the eventual abolition of imprisonment for fine default. There are imaginative non-criminal means for the recuperation of debts. This approach is consistent with one that our Commission is developing in a forthcoming Working Paper on *Costs in Criminal Cases*.

187. See *Justice on Trial, supra*, note 14 at 6-40 to 6-42.

188. Such orders are made under *Criminal Code* s. 737(2)(*h*), which allows a court to attach "reasonable conditions" to a probation order. Apparently the only Canadian jurisdiction not providing for CSOs is New Brunswick. See *Taking Responsibility, supra*, note 171 at 79.

189. See LRC, Report 2, *supra*, note 175 at 23-24.

190. *Taking Responsibility, supra*, note 171 at 80.

191. Barkwell et al., *supra*, note 18 at 138.

192. "Indicators of success or failure do not emerge": Margaret Jackson and John W. Ekstedt, *Alternatives to Incarceration/Sentencing Option Programmes: What Are the Alternatives?*, Research Report of the Canadian Sentencing Commission (Ottawa: Dept. of Justice, 1988) at 26.

experience to date. To be successful, considerably greater resources must be devoted to the monitoring and design of these community-based programs. By the same token, the scarcity of administrative resources can result in a theoretically beneficial program becoming a nuisance to the very community that administers the program. As with other alternative programs, a CSO program must enjoy the support of the affected community.

RECOMMENDATION

13. (9) Community service order programs should be created in communities that wish to institute them. The programs should be provided with resources adequate to determine what kind of community service work could be performed and what resources the community needs to make such programs succeed. Much greater care must be taken in the design of these programs, and the enabling statute or regulation should clearly set out the purposes of the programs. There must be appropriate education of the judiciary, Crown prosecutors and defence counsel about the purposes and availability of the programs.[193] While its use should be encouraged, the *Criminal Code* should provide that a community service order will only be imposed after the court has ascertained from the community the opportunities for community service and the willingness of the community to accept the offender.

B. Probation

Probation is used mainly to supervise convicted offenders who are allowed to remain at liberty or who are returned to the community after serving a period of imprisonment. It also provides a mechanism for extending treatment or other assistance to sentenced individuals.

The terms and conditions typically included in probation orders are not always appropriate to Aboriginal persons. The obligation to report regularly to a probation officer can create difficulties when the offender lives in an isolated community. Many treatment programs are not designed with Aboriginal persons in mind. Some non-association orders can be difficult to comply with in small communities and may almost amount to banishment.

Greater local control over probation would help.[194] The stumbling block would be enlisting sufficient community support. Nevertheless, if selected members of communities were trained as probation officers, there would be far fewer reporting difficulties. Even in communities with no trained probation officers, many tasks could be performed by

---

193. Jackson and Ekstedt, *ibid.*, indicate, at 25, that some judges misunderstood the nature of the CSO, thus undermining its value and utility.

194. What must be provided are specialized correctional institutions and programs modified to meet the needs of Aboriginal offenders. Issues such as the location of probation facilities and the training of staff to be employed in correctional institutions and in probation, parole, rehabilitation and after-care services also must be addressed. There are some lessons to be cognizant of in this area. Note especially the experience with the unimplemented 1975 James Bay Agreement and see the critique of it contained in Jackson, *supra*, note 18 at 257-60.

respected community members under the guidance of a probation officer located elsewhere.[195] Further, reporting requirements should be interpreted to maximize the offender's ability to maintain a productive life-style. For hunters, this could mean assigning a local person to hunt with one or several offenders or simply postponing the reporting requirement.

RECOMMENDATION

13. (10) Probation services, modified to meet the needs of Aboriginal offenders, should be provided in a wide range of Aboriginal communities. More use should be made of community resources, coupled with a commitment to train individuals from the communities to serve as probation officers.

Sentencing judges, when considering a probation order, have repeatedly lamented the fact that appropriate facilities and treatment programs do not exist, and that it is impossible to place people into the programs that do exist. Additional resources are necessary to provide appropriate facilities, trained staff and a variety of useful treatment programs. Only if such resources are available will the sentencing court be in a position to impose a meaningful disposition.

It is often asserted that Aboriginal offenders are generally not regarded by judges as good candidates for probation.[196] While the reasons for this are complex, the cultural factor is important. Judges must come to recognize that "our techniques of rehabilitation, of 'healing,' may not only be very different, but also traditionally improper."[197]

RECOMMENDATION

13. (11) The criteria governing eligibility for probation should be formulated to have proper regard for cultural differences and to meet the needs of Aboriginal offenders and communities. In addition, probation reports should give greater emphasis to factors such as the offender's skills, potential employability and preparedness to enrol in treatment or training programs. The community's willingness to become involved in the probation and supervision of the offender should also take on added importance.

---

195. See *Justice on Trial, supra,* note 14 at 6-42 to 6-43. In Ontario, the Ministry of Correctional Services employs assistants to probation officers who reside in Aboriginal communities and act as friend and counsellor to probationers and parolees: Stan Jolly, C. Peters and S. Spiegel, *Progress Report on Government Action Taken Since the 1975 Federal-Provincial Conference on Native Peoples and the Criminal Justice System,* Report prepared for the Ontario Native Council on Justice (Toronto: The Council, 1979).

196. See the sources cited in Susan V. Zimmerman, *The Revolving Door of Despair: Native Involvement in the Criminal Justice System* (Paper prepared for the Law Reform Commission of Canada, 1991) at 46-49 [unpublished]. This perception is questioned by LaPrairie, *supra,* note 168 at 433.

197. Ross, *supra,* note 21 at 10.

C. Structural Adjustments and Process Reforms

(1) The Need for a Revised Sentencing Structure

Canada's current sentencing laws are archaic and inadequate. The *Criminal Code* lacks a coherent sentencing philosophy and provides little or no direction to sentencing judges. These defects result in serious sentencing disparities. In our view, the current regime fails to respect the *Charter's* guarantees of equality and fundamental justice in a number of important respects. To rectify these shortcomings, we have elsewhere recommended a major reclassification of current sentencing practices, bench-mark sentences, the abolition of parole and the creation of a permanent Sentencing Commission.[198] In addition, proposals for structural change made elsewhere in this Report, such as for the creation of an Aboriginal Justice Institute, increased involvement of Elders and courtworkers and formal community liaison, offer potential benefits for Aboriginal persons in the sentencing process.

(2) Racism, Discrimination and Sentencing Practices

Racism was a matter of pressing concern to our consultants. Anecdotal evidence of racism exists but is often discounted because proof in accordance with the standards of the social sciences is elusive.[199] Overt racism is difficult to prove, in part because the culpable actors are sufficiently sophisticated to mask this motivation. Also, regarding both overt racism and systemic discrimination, "the lack of a solid empirical base has inhibited any real understanding of whether bias exists in the conviction and sentencing of Aboriginal accused."[200]

RECOMMENDATION

13. (12) Further research should be conducted into whether Aboriginal persons receive harsher sentences than non-Aboriginal persons, and, if so, the causes of that disparity.

Although sentences that are harsher based on race or culture are repugnant, we do not suggest that racial or cultural factors should always be irrelevant at sentencing. The Canadian Sentencing Commission, in *Sentencing Reform*, proposed national sentencing guidelines, which would only be departed from where aggravating or mitigating factors

---

198. See, *e.g.*, our Report 2, *supra*, note 175. The 1987 Report of the Canadian Sentencing Commission, *supra*, note 176 and the 1988 Report, *Taking Responsibility*, *supra*, note 171, also advocated the creation of a permanent Sentencing Commission.

199. See LaPrairie, *supra*, note 168 at 436.

200. *Ibid.* at 432, citing Clark.

set forth in a statutory scheme come into play.[201] Mitigating factors, such as whether restitution or compensation was made by the offender, are contemplated under the Sentencing Commission's proposal. Given this approach or, indeed, current sentencing practices, the race or culture of the offender could also be relevant in mitigation of sentence, provided other features are present.

RECOMMENDATION

13. (13) A list of factors should be enunciated which, in conjunction with other circumstances, would mitigate sentence where the offender is an Aboriginal person. For example, where an offender is an Aboriginal person, the sentence to be imposed should be reduced if the offender has already been, or will be, subject to traditional sanctions imposed by the community.

Such mitigating factors could be coupled with others that are generally accepted, such as evidence of the offender's acknowledgement of responsibility towards the victim and his or her community. This approach is consistent with the principle that incarceration should only be used as a last resort, and accords with the need to promote more appropriate individualization in sentencing.

(3)   Plea Bargaining

Plea bargaining includes agreements to plead guilty in exchange for a prosecutor's withdrawing some charges or making certain representations on sentence. Our consultants suggest, and surveys confirm, that Aboriginal persons perceive plea bargains as often being reached without their conscious participation.[202] Obviously, this situation is unacceptable.

Knowledge of the effect of race and culture on plea bargaining is limited, and studies do not agree about the extent to which Aboriginal persons are subject to that effect.[203] One study shows a disturbing lack of understanding on the part of Aboriginal persons; often no one, including defence counsel, explained the plea-bargaining process to them.[204] Openness in the process and a clearer articulation of the proper roles to be played by defence counsel, Crown attorneys and judges could do much to rectify this situation.

---

201. *Supra*, note 176 at 320ff.

202. See Morse and Lock, *supra*, note 89.

203. Compare John Hagan, ''Parameters of Criminal Prosecution: An Application of Path Analysis to a Problem of Criminal Justice'' (1974) 65 J. Crim. L. & Criminology 536 at 542; and Derek F. Wynne and Timothy F. Hartnagel, ''Race and Plea Negotiation: An Analysis of Some Canadian Data'' (1975) 1:2 Can. J. Soc. 147 at 149.

204. Morse and Lock, *supra*, note 89 at 40.

Our Working Paper 60, *Plea Discussions and Agreements*,[205] argues that an open and accountable process of plea discussions and agreements is appropriate to the criminal justice system. We proposed the development of a process resting on a framework of statutory rules and published guidelines. Under this scheme, the negotiation is disclosed to the court and pains are taken to ensure that the accused (and also the victim and the public) understands the exact nature of what has occurred. These proposals would go some distance toward ensuring that the Aboriginal offender is properly informed about the nature of the process.

RECOMMENDATION

13. (14) As we have previously recommended, a well-structured, visible and responsible process of plea discussion and agreement should be established.

(4) The Preparation of Pre-sentence Reports

The bare power of the sentencing judge to obtain a pre-sentence report is contained in subsection 735(1) of the *Criminal Code*. These reports can be valuable but should be improved.

RECOMMENDATION

13. (15) The *Criminal Code* provisions pertaining to pre-sentence reports should be considerably more detailed than at present. At a minimum, the contents of those reports and the circumstances in which they are to be ordered should be the subject of clear statutory provisions.

Characteristically a pre-sentence report supplies information concerning the offender's age, employment, family situation, personal history, education and financial situation. These are useful categories of information which ought to be set out in the legislation stipulating the contents of such reports. However, chronic unemployment in Aboriginal communities, family environments that have been disrupted, substandard educational facilities and general conditions of poverty in the area militate against relying on a report that only supplies the information required at present.

RECOMMENDATION

13. (16) The *Criminal Code* should provide that pre-sentence reports shall set out and consider the special circumstances of Aboriginal offenders.

The views of the community regarding the offender's potential for reintegration into that community should be considered. Any rehabilitative measures undertaken or planned by the offender in conjunction with the community should be mentioned. Also, the suitability of the offender for any particular disposition or programs ought to be considered.

---

205. LRC, *Plea Discussions and Agreements*, Working Paper 60 (Ottawa: The Commission, 1989).

These suggestions may accord with current practice in some parts of the country. However, to encourage greater uniformity and to remove any ambiguity, we are calling for statutory amendments to promote a positive and lasting reform of the process. In addition, in view of the sensitive content of the pre-sentence reports, we attach the utmost importance to the following requirement.

RECOMMENDATION

13. (17) Only persons familiar with the general condition of Aboriginal peoples and with their customs, culture and values should prepare pre-sentence reports.

Further, the case law reveals difficulties when a court incarcerates offenders in the absence of a pre-sentence report.[206]

RECOMMENDATION

13. (18) Where incarceration of an offender is being considered for the first time (and incarceration is not required by law), the court should be expressly obliged to order a pre-sentence report. Moreover, the statute should direct that, whenever incarceration is contemplated, the judge should consider ordering a report.

A pre-sentence report should not merely depend on the request of the offender or defence counsel.

We also believe that the assistance of counsel prior to the preparation of a pre-sentence report can be vital.

RECOMMENDATION

13. (19) Where a pre-sentence report is to be prepared, the court should ensure that any unrepresented offender is advised of the possible benefits of having counsel.

This task need not be performed by the judge personally. Rather, the court should draw on the resources of the community, perhaps through the use of Aboriginal court-workers.

(5) Weapons Bans

Many members of Aboriginal communities rely on hunting, fishing and trapping as means of livelihood. Typically, treaties preserved Aboriginal hunting and fishing rights in perpetuity, and "[t]he exercise of hunting and fishing rights is as central an element of Aboriginal culture as any characteristic of Aboriginal people."[207] Some conflicts arise from the inherent requirements of this life-style. Specifically, the possession of weapons is of particular importance to Aboriginal persons.

---

206. See, *e.g.*, *R.* v. *Young* (1982), 39 Nfld & P.E.I.R. 76 (P.E.I.S.C.).
207. IBA, *supra*, note 24 at 42-43.

Section 100 of the *Criminal Code* prohibits an offender convicted of certain crimes from possessing firearms for a fixed period. The purported equal application of this section can cause inequity. A weapons ban has a much greater impact on Aboriginal persons who support themselves, as their treaties allow, through hunting and trapping and have no alternative occupations to pursue. Two courts of appeal have nonetheless found that a weapons ban does not create a *Charter* violation.[208] By contrast, *R. v. Chief* holds that "[i]n the case of a trapper in the Yukon, . . . [a ban] is a virtual prohibition against employment in the only vocation that may be open to him,"[209] and violates section 12 of the *Charter*. Consequently, the court granted the offender a "constitutional exemption" from the absolute prohibition, allowing him to have a weapon while hunting.[210]

We favour the approach in *Chief*.

RECOMMENDATION

13. (20) Subsection 100(1) of the *Criminal Code* should be amended to allow for a limited exemption to the mandatory prohibition on the possession of weapons, where a judge is satisfied that the prohibition would be oppressive and unfair and that allowing the offender to have access to weapons for the purpose of making a living would not cause any threat to public safety.

VII. Corrections

In recent years, the National Parole Board and the Correctional Service of Canada have made valuable efforts to address the concerns and needs of Aboriginal offenders, but this process is in its infancy and much remains to be done. Generally speaking, Aboriginal offenders are incarcerated in prisons that are geographically and culturally far removed from their communities. The programs and services at those institutions have not been sensitive to the culture of Aboriginal inmates and, in particular, to their spiritual needs. Few Aboriginal persons work within the correctional system. Native brotherhoods and sisterhoods have done important work, but they suffer from inadequate recognition and insufficient resources. Further, Aboriginal offenders must satisfy parole and early release criteria that, in some respects, appear to be culturally inappropriate.[211] Also, many reports have commented on the inadequacy of after-care facilities for Aboriginal offenders, in their own communities and elsewhere.[212]

---

208. See *R. v. Tobac* (1985), 60 A.R. 253 (N.W.T. C.A.); *R. v. Weyallon* (1985), 60 A.R. 79 (N.W.T. C.A.); and *R. v. Kelly* (1990), 80 C.R. (3d) 185 (Ont. C.A.). The latter case considers, but is not itself, a "trapper case."

209. *Supra*, note 159 at 270-71.

210. See *McGillivary, supra*, note 159, to the same effect.

211. National Parole Board, *Final Report: Task Force on Aboriginal Peoples in Federal Corrections* (Ottawa: Supply and Services Canada, 1988) recommended, at 36, that: "The current assessment tools, criteria, and procedures being used should be evaluated as to their validity for Aboriginal offenders."

212. See, *e.g.*, Marshall Inquiry, vol. 1, *supra*, note 14 at 181; *Justice on Trial, supra*, note 14 at 6-18 to 6-21; National Parole Board, *supra*, note 211 at 67.

A.   Spirituality and Elders

The importance of spirituality and Elders in the rehabilitation of Aboriginal offenders has generally been recognized in principle. In practice, however, Elders seem to be given less freedom and trust than other spiritual leaders: they are required to have their ceremonies and activities supervised. Even Elders known to prison officials and regarded as posing no real threat have their medicine bundles searched when they enter the institution.[213] Further, the use of sweetgrass is associated with drug use by correctional officials, and sweat lodges are looked on with suspicion.[214]

RECOMMENDATION

14. (1) Aboriginal spirituality should, by legislation, be given the same recognition as other religions, and Aboriginal Elders should be given the same status and freedom as prison chaplains.[215]

On occasion, this may mean releasing a prisoner on a day pass into the custody of members of the community to attend ceremonies outside the prison.

B.   Program Development and Delivery

Generally, the programs and services offered at federal and provincial correctional facilities have, until very recently, provided little that is culturally relevant and responsive to Aboriginal offenders. The cost to society of maintaining an offender in prison — already high — is that much greater if there is no discernible benefit to the inmate from the programs and services provided there.

RECOMMENDATION

14. (2) A review of all programming should be undertaken, in co-operation with Aboriginal persons and organizations, to develop programs and services that are culturally relevant to Aboriginal inmates. Aboriginal service organizations and prisoners' support groups should be systematically involved in program and service delivery and should be appropriately funded in this regard.

---

213. *Justice on Trial, supra*, note 14 at 6-27.

214. Jackson, *supra*, note 18 at 289. See also *Correctional Issues Affecting Native Peoples, supra*, note 166 at 33: "[S]ince complaints continue to arise about the recognition of Native spirituality as a religion, and about the particulars of Native spiritual observance, some critics would support special guarantees."

215. See the similar suggestion in *Correctional Issues Affecting Native Peoples, supra*, note 166 at 34.

C. Parole

Aboriginal offenders are less likely to be released on parole: in 1987, 9.5 per cent of Aboriginal offenders were released on parole, compared to 24 per cent of non-Aboriginal offenders.[216] Aboriginal offenders granted parole are more likely to find themselves back in prison,[217] and there is some concern that they waive their right to a parole hearing more frequently than do non-Aboriginal offenders.[218]

Many explanations have been offered for these phenomena. Aboriginal offenders may not understand the system well enough to assert their rights fully.[219] Very few case management officers are of Aboriginal origin or have been adequately trained to recognize Aboriginal needs, and so might misjudge an aboriginal inmate's readiness for conditional release.[220] Certain parole criteria are inherently weighted against Aboriginal offenders;[221] consequently, Aboriginal inmates may be detained owing to an inappropriate analysis of their behaviour or of the risk they represent to society.[222] It has also been suggested that release conditions are enforced more stringently against Aboriginal persons, and that they have inadequate support upon release.[223]

In other parts of this Report, we have made recommendations for greater cross-cultural training, increased hiring of Aboriginal persons, greater liaison with Aboriginal communities and consultation on release criteria and plans: all of those proposals are relevant here. In addition, steps should be taken to guard against waiver of parole applications or hearings caused by case management officers' subtle encouragement.[224]

---

216. National Parole Board, *supra*, note 211, Table 7 at 29.

217. A 1986 study found that Native penitentiary inmates had the worst total release supervision success rate — 55.9%. White inmates had a 66.2% success rate, while inmates of other races had a 74.2% success rate. William G. Harman and Robert G. Hann, *Release Risk Assessment: An Historical Descriptive Analysis*, User Report No. 1986-32 (Ottawa: Solicitor General Canada, 1986) at 2-9 and 4-4.

218. National Parole Board, *supra*, note 211 at 29.

219. *Taking Responsibility*, *supra*, note 171 at 214.

220. See National Parole Board, *Pre- and Post-Release Decision Policies* (Ottawa: The Board, 1989) Appendix A, where its general recidivism prediction scoring system is not applied to Aboriginal offenders because of insufficient data relating to Aboriginal persons in development of the test. No alternative measures appropriate to Aboriginal persons have been developed. See, however, Robert G. Hann and William G. Harman, *Release Risk Prediction: Testing the Nuffield Scoring System for Native and Female Inmates*, User Report No. 1989-4 (Ottawa: Solicitor General Canada, 1989) at 6, holding that except for one category, "the Nuffield scoring system seems to differentiate between the low and high risk inmates at least as well for Native and for non-Native inmates," and, at 9, that "[b]asing parole release decisions for *Natives* solely on Nuffield scores would have resulted in a significant increase in the parole release rate for Natives — from 12% to 41%."

221. *E.g.*, using employment prospects as a criterion works against Aboriginal persons: see Marshall Inquiry, vol. 3, *supra*, note 18 at 44. Our consultants point out that a prohibition against association with anyone having a criminal record causes difficulties owing to the high percentage of Aboriginal persons with a criminal record: see also *Taking Responsibility*, *supra*, note 171 at 215.

222. See Canada, House of Commons, *Minutes and Proceedings of the Standing Committee on Justice and the Solicitor General*, Issue No. 57 at 57:10-57:11 (18 December 1990) in the submission of the Indigenous Bar Association to the Committee.

223. National Parole Board, *supra*, note 211 at 31.

224. *Ibid.* at 47.

RECOMMENDATION

14. (3) The National Parole Board and the Correctional Service of Canada should develop a national policy and guidelines concerning waiver of parole applications, parole hearings and reviews, and appropriate training should be provided to correctional staff. Information as to the national policy and guidelines should be made available to inmates.[225]

D. After-care

Aboriginal involvement in the criminal justice system has to do not only with offending but also with reoffending. Reintegration into society is the surest way to guard against recidivism, but reintegration depends on the availability of appropriate after-care facilities and programs. Specifically, there must be half-way houses, substance abuse treatment programs and employment and life skills programs which are sensitive to the particular needs of Aboriginal persons. Mainstream programs and facilities are not designed by or for Aboriginal people: the most effective means of providing for these needs of Aboriginal offenders is to involve Aboriginal communities and service organizations in after-care.

Where an offender returns to an Aboriginal community, that community can play a role in formulating and delivering after-care services.[226] Aboriginal inmates going to an urban setting require a similar social structure, which might be provided by Native friendship centres, Métis community organizations and Aboriginal women's groups. If they choose, these organizations might offer the structure and leadership that band councils provide on reserves and in remote communities.[227] At present, these organizations generally operate on shoe-string budgets, and have too many demands on their resources to be able to take on the supervision of paroled offenders. With appropriate financial support and training from correctional services, however, suitable programs could be developed.

---

225. See *ibid.*, Rec. 17, for similar proposals.

226. See also the discussion, above, in chap. 5 at 34, under "IV. Increasing Community Involvement with the Justice System." We are told that some groups of communities have pooled their resources: five or six communities may jointly support half-way houses, shelters, and so on, with each facility located in a different community. Of course, not all communities will wish to be involved in after-care, and these programs can only be instituted where there is local support.

227. *E.g.*, the Grierson Centre in Edmonton, administered by Native Counselling Services of Alberta since the fall of 1989, has been praised as a "fine example" of the federal and provincial governments working together with a Native service organization: remarks of Carola Cunningham in *Sharing Our Future: A Conference of Aboriginal Leaders and Correctional Service Managers*, held at Kananaskis, Alberta, February 11-13, 1991 (Ottawa: Correctional Service of Canada, 1991). See also the discussion of the Native Counselling Services of Alberta in *Correctional Issues Affecting Native Peoples*, *supra*, note 166 at 27-28.

RECOMMENDATION

14. (4) Aboriginal community organizations should be funded to design and administer after-care programs for Aboriginal people. In particular, the use of alternative residential facilities for Aboriginal offenders in areas where half-way houses are neither available nor economically feasible should be promoted.[228]

E. Regional and Local Facilities

Family, community, culture and spirituality are significant to the rehabilitation of all offenders. However, while for most non-Aboriginal offenders prison does not mean incarceration in a foreign cultural milieu, for many Aboriginal offenders it does. Thus, it is important to the rehabilitation of Aboriginal offenders that they be located as near as possible to their communities, to have access to families, Elders and community support.

Case management officers do consider an offender's community of origin and, in many cases, transfer agreements allow offenders to be located as near as possible to home. However, Aboriginal offenders from the North sometimes cannot be transferred because of shortage of space; female Aboriginal federal offenders are often placed far from home, because there is only one federal prison for women.[229]

RECOMMENDATION

14. (5) Smaller local correctional facilities should be created and Aboriginal communities should exercise control over those facilities.[230]

In some areas, we are told, programs to send Aboriginal offenders out on trap-lines rather than incarcerating them have been instituted. As we have noted above, in our discussions under "VI. Sentencing," we support the use of such alternatives.

Aboriginal women account for 20 to 30 per cent of inmates at Kingston's Prison for Women (P4W), currently the only federal facility for female offenders. In recent years, four of them have committed suicide in the prison, and a fifth did so shortly after her

---

228. Note, *e.g.*, the recommendation concerning the use of private homes, with indirect supervision of parolees, in National Parole Board, *supra*, note 211, Rec. 37 at 68.

229. Recent Government policy indicates that five regional prisons for women will be opened in the future. This will ameliorate to some extent the particular hardship facing female Aboriginal federal offenders.

230. See *Justice on Trial*, *supra*, note 14 at 6-28, and Osnaburgh/Windigo Report, *supra*, note 43 at 65. Note also the observation in *Correctional Issues Affecting Native Peoples*, *supra*, note 166 at 27, that legislation will "need to be open-ended enough to take into account a wide variety of correctional arrangements . . . . In an effort to develop a culturally-based system or systems, Native groups may propose correctional facilities or services which are very different from existing structures."

release. The particularly harsh effect on Aboriginal women of conditions at P4W has led at least one judge to rule that sending an Aboriginal woman to serve her sentence at P4W constitutes cruel and unusual punishment, in violation of her *Charter* rights.[231]

The Task Force on Federally Sentenced Women recently recommended the creation of an Aboriginal healing lodge as one of five regional facilities to replace P4W. The success of the healing lodge will depend upon the extent to which Aboriginal women have an effective voice in the design and control of that facility.

RECOMMENDATION

14. (6) In establishing the Aboriginal healing lodge, the Correctional Service of Canada should ensure that it does so in accordance with the recommendation of the Task Force on Federally Sentenced Women. Aboriginal peoples should be consulted and given effective control over the process.[232]

---

231. *R.* v. *Daniels*, [1990] 4 C.N.L.R. 51 (Sask. Q.B.), overturned on appeal on jurisdictional grounds, June 6, 1991.

232. Issues unique to Aboriginal women, particularly correctional issues, are noted in our agenda for future action as especially important matters requiring further research.

CHAPTER SEVEN
Ensuring Progress

Highlights

We call for the creation of an Aboriginal Justice Institute. This Institute should have a broad mandate to deal with any matters relating to Aboriginal persons in the criminal justice system, including collecting data, developing programs within the justice system or as alternatives to it, providing assistance to Aboriginal communities in establishing programs, and developing policy options regarding Aboriginal justice issues. An Aboriginal Justice Institute should be staffed, operated and controlled by Aboriginal persons to the fullest extent possible.

Informed readers will recognize that many of our recommendations are not new, but are similar to recommendations made in previous reports over many years. One report prepared for us has noted that:

> In 1975, the National Conference on Native Peoples held in Edmonton made a number of recommendations that were easily achievable. They recommended that courts sit in Native communities, that provision be made for judges to increase their awareness of the Native communities, and that resident judges or justices of the peace be appointed from within Native communities. Sixteen years later, in 1991, the Alberta Task Force on the impact of the criminal justice system on the Indian and Métis people of Alberta found it necessary to make essentially the same recommendations.[233]

It is clear that a major difficulty in solving Aboriginal criminal justice problems lies not in finding the solutions, but in instituting them. For that reason, we feel it necessary to make particular recommendations in this regard.

---

233. IBA, *supra*, note 24 at 12.

I. Ascertaining the Costs of Change

Clearly, one issue is cost. One is likely to conclude that large sums of money would be required to institute our recommendations. That additional resources are required cannot be denied, but not all of our proposals are costly. Some would result in decreased cost: many of our suggestions would improve or simplify procedures generally, and simplified procedures are less expensive procedures. Many of our proposals are cost-neutral, resulting in neither increased savings nor increased expenditures. Further, other proposals could be accommodated with no noticeable increase in current budgets. (In some cases, the prudent reallocation of existing budget resources would accomplish the objective.) Nonetheless, many of our proposals would involve additional cost. Supporting Aboriginal justice systems in particular would require additional resources.

Funding for various Aboriginal justice programs is currently drawn from several sources. Federal departments — Indian Affairs and Northern Development, Justice, Solicitor General, Secretary of State — all provide resources, as do many provincial government departments and other bodies such as bar associations and universities. We suggest that the level of resources currently devoted to Aboriginal justice issues, including provincial resources, should be precisely identified and evaluated. Expenditure priorities should be established in consultation with Aboriginal peoples to decide the best ways to deploy resources and eliminate unnecessary duplication.[234] This process should include not only "Aboriginal-specific" programs, but also the portion of spending that in large part concerns Aboriginal people, such as funding for correctional facilities or policing. Comprehensive cost-feasibility studies should be immediately undertaken in respect of all proposals carrying resource implications that are advanced in this Report.

The historical disadvantage suffered by Aboriginal persons in the justice system has been too long ignored. If needed reforms have not been made in a timely fashion, we cannot now plead poverty as an excuse for continued inaction.[235]

RECOMMENDATION

15. (1) The level of resources currently devoted to Aboriginal justice issues, including provincial resources, should be precisely identified and evaluated. Expenditure priorities should be established in consultation with Aboriginal peoples to decide the best ways to deploy resources and eliminate unnecessary duplication. Comprehensive cost-feasibility studies should be immediately undertaken in respect of all proposals carrying resource implications that are advanced in this Report.

---

234. This process was begun with the work undertaken by the Nielsen Task Force in 1985: See Task Force on Program Review, *Improved Program Delivery: Indians and Natives*, a Study Team Report (Ottawa: The Task Force, 1985) (Chair: Eric Nielsen). One focus of this study was on areas of duplication and fragmentation between federal departments and agencies. Provincial programming was also examined.

235. The Prime Minister has spoken approvingly of Government decisions to increase spending on Aboriginal issues, saying that "we have made these decisions because they are right": The Rt. Hon. Brian Mulroney, Address (First Nations Congress, Victoria, B.C., 23 April 1991) at 6 [unpublished].

Further, although funds must be allocated immediately, a short-term perspective is not appropriate. Aboriginal justice systems may be expensive in the short term, but in the long term, there would be a return on the investment.[236] The expense can be rationalized by looking at the saving that would come partly from the fact that the rest of the justice system, the correctional system in particular, would be required to deal with fewer Aboriginal persons. But beyond that, restoring social control to communities could help to reverse the process of colonization that has created the problems Aboriginal persons face in the justice system. Their increased social control should result in lower crime rates and a lessened need for the use of any justice system.

In addition to providing funding, further steps are necessary to ensure the enactment of reforms.

II. Creating an Aboriginal Justice Institute

We suggest that an Aboriginal Justice Institute should be created specifically to deal with Aboriginal criminal justice issues and to oversee the implementation of these recommendations. That Institute could perform a number of valuable functions.[237]

First, the Institute could direct future empirical research. Despite the extensive study of Aboriginal justice issues that has taken place, there are major gaps in our knowledge. It is not clear, for example, whether racial bias plays a role in the sentencing of Aboriginal offenders.[238] Indeed, some people challenge whether Aboriginal persons really are over-represented in prisons — the claim that, to many eyes, justifies the need for studies such as this.

Over-representation is an important issue in Aboriginal justice questions,[239] and more data about certain questions would be useful. Does a lower income and a younger average age account for Aboriginal representation in prison?[240] Would Aboriginal persons still

---

236. A Gitksan and Wet'suwet'en request for funding to research, design and implement a dispute settlement project points out that "the problems that western justice systems have with Aboriginal people have been vividly recounted in a number of enquiries across Canada, any one of which would cost more than [this] project": Jackson, *supra*, note 28 at 94-95.

237. In particular, creating such an Institute would help ensure that Aboriginal peoples would be more closely and significantly involved in the reform process, a step which we agree is important: see IBA, *supra*, note 24 at 52, 58-59.

238. LaPrairie, *supra*, note 168.

239. Many problems facing Aboriginal persons — translation, understanding the criminal process, obtaining counsel, bail and probation conditions — would need to be addressed even were Aboriginal persons incarcerated only at the same rate as the rest of the population.

240. There is some evidence that Aboriginal prisoners are older on average: see Alberta, Board of Review on the Administration of Justice in the Provincial Courts of Alberta, *Native People in the Administration of Justice in the Provincial Courts of Alberta*, Report No. 4 (Edmonton: The Board, 1978) (Chair: W. J. C. Kirby). This result suggests that the average younger age of the Native population is not a factor accounting for the high proportion of Aboriginal offenders.

be over-represented in provincial prisons if all fine-defaulters were removed from the equation? The answers cannot show that no problem exists — that a sixteen-year-old Aboriginal boy has a 70-per-cent chance of going to prison[241] is a problem whatever the cause — but can help isolate the causes of the problem. Figures on whether there are differences in the rate at which Aboriginal persons are charged with crimes, plead guilty, are convicted or are imprisoned could help show whether solutions are needed throughout the process or in specific areas.[242]

Beyond simply gathering data, however, an Aboriginal Justice Institute should play a role in formulating policy. The Institute could look at broad questions of principle regarding sentencing, and develop sentencing guidelines or propose modifications or alternatives to the sentencing process. Similarly, it could question the view that sentencing guidelines must be laid down province-wide, and develop guidelines concerning when cultural and local differences should affect general principles of sentencing. In part, the Institute could operate as an Aboriginal Sentencing Commission.

The Institute ought also to be closely involved in implementing the recommendations in this Report and those of other Aboriginal criminal justice initiatives. The Institute could conduct or commission research into customary law. It could help train Aboriginal justices of the peace. It could help establish cross-cultural training programs or training programs for legal interpreters. It could advise on holding court sittings in Aboriginal communities. It could develop criteria for granting bail or parole that take the special situation of Aboriginal persons into account.

The Institute could also evaluate existing measures such as diversion, fine option or community service programs. The Institute could formulate programs of its own, provide expert assistance to communities wishing to create such programs and assist in making funding applications. Another possibility is to give the Institute the ability to fund those programs itself. This step could make implementation of programs easier and more efficient — services and resources might be more economically arranged on a large scale — but might also create other problems. We therefore make no recommendation on this point at the moment.

---

241. John Hylton, "Locking Up Indians in Saskatchewan," discussed in Jackson, *supra*, note 18 at 216.

242. Some information is available concerning these types of questions: see, *e.g.*, LaPrairie, *supra*, note 168, and the sources discussed there; Nova Scotia, Royal Commission on the Donald Marshall, Jr., Prosecution, *Discrimination against Blacks in Nova Scotia* by Wilson Head and Don Clairmont, vol. 4 (Halifax: The Commission, 1989) (Chair: T. A. Hickman); or Hagan, *supra*, note 203, but more is required. Data-collection practices vary considerably across the country: some jurisdictions keep very limited data on race, or are unable to correlate it to data such as type of offence. Also, the Canadian Centre for Justice Statistics has decided not to collect data based on ethnicity: some people argue that such data may be misinterpreted to mean that particular races are especially prone to criminal behaviour. The absence of such data makes it difficult to determine whether members of various races are treated unfairly: How can one argue that *too* many Blacks are charged, for example, without knowing *how* many Blacks are charged?

RECOMMENDATIONS

15. (2) An Aboriginal Justice Institute should be created and should have a broad mandate to deal with any matters relating to Aboriginal persons in the criminal justice system, including:

(a) conducting empirical research;

(b) collecting data;

(c) developing and evaluating programs within the justice system or as alternatives to it;

(d) providing assistance to Aboriginal communities in establishing programs; and

(e) developing policy options regarding Aboriginal justice issues.

(3) The Aboriginal Justice Institute should be instrumental in the design, implementation and monitoring of initiatives concerning criminal justice deriving from proposals advanced in this Report as well as those generated by the commissions of inquiry. The Aboriginal Justice Institute should be staffed, operated and controlled by Aboriginal persons to the fullest extent possible.

CHAPTER EIGHT
Conclusion

I.   Agenda for Future Action

Given the constraints on the preparation of this Report, there are of course many areas that we were either unable to address or not able to address in sufficient detail. It is appropriate, therefore, to indicate some of the areas in which further work is required.

We have chosen to defer two issues, namely, trial by jury and police harassment, for subsequent consideration in our second Report under this Reference, which will deal with religious minorities and multicultural justice issues. This decision was based on our belief that the interests of Aboriginal peoples and those of ethnic and religious minorities with regard to trial by jury and police harassment are not significantly different.

One purpose of a jury is to allow an accused to be tried by his or her peers.[243] Fundamental to that purpose is the possibility that jury members and the accused will have something in common. If jury members share none of the cultural background and experiences of the accused, then the potential benefits may well be lost. However, the issue becomes more complicated when one also considers that the jury is intended to represent the community. Whose interests is it most important to protect, and how are competing interests to be balanced?

The police have sometimes been accused of using their vast discretionary powers simply for harassment: recently, for example, the systematic stopping of many Kahnawake motorists by the Quebec Police Force, ostensibly for highway traffic purposes, has heightened tensions in the wake of the Oka crisis.[244] In due course we will be canvassing various methods for responding to these complaints — for example, through police complaint procedures, court action or human rights legislation — but we are not yet in a position to make a firm recommendation.

As this Report reveals, much additional work, specific to Aboriginal peoples, is required and should be undertaken as part of the implementation of this Report's recommendations. Still needed are research into customary law, a review of legal aid eligibility

---

243. A 1989 study reported that there had not yet been a single jury trial in Nova Scotia in which an Aboriginal person has served as a juror: Marshall Inquiry, vol. 3, *supra*, note 18 at 48.

244. See "Armed Mohawks, Police Clash Violently" *The [Toronto] Globe and Mail* (9 January 1991) A1-A2; "Issue of Policing at Centre of Storm," "Police Patrols Increased on Reserve" and "Oka Lesson Ignored, Natives Say" *The [Toronto] Globe and Mail* (10 January 1991) A5.

guidelines and the creation of special interrogation rules. We have also suggested that an Aboriginal Justice Institute should commission empirical studies into certain areas, such as sentencing disparity.

Among our proposals is a call for special rules regarding Aboriginal offenders in a number of situations. The details of those individual rules, and in addition more general issues, need to be decided. Will the rules be legislated or introduced through guidelines? Will they apply to all Aboriginal persons? Whose responsibility will it be to raise a rule? What consequences will flow from failing to follow the rules? These are matters calling for separate, sustained and detailed study.

Beyond this, other areas need further research. One especially important issue is the situation regarding Aboriginal women. Aboriginal persons are incarcerated in a much higher percentage than their proportion in the population, and this disproportion is especially pronounced for Aboriginal women.[245] Aboriginal women are also more likely to be incarcerated far from home. Other correctional issues affecting these women also arise: Are the standards applied in deciding the security classification of female offenders, or in assessing transfer applications, for example, inherently biased against Aboriginal women? There are also several notorious examples of the justice system failing Aboriginal women who have been victims.[246] Specific study of Aboriginal women in the criminal justice system is therefore called for. For similar reasons, particular consideration of Aboriginal young offenders is also required.

The quality and the quantity of legal services Aboriginal persons receive have often been raised as a concern. Should there be a national role in setting minimum standards, either through legal aid funding (which covers only some lawyers) or some other means? A study on this subject should be mounted.

We have proposed local control of police forces: in that regard, questions requiring study arise. To whom in the community would such police forces be accountable? Would they have any accountability beyond the local level? Would such safeguards be necessary to prevent the political use of local police forces?

It has also been suggested to us that some type of mechanism to allow communities a say in which judges are assigned to work there would be appropriate. We agree that the idea deserves consideration, but an exploration into its ramifications would be required before we could be in a position to make a recommendation. In the same vein, recommendations regarding the appointment process for judges also might be appropriate, but we have not as yet made any suggestions in this area. Further investigation is required.

---

245. According to the Canadian Centre for Justice Statistics, ''Adult Female Offenders in the Provincial/Territorial Corrections Systems, 1989-90'' (1991) 11:6 Juristat 1 at 5, 29.1% of women in provincial/territorial facilities were Aboriginal, while 16.9% of male prisoners were Aboriginal, and ''[s]ince 1986-87 these proportions have remained stable.''

246. The murder of Helen Betty Osborne is the best-known example.

Cross-cultural training programs increase the level of knowledge that actors in the criminal justice system have concerning Aboriginal persons, but they are not designed to change underlying attitudes. Changing those attitudes, especially through short-term programs, is a much more difficult task. Further research into effective methods of anti-racism training is therefore necessary.

The number of female Aboriginal offenders who commit suicide in prison is disturbing, as is the much higher suicide rate among Aboriginal people generally.[247] Examination of Aboriginal suicide and its relationship to incarceration or to the criminal justice system is called for.

These are a few of the areas that clearly justify additional research and study. Some of this could be done by an Aboriginal Justice Institute and, as noted, it is our hope to carry some of it out ourselves. However, this agenda for future research and study should not in any way prevent the immediate implementation of other valuable reforms, where possible. Some of our recommendations require no further detail, while others need filling in and refinement through negotiation or implementation. Most importantly, although more study can always be justified, action is needed and is possible, now.

II. Some Final Observations

The system that many Aboriginal people would replace or drastically alter is much admired the world over, because it is generally characterized by humanity and a respect for human dignity. However, as we have reported, this has not been the experience of Aboriginal peoples with the system.

History records that Canada's Aboriginal peoples have suffered terrible and devastating wrongs. As a result, traditional Aboriginal life has been drastically altered and, in some communities, distorted beyond recognition. The conclusion has been drawn that "the original lifestyle of Aboriginal society, characteristic of pre-European contact, will never again be fully reached."[248] Whether this is true or not is ultimately irrelevant insofar as Aboriginal aspirations and political strivings are concerned. Aboriginal peoples have consistently voiced their desire to establish systems of justice that incorporate their own values, customs, traditions and beliefs but that permit the adaptation of these features to the realities of the modern age. They have well-articulated and amply documented reasons for preferring their vision to the present criminal justice system — a system to which, they contend, they have never consented and that can never command their respect.

---

247. In 1986, 34 Status Indians, 54 Inuit but only 15 in 100,000 of all Canadians committed suicide: see Standing Committee on Aboriginal Affairs, *Unfinished Business: An Agenda for All Canadians in the 1990's*, Second Report (Ottawa: The Committee, 1990) Appendix C.

248. Osnaburgh/Windigo Report, *supra*, note 43 at 37.

The Canadian people have reached a better understanding of the Aboriginal reality and have come to acknowledge the legitimacy of Aboriginal historical grievances.[249] That recognition is now supplemented by a willingness among Canadians to attempt to redress past injustices.[250]

Substantial changes to the present system are urgently required. Our own work over a period of twenty years in the fields of criminal law and procedure bears sufficient testimony to this fact. The many system alterations which we propose in this Report are, in our view, necessary to provide as much effective, remedial relief as possible. We believe that these proposals can facilitate the creation of the kind of plural legal reality that Aboriginal peoples desire and our Constitution is able to accommodate.

We accept the necessity to effect fundamental changes to the criminal justice system in order to ensure that Aboriginal persons are treated equitably and with respect. Equal access to justice in this context means equal access to a system that is sensitive to the needs and aspirations of Aboriginal people. That system, as we have repeatedly emphasized throughout this Report, is not uniform. Nor does it invariably require a marked departure from the present one. It must, however, be a system that the Aboriginal peoples themselves have shaped and moulded to their particular needs.

---

249. See *Citizens' Forum on Canada's Future: Report to the People and Government of Canada* (Ottawa: Supply and Services Canada, 1991) at 74-85.

250. *Ibid.* at 120-21.

Summary of Recommendations

The Meaning of Equal Access to Justice, Equitable Treatment and Respect

1. The criminal justice system must provide the same minimum level of service to all people and must treat Aboriginal persons equitably and with respect. To achieve these objectives, the cultural distinctiveness of Aboriginal peoples should be recognized, respected and, where appropriate, incorporated into the criminal justice system.

The Desirability of Aboriginal Justice Systems

2. Aboriginal communities identified by the legitimate representatives of Aboriginal peoples as being willing and capable should have the authority to establish Aboriginal justice systems. The federal and provincial governments should enter into negotiations to transfer that authority to those Aboriginal communities.

Criminal Justice System Recruitment and Training

3. (1) Programs should be established to bring more Aboriginal persons into all aspects of the criminal justice system, including as police, lawyers, judges, probation officers and correctional officials. More specifically, the following steps should be taken:

(a) police forces and correctional services should hire Aboriginal persons through affirmative action if necessary, and an affirmative action policy should be carried over into access to training and promotion decisions;

(b) recruitment programs to draw more Aboriginal persons into law schools should be financially supported to a greater extent than is presently the case; and

(c) Aboriginal persons should be appointed as judges at all levels of the judiciary, based on consultation with Aboriginal communities to identify appropriate candidates.

(2) Aboriginal courtworker programs should be expanded, and their functions should include involvement with Aboriginal accused persons at all stages of the investigation and prosecution process, particularly where a lawyer is not immediately and continuously available.

(3) Cross-cultural training for all participants in the criminal justice system, including police, lawyers, judges, probations officers and correctional officials, should be expanded and improved. This training should be mandatory and ongoing for those whose regular duties bring them into significant contact with Aboriginal persons. Local Aboriginal groups should be closely involved in the design and implementation of the training.

(4) Information concerning Aboriginal culture should be incorporated into law school programs.

(5) Legal aid services should make arrangements to allow some lawyers to specialize in representing Aboriginal persons.

Overcoming Language Difficulties and Cultural Barriers

4. (1) The right of Aboriginal peoples to express themselves in their own Aboriginal languages in all court proceedings should be statutorily recognized. Qualified interpreters should be provided at public expense to all Aboriginal persons who need assistance in court proceedings.

(2) Legislation should provide that interpreters be provided during the pre-trial stage of a police-conducted investigation, including questioning, to any suspect who needs assistance.

(3) The *Criminal Code* and the *Canada Evidence Act* should provide that the costs of interpreter services rendered to accused persons at any stage of the criminal process must be borne by the state.

(4) Notices should be prominently posted, in languages frequently used in the community, in each court house or preferably outside of each courtroom, explaining the section 14 *Charter* right to an interpreter. These notices should set out:

(a) the requirements for obtaining an interpreter;

(b) that an accused or witness who speaks some English or French may still be entitled to an interpreter; and

(c) that, if an interpreter is ordered, the accused or witness will not be required to pay for it.

(5) Duty counsel should be instructed to pay particular attention to the language abilities of Aboriginal accused.

(6) Unless advised by counsel that it is unnecessary, judges should satisfy themselves on first appearance that Aboriginal accused or witnesses speak and understand the language in which the proceedings are to be conducted.

(7) The need for, the feasibility and the cost of providing simultaneous translation services to members of the Aboriginal public attending court hearings on or near reserves should be examined.

(8) A system should be established to train independent, competent professional interpreters for criminal cases. As a general rule, only such interpreters should qualify to assist in criminal cases.

Increasing Community Involvement with the Justice System

5. (1) Consideration should be given to making "Peacemakers" a formal aspect of the justice system to mediate disputes.

(2) Permanent liaison mechanisms should be established between local Crown prosecutors and Aboriginal communities and leaders.

(3) Representatives of the accused's community should be allowed to give evidence, at bail hearings, of available alternatives to custody pending trial.

(4) Lay assessors (Elders or other respected members of the community) should be permitted by express statutory provision to sit with a judge to advise on appropriate sentences.

(5) A process of ongoing consultation between Aboriginal service providers and officials of the Correctional Service of Canada and the National Parole Board should be established.

(6) Aboriginal communities should be involved in the preparation of release plans for Aboriginal offenders and the supervision of those persons in their communities following release.

Applying Customary Law and Practices

6. The federal government should provide funding for research into Aboriginal customary law.

7. Governments should develop clear and public policies concerning the preferred methods for determining Aboriginal and treaty rights. These policies should encourage identifying areas of conflict through discussion with Aboriginal communities, for the purpose of negotiating agreements about those issues with the affected parties. Where litigation is necessary, declaratory relief or court references should be preferred to the laying of charges, but if prosecutions are commenced, multiple proceedings should be vigorously discouraged and only a single test case pursued.

The Police

8. (1) The police must be more involved in and accountable to the communities they serve.

(2) Community-based policing should be facilitated to the fullest extent in Aboriginal communities that wish to continue to have external police services.

(3) The federal and provincial governments should facilitate autonomous Aboriginal police forces wherever local communities desire them. No single structure or role for that police force should be demanded. If the force is to be autonomous, then its structure and its role must be determined by the community.

(4) Funding for autonomous police services should not be limited to programs that are directly analogous to existing agencies.

(5) Although police officers should retain the discretion to decide when to lay charges, they should routinely seek advice from Crown prosecutors, including advice as to whether it is appropriate to lay charges at all.

(6) The police should take special care, when presenting an Aboriginal person with an appearance notice, to confirm that that person understands the significance of failing to appear in court and is clearly made aware of the appearance date; in particular, the officer should inquire whether there is any reason the person will be unavailable and make reasonable accommodations concerning the date. Instruction manuals and training courses should be altered so as to give effect to this recommendation. It should be emphasized, however, that no accused should be unnecessarily detained simply to comply with this recommendation.

(7) Police forces should be encouraged to use forms translated into the language of the relevant community where possible and where the nature and extent of police contact with the community justifies the practice.

Prosecutors

9. **(1) All public criminal prosecutions should be conducted by a lawyer responsible to and under the supervision of the Attorney General.**

(2) No person other than a lawyer responsible to and under the supervision of the Attorney General should be entitled to conduct prosecutions of hunting, trapping and fishing offences.

(3) Prosecutors should be clearly instructed, by directive and through training, that they are to exercise their discretion independent of police influence or pressure and that their advice to the police must remain dispassionate and impartial.

(4) A clearly stated policy should be published and implemented concerning the public interest factors that should and should not be taken into consideration in decisions on whether to commence or stop a prosecution.

(5) The *Criminal Code* should be amended to provide for a statutory duty of complete and timely disclosure in all prosecutions.

(6) Federal and provincial attorneys general should adopt a policy of early post-charge screening of charges by Crown prosecutors.

Defence Counsel

10. **(1) Provincial bar associations and legal aid societies should make public legal education materials — in particular, information about how to obtain legal aid — readily available to Aboriginal persons. Where necessary, video technology should be used or materials should be produced in Aboriginal languages.**

(2) Legal aid eligibility guidelines should be reviewed to ensure that they do not have an unequal impact on Aboriginal persons. The governments concerned should ensure that funding is available to provide necessary legal services to all Aboriginal persons who require assistance.

(3) Special interrogation rules governing the taking of statements from Aboriginal persons should be created, including rules concerning the presence of counsel or some other person during questioning.

The Courts

11. **(1) Courtrooms serving Aboriginal communities should be physically set up in a way that is sensitive to Aboriginal culture and tradition.**

(2) Federal legislation should give federally appointed justices of the peace jurisdiction to deal with all matters conferred on justices of the peace under both the *Criminal Code* and the *Indian Act*. Greater use should be made of this federal appointment power so as to appoint more Aboriginal justices of the peace.

(3) The right of Aboriginal persons to swear an oath in a traditional way when giving evidence in court should be recognized.

(4) Court dates for Aboriginal accused persons should be scheduled to avoid, where possible, hunting and trapping seasons. Chief justices of the affected courts should develop scheduling policies in conjunction with and on the advice of community representatives.

(5) Statutory authority should allow for appearances to be made through electronic means.

(6) An accused who is released by a court some distance from the place where the arrest was made should, in the discretion of the court, be returned home or to such other place as is reasonably designated by the accused. The *Criminal Code* should contain a statutory direction requiring the judge to inquire into this issue. The cost of transportation should be borne by the state.

(7) The *Code* should provide that a detainee who is released "unconditionally" (that is, without charges being laid) should automatically be returned to the place of arrest or to such other place as is reasonably designated by the detainee.

(8) Where court hearings are not held in or near an Aboriginal community, accused persons and witnesses under subpoena should be provided with transportation to and from court hearings or sufficient conduct money to cover the cost of transportation.

(9) Wherever possible and desired by the community, the court sitting should occur in or near the Aboriginal community in which the offence was committed.

(10) Because fly-in courts do not provide remote communities with legal services equal to those available elsewhere, they should be phased out where possible. Where fly-in courts are used, steps should be taken to guarantee that

(a) defence counsel is available to all accused persons on a date meaningfully in advance of the court hearing;

(b) Crown prosecutors consult with the affected communities enough in advance of court hearings to ensure that the public interest is protected; and

(c) sufficient resources, including additional judicial appointments, if necessary, are provided to ensure that court hearings need not be rushed and can be held within a reasonable time after the offence.

12. (1) An endorsement permitting a peace officer to release an arrested person on an appearance notice should be available for all crimes. Legislation should expressly require a justice to consider making an endorsement when issuing an arrest warrant.

(2) Any peace officer should have the discretion to release a person arrested for any crime, by means of an expanded appearance notice which could include conditions that, at present, only the officer in charge can impose. A peace officer should be required to release the person unless specific grounds of detention are satisfied.

(3) Bail legislation should specifically provide that, in assessing the reasonableness of any condition of release, the justice must consider:

(a) an accused's occupation, place of residence and cultural background;

(b) the geographical location and size of the community to which the accused belongs; and

(c) the special requirements of traditional Aboriginal pursuits.

(4) A condition requiring an accused to refrain from the use of alcohol should only be attached if the use of alcohol contributed to the offence with which the accused is charged.

(5) There should be no criminal liability for breaching non-monetary conditions of release.

(6) Bail legislation should be amended to provide that, in considering the suitability of an intended surety, a justice shall consider:

(a) the financial resources the intended surety has or may reasonably be expected to have;

(b) his or her character and the nature of any previous convictions;

(c) his or her proximity (whether in kinship, place of residence or otherwise) to the accused; and

(d) any other relevant matter.

(7) A justice should only be allowed to require a surety to deposit cash or other security if the justice is satisfied that exceptional circumstances related to the surety require such an order — for example, where the intended surety resides in another jurisdiction.

(8) A surety should be under a duty to take all reasonable steps to ensure the attendance of the accused in court. The surety should not be liable to forfeiture for the accused's breach of other bail conditions.

(9) If a justice orders a person to obtain a surety and that condition is not met within twenty-four hours, the imposition of that condition should be reconsidered.

(10) The requirement of a cash deposit by the accused should either be abolished or be subject to greater restriction, such as requiring a cash deposit only where the justice believes on reasonable grounds that the deposit is necessary to prevent the accused from leaving the country.

Sentencing

13. (1) Alternatives to imprisonment should be used whenever possible. The *Criminal Code* provisions creating such alternatives should ensure that those alternatives are given first consideration at sentencing. A judge imprisoning an Aboriginal person for an offence amenable to the use of alternative dispositions should be required to set forth the reasons for using imprisonment rather than a non-custodial option.

(2) Programs providing alternatives to incarceration should, to the extent possible, be universally available. To pursue this goal, adequate financial and human resources must be made available and comprehensive cost-feasibility studies should be undertaken immediately.

(3) Research must be accompanied by monitoring of the programs, together with policy analyses, to allow for structural readjustment as experience is gathered.

(4) Victim-offender reconciliation programs should be expanded and ought to be evaluated more thoroughly than has been done to date. Federal and provincial governments should provide the necessary financial support to ensure that community programs are made more generally available and to encourage their greater use.

(5) The *Criminal Code* should contain a counterpart to the "alternative measures" provisions in the *Young Offenders Act*, for disposing of and diverting cases against adult Aboriginal offenders.

(6) Fine option programs should be created in communities that wish to institute them. The programs should be provided with resources adequate to allow the community to mount projects that will promote a sense of accomplishment and self-worth. Special measures should be taken to make these programs accessible to Aboriginal women.

(7) The provinces should be encouraged to institute pilot projects on the use of day-fine systems, and Aboriginal communities ought to be among the first beneficiaries of such projects.

(8) Incarceration for non-payment of fines should only occur upon a refusal or wilful default to pay a fine, not upon an inability to pay. An offender should not be imprisoned unless the following alternatives have been tried:

(a) show-cause hearings over why the offender has not paid the fine;

(b) attachment of wages, salaries and other moneys;

(c) seizure of the offender's property;

(d) community service equal to the fine; and

(e) alternative community sanctions.

(9) Community service order programs should be created in communities that wish to institute them. The programs should be provided with resources adequate to determine what kind of community service work could be performed and what resources the community needs to make such programs succeed. Much greater care must be taken in the design of these programs, and the enabling statute or regulation should clearly set out the purposes of the programs. There must be appropriate education of the judiciary, Crown prosecutors and defence counsel about the purposes and availability of the programs. While its use should be encouraged, the *Criminal Code* should provide that a community service order will only be imposed after the court has ascertained from the community the opportunities for community service and the willingness of the community to accept the offender.

(10) Probation services, modified to meet the needs of Aboriginal offenders, should be provided in a wide range of Aboriginal communities. More use should be made of community resources, coupled with a commitment to train individuals from the communities to serve as probation officers.

(11) The criteria governing eligibility for probation should be formulated to have proper regard for cultural differences and to meet the needs of Aboriginal offenders and communities. In addition, probation reports should give greater emphasis to factors such as the offender's skills, potential employability and preparedness to enrol in treatment or training programs. The community's willingness to become involved in the probation and supervision of the offender should also take on added importance.

(12) Further research should be conducted into whether Aboriginal persons receive harsher sentences than non-Aboriginal persons, and, if so, the causes of that disparity.

(13) A list of factors should be enunciated which, in conjunction with other circumstances, would mitigate sentence where the offender is an Aboriginal person. For example, where an offender is an Aboriginal person, the sentence to be imposed should be reduced if the offender has already been, or will be, subject to traditional sanctions imposed by the community.

(14) As we have previously recommended, a well-structured, visible and responsible process of plea discussion and agreement should be established.

(15) The *Criminal Code* provisions pertaining to pre-sentence reports should be considerably more detailed than at present. At a minimum, the contents of those reports and the circumstances in which they are to be ordered should be the subject of clear statutory provisions.

(16) The *Criminal Code* should provide that pre-sentence reports shall set out and consider the special circumstances of Aboriginal offenders.

(17) Only persons familiar with the general condition of Aboriginal peoples and with their customs, culture and values should prepare pre-sentence reports.

(18) Where incarceration of an offender is being considered for the first time (and incarceration is not required by law), the court should be expressly obliged to order a pre-sentence report. Moreover, the statute should direct that, whenever incarceration is contemplated, the judge should consider ordering a report.

(19) Where a pre-sentence report is to be prepared, the court should ensure that any unrepresented offender is advised of the possible benefits of having counsel.

(20) Subsection 100(1) of the *Criminal Code* should be amended to allow for a limited exemption to the mandatory prohibition on the possession of weapons, where a judge is satisfied that the prohibition would be oppressive and unfair and that allowing the offender to have access to weapons for the purpose of making a living would not cause any threat to public safety.

Corrections

14. (1) Aboriginal spirituality should, by legislation, be given the same recognition as other religions, and Aboriginal Elders should be given the same status and freedom as prison chaplains.

(2) A review of all programming should be undertaken, in co-operation with Aboriginal persons and organizations, to develop programs and services that are culturally relevant to Aboriginal inmates. Aboriginal service organizations and prisoners' support groups should be systematically involved in program and service delivery and should be appropriately funded in this regard.

(3) The National Parole Board and the Correctional Service of Canada should develop a national policy and guidelines concerning waiver of parole applications, parole hearings and reviews, and appropriate training should be provided to correctional staff. Information as to the national policy and guidelines should be made available to inmates.

(4) Aboriginal community organizations should be funded to design and administer after-care programs for Aboriginal people. In particular, the use of alternative residential facilities for Aboriginal offenders in areas where half-way houses are neither available nor economically feasible should be promoted.

(5) Smaller local correctional facilities should be created and Aboriginal communities should exercise control over those facilities.

(6) In establishing the Aboriginal healing lodge, the Correctional Service of Canada should ensure that it does so in accordance with the recommendation of the Task Force on Federally Sentenced Women. Aboriginal peoples should be consulted and given effective control over the process.

Ensuring Progress

15. (1) The level of resources currently devoted to Aboriginal justice issues, including provincial resources, should be precisely identified and evaluated. Expenditure priorities should be established in consultation with Aboriginal peoples to decide the best ways to deploy resources and eliminate unnecessary duplication. Comprehensive cost-feasibility studies should be immediately undertaken in respect of all proposals carrying resource implications that are advanced in this Report.

(2) An Aboriginal Justice Institute should be created and should have a broad mandate to deal with any matters relating to Aboriginal persons in the criminal justice system, including:

(a) conducting empirical research;

(b) collecting data;

(c) developing and evaluating programs within the justice system or as alternatives to it;

(d) providing assistance to Aboriginal communities in establishing programs; and

(e) developing policy options regarding Aboriginal justice issues.

(3) The Aboriginal Justice Institute should be instrumental in the design, implementation and monitoring of initiatives concerning criminal justice deriving from proposals advanced in this Report as well as those generated by the commissions of inquiry. The Aboriginal Justice Institute should be staffed, operated and controlled by Aboriginal persons to the fullest extent possible.

APPENDIX A

Unpublished Studies Commissioned for This Report

Doob, Anthony N., and Philip C. Stenning. *Report to the Law Reform Commission of Canada on the Aboriginal Reference from the Minister of Justice, Canada.* 1991.

Indigenous Bar Association. *The* Criminal Code *and Aboriginal People.* 1991.

Jackson, Michael. *In Search of the Pathways to Justice: Alternative Dispute Resolution in Aboriginal Communities.* 1991.

Kaiser, H. Archibald. *The* Criminal Code *of Canada: A Review Based on the Minister's Reference.* 1991.

Monture, Patricia A., and Mary Ellen Turpel, eds. *Aboriginal Peoples and Canadian Criminal Law: Rethinking Justice.* 1991.

Zimmerman, Susan V. *The Revolving Door of Despair: Native Involvement in the Criminal Justice System.* * 1991.

The last five of the above studies will be published under separate cover.

---

* This study was developed in conjunction with the Aboriginal Justice Inquiry of Manitoba, and derives in part from a background study prepared by Kenneth Chasse.

APPENDIX B

Consultants

On March 18 and 19, 1991, the Commission met with a group of consultants in Edmonton, Alberta. Present at that consultation were:

Mr. Daniel Bellgarde,
First Vice-Chief,
Federation of Saskatchewan Indian Nations

Ms. Marion Buller,
Barrister and Solicitor,
Member, Indigenous Bar Association

Mr. Dennis Callihoo,
Barrister and Solicitor

Mr. Larry Chartrand,
Chair,
Indigenous Bar Association Justice
    Committee

Professor Paul Chartrand,
Department of Native Studies,
University of Manitoba

Professor Michael Jackson,
Faculty of Law,
University of British Columbia

Ms. Deborah Jacobs,
Associate Director of Education,
Squamish Nation

Professor Archibald Kaiser,
Dalhousie Law School

Ms. Joan Lavalee,
Elder

Mr. Tony Mandamin,
Barrister and Solicitor

Mr. Ovide Mercredi,
Barrister and Solicitor,
Vice-Chief,
Assembly of First Nations

Professor Patricia Monture,
Dalhousie Law School

Ms. Eileen Powless,
Barrister and Solicitor,
Indian Association of Alberta

Ms. Carol Roberts,
Legal Counsel,
Department of Justice (Northwest
    Territories)

Professor Philip C. Stenning,
Centre of Criminology,
University of Toronto,
Former Consultant to Marshall Inquiry

Ms. Fran Sugar,
Task Force on Federally Sentenced
    Women

Mr. Allan Torbitt,
Political Co-ordinator,
Assembly of Manitoba Chiefs

Ms. Rosemary Trehearne,
Manager, Justice Programs,
Council for Yukon Indians

On March 25 and 26, 1991, a consultation was held in Toronto, Ontario. Present at that consultation were:

Mr. Jerome Berthellete,
Executive Director,
National Association of Friendship Centres
   of Canada

Mr. Ian Cowie,
Barrister and Solicitor,
Consultant

Sergeant Bob Crawford,
Metro Toronto Police Force

Mr. Chester Cunningham,
Executive Director,
Native Counselling Services of Alberta

Mr. Ab Currie,
Department of Justice

Professor Anthony N. Doob,
Centre of Criminology,
University of Toronto,
Former Member,
Canadian Sentencing Commission,
Consultant to the Nishnawbe-Aski Legal
   Services Corporation

Grand Chief Phil Fontaine,
Association of Manitoba Chiefs

Mr. John Giokas,
Department of Justice

Mr. Roger Jones,
Barrister and Solicitor,
Former President,
Indigenous Bar Association

Ms. Rosemarie Kuptana,
Former Vice-President,
Inuit Circumpolar Conference

Mr. Harry Laforme,
Commissioner,
Indian Commission of Ontario

Mr. Ovide Mercredi,
Barrister and Solicitor,
Vice-Chief,
Assembly of First Nations

Chief Henry Mianscum,
Mistissini Band (Cree)

Professor Patricia A. Monture
Dalhousie Law School

Grand Chief Mike Mitchell,
Mohawk Council,
Territory of Akwesasne

Mrs. Carole V. Montagnes,
Executive Director,
Ontario Native Council on Justice

Professor Graydon Nicholas,
Chair, Native Studies,
St. Thomas University,
Former President,
Union of New Brunswick Indians

Mr. Moses Okimaw,
Barrister and Solicitor,
Association of Manitoba Chiefs

Chief Violet Pachanos,
Chisasibi Band (Cree)

Mr. Gordon Peters,
Ontario Regional Chief,
Chiefs of Ontario

Ms. Viola Robinson,
President,
Native Council of Canada

Chief Tom Sampson,
Chair,
First Nations of the South Island Tribal
   Council
British Columbia

Mr. Art Solomon,
Elder

Mr. Lewis Staats,
Member,
Six Nations Police Commission

Professor Philip C. Stenning,
Centre of Criminology,
University of Toronto,
Former Consultant to Marshall Inquiry

Mr. Paul Williams,
Counsel to Iroquois Confederacy,
Barrister and Solicitor practising
   exclusively Aboriginal Law

Chief Bill Wilson,
Barrister and Solicitor,
First Nations Congress

On April 30, 1991, the Commission, responding to a request for a meeting from the Métis National Council, consulted with members of the Council in Winnipeg, Manitoba. Present at that consultation were:

Ms. Cynthia Bertolin,
Barrister and Solicitor

Mr. David Chartrand,
Manitoba Métis Federation

Professor Paul L. A. H. Chartrand,
Department of Native Studies,
University of Manitoba

Mr. Norman Evans,
Barrister and Solicitor

Mr. David Gray,
Legal Counsel,
Manitoba Métis Federation

Mr. Ron Rivard,
Executive Director,
Métis National Council

Mr. Edward Swain,
Manitoba Métis Federation

On July 25, 26, and 30, 1991, the Commission met in Ottawa with a group of reviewers to receive advice and comments on a draft of the Report. Present at those meetings were:

Professor Jean-Paul Brodeur,
International Centre for Comparative
   Criminology,
University of Montreal

Ms. Marion Buller,
Barrister and Solicitor,
Member, Indigenous Bar Association

Professor Paul L. A. H. Chartrand,
Department of Native Studies,
University of Manitoba

Professor Michael Jackson,
Faculty of Law,
University of British Columbia

Mr. Roger Jones,
Barrister and Solicitor,
Former President,
Indigenous Bar Association

Ms. Rosemary Trehearne,
Manager, Justice Programs,
Council for Yukon Indians

Mr. Paul Williams,
Counsel to Iroquois Confederacy,
Barrister and Solicitor practising
   exclusively Aboriginal Law

600587

Rapports et documents de travail de la Commission de réforme du droit du Canada

Rapports au Parlement

1. *La preuve** (19 déc. 1975)
2. *Principes directeurs — Sentences et mesures non sentencielles dans le processus pénal** (6 févr. 1976)
3. *Notre droit pénal* (25 mars 1976)
4. *L'expropriation** (8 avril 1976)
5. *Le désordre mental dans le processus pénal** (13 avril 1976)
6. *Le droit de la famille** (4 mai 1976)
7. *L'observance du dimanche** (19 mai 1976)
8. *La saisie des rémunérations versées par la Couronne du chef du Canada** (19 déc. 1977)
9. *Procédure pénale — Première partie : amendements divers** (23 févr. 1978)
10. *Les infractions sexuelles** (29 nov. 1978)
11. *Le chèque** (8 mars 1979)
12. *Le vol et la fraude** (16 mars 1979)
13. *Les commissions consultatives et les commissions d'enquête** (18 avril 1980)
14. *Le contrôle judiciaire et la Cour fédérale** (25 avril 1980)
15. *Les critères de détermination de la mort** (8 avril 1981)
16. *Le jury** (28 juill. 1982)
17. *L'outrage au tribunal** (18 août 1982)
18. *L'obtention de motifs avant la formation d'un recours judiciaire — Commission d'appel de l'immigration** (16 déc. 1982)
19. *Le mandat de main-forte et le télémandat** (22 juill. 1983)
20. *Euthanasie, aide au suicide et interruption de traitement* (11 oct. 1983)
21. *Les méthodes d'investigation scientifiques : l'alcool, la drogue et la conduite des véhicules** (10 nov. 1983)
22. *La communication de la preuve par la poursuite** (15 juin 1984)
23. *L'interrogatoire des suspects* (19 nov. 1984)
24. *Les fouilles, les perquisitions et les saisies* (22 mars 1985)
25. *Les techniques d'investigation policière et les droits de la personne* (12 juin 1985)
26. *Les organismes administratifs autonomes** (23 oct. 1985)
27. *La façon de disposer des choses saisies* (24 avril 1986)
28. *Quelques aspects du traitement médical et le droit pénal** (12 juin 1986)
29. *L'arrestation* (6 nov. 1986)
30. *Pour une nouvelle codification du droit pénal : Volume 1* (3 déc. 1986)
31. *Pour une nouvelle codification du droit pénal — Édition révisée et augmentée du rapport n° 30* (19 mai 1988)
32. *Notre procédure pénale* (21 juin 1988)
33. *Pour une nouvelle codification de la procédure pénale, Volume premier, Titre premier* (27 février 1991)

Documents de travail

1. *Le tribunal de la famille** (1974)
2. *La notion de blâme — La responsabilité stricte** (1974)
3. *Les principes de la détermination de la peine et du prononcé de la sentence** (1974)
4. *La communication de la preuve** (1974)
5. *Le dédommagement et l'indemnisation** (1974)
6. *L'amende** (1974)
7. *La déjudiciarisation** (1975)
8. *Les biens des époux** (1975)
9. *Expropriation** (1975)
10. *Les confins du droit pénal : leur détermination à partir de l'obscénité** (1975)
11. *Emprisonnement — Libération** (1975)
12. *Les divorcés et leur soutien** (1975)
13. *Le divorce** (1975)
14. *Processus pénal et désordre mental** (1975)
15. *Les poursuites pénales : responsabilité politique ou judiciaire** (1975)
16. *Responsabilité pénale et conduite collective** (1976)
17. *Les commissions d'enquête — Une nouvelle loi** (1977)
18. *La Cour fédérale — Contrôle judiciaire** (1977)
19. *Le vol et la fraude — Les infractions** (1977)
20. *L'outrage au tribunal — Infractions contre l'administration de la justice** (1977)
21. *Les paiements par virement de crédit** (1978)
22. *Infractions sexuelles** (1978)
23. *Les critères de détermination de la mort** (1979)
24. *La stérilisation et les personnes souffrant de handicaps mentaux** (1979)
25. *Les organismes administratifs autonomes** (1980)
26. *Le traitement médical et le droit criminel** (1980)
27. *Le jury en droit pénal** (1980)
28. *Euthanasie, aide au suicide et interruption de traitement* (1982)
29. *Partie générale : responsabilité et moyens de défense* (1982)
30. *Les pouvoirs de la police : les fouilles, les perquisitions et les saisies en droit pénal** (1983)
31. *Les dommages aux biens — Le vandalisme* (1984)
32. *L'interrogatoire des suspects** (1984)
33. *L'homicide** (1984)
34. *Les méthodes d'investigation scientifiques** (1984)
35. *Le libelle diffamatoire* (1984)
36. *Les dommages aux biens — Le crime d'incendie* (1984)
37. *La juridiction extra-territoriale* (1984)
38. *Les voies de fait** (1984)
39. *Les procédures postérieures à la saisie* (1985)

---

* Ces documents sont épuisés mais ils peuvent être consultés dans de nombreuses bibliothèques.

La Commission a également publié au-delà de soixante-dix documents d'étude portant sur divers aspects du droit. Pour obtenir le catalogue des publications, écrire à : Commission de réforme du droit du Canada, 130, rue Albert, Ottawa (Ontario) K1A 0L6, ou Bureau 310, Place du Canada, Montréal (Québec) H3B 2N2.

---

* Ces documents sont épuisés mais ils peuvent être consultés dans de nombreuses bibliothèques.

LES PEUPLES AUTOCHTONES

ET LA JUSTICE PÉNALE

RAPPORT

SUR

LES PEUPLES AUTOCHTONES

ET LA JUSTICE PÉNALE

Égalité, respect et justice à l'horizon

Préparé à la demande de
la Ministre de la Justice
en vertu du paragraphe 12(2)
de la *Loi sur la Commission
de réforme du droit*

Données de catalogage avant publication (Canada)

Commission de réforme du droit du Canada

Les peuples autochtones et la justice pénale : égalité, respect et justice à l'horizon

(Rapport ; 34)
Texte en français et en anglais disposé tête-bêche.
Titre de la p. de t. addit. : Égalité, respect et justice à l'horizon
Comprend des références bibliographiques.
ISBN 0-662-58641-7
No de cat. MAS J31-58/1991

1. Indiens — Amérique du Nord — Canada — Système pénal. 2. Justice pénale — Administration — Canada. 3. Procédure pénale — Canada. I. Titre. II. Titre : Report on aboriginal
peoples and criminal justice. III. Coll. : Commission de réforme du droit du Canada.
Rapport ; 34.

KE7722.C75L38 1991   345.71'05   C91-098750-5F

On peut obtenir ce document gratuitement en écrivant à :

Commission de réforme du droit du Canada
130, rue Albert, 7ᵉ étage
Ottawa, Canada
K1A 0L6

ou

Bureau 310
Place du Canada
Montréal (Québec)
H3B 2N2

Commission de réforme du droit du Canada 1991
Nᵒ de catalogue J31-58/1991
ISBN 0-662-58641-7

Décembre 1991

L'Honorable A. Kim Campbell, c.p., députée
Ministre de la Justice
   et Procureure générale du Canada
Ottawa, Canada

Madame la Ministre,

Comme suite à la demande que vous nous avez faite en vertu du paragraphe 12(2) de la *Loi sur la Commission de réforme du droit*, et conformément à l'article 16 de la même loi, nous avons l'honneur de vous présenter le rapport résultant des recherches effectuées sur les peuples autochtones et la justice pénale par la Commission de réforme du droit du Canada.

Veuillez agréer, Madame la Ministre, l'assurance de notre très haute considération.

Gilles Létourneau
président

Ellen Picard
vice-présidente

John Frecker
commissaire

Jacques Frémont
commissaire

La Commission

Me Gilles Létourneau, président
Mme la juge Ellen Picard, vice-présidente*
Me John Frecker, commissaire
M. le professeur Jacques Frémont, commissaire**

Secrétaire

François Handfield, *B.A.*, *LL.L.*

Directeur du projet de recherche, Renvoi de la Ministre

Stanley A. Cohen, *B.A.*, *LL.B.*, *LL.M.*

Directeurs adjoints du projet

John E.S. Briggs, *B.A.*, *LL.B.*
Stephen G. Coughlan, *B.A.*, *M.A.*, *LL.B.*, *Ph.D.*

Conseillers

Jean-Paul Brodeur, *M.A.* (Phil.), *M.A.* (Crim.), *Ph.D.*
Marion Buller, *B.A.*, *LL.B.*
Paul L.A.H. Chartrand, *B.A.*, *LL.B.*, *LL.M.*
Glenn A. Gilmour, *B.A.*, *LL.B.*
Michael Jackson, *LL.B.*, *LL.M.*
Roger Jones, *B.A.*, *LL.B.*
H. Archibald Kaiser, *B.A.*, *LL.B.*, *LL.M.*
Leonard (Tony) Mandamin, *B.Sc.*, *LL.B.*
Patricia A. Monture-OKanee, *B.A.*, *LL.B.*
David L. Pomerant, *B.A.*, *LL.B.*
Rosemary Trehearne
Mary Ellen Turpel, *B.A.*, *LL.B.*, *LL.M.*, *J.S.D.*
Paul Williams, *LL.B.*, *LL.M.*
Susan V. Zimmerman, *B.A.*, *B.C.L.*, *LL.B.*

---

* N'était pas membre de la Commission lorsque le présent rapport a été approuvé.

** N'était pas membre de la Commission lorsque les consultations ont eu lieu.

Note de la rédaction

Conformément à la recommandation formulée dans le document intitulé *Égalité pour tous — Rapport du Comité parlementaire sur les droits à l'égalité*, nous nous sommes fait un devoir de rédiger notre rapport dans une langue non sexiste. Dans cette optique, et puisque le mandat de la Commission consiste à formuler des propositions en vue de moderniser les lois fédérales canadiennes, nous nous sommes conformés aux principes énoncés dans l'ouvrage publié sous le titre *Cap sur l'égalité — Réponse au Rapport parlementaire sur les droits à l'égalité*, relativement à la rédaction des lois, tant en français qu'en anglais.

Table des matières

Remerciements

Au cours des travaux qui ont mené à l'élaboration du présent rapport, nous avons eu le privilège de consulter des personnes ayant une vaste expérience au sein de la communauté autochtone qui se sont engagées à défendre et à promouvoir les droits des peuples autochtones. Nous avons également pu bénéficier des commentaires et des conseils que nous ont prodigués des experts œuvrant dans différentes sphères d'activité, soit la police et l'application de la loi, l'enseignement du droit, l'exercice du droit, la magistrature et le système correctionnel. Nous avons aussi consulté des représentants des Administrations fédérale et provinciales ainsi que les membres de commissions d'enquête provinciales sur la justice pénale et les peuples autochtones. Nous tenons à remercier toutes ces personnes et à souligner la contribution marquée de ces groupes à nos travaux.

Il serait impossible de nommer ici toutes les personnes qui ont été consultées dans le contexte de ce rapport, mais nous tenons à remercier plus particulièrement les personnes dont le nom figure à l'annexe B.

CHAPITRE PREMIER

Introduction

I. La nature du renvoi de la Ministre

Dans une lettre en date du 8 juin 1990, la ministre de la Justice priait la Commission, aux termes du paragraphe 12(2) de la *Loi sur la Commission de réforme du droit*[1], d'accorder une priorité spéciale à l'étude du *Code criminel*[2] et de la législation connexe, afin de déterminer la mesure dans laquelle ces textes de loi assurent un accès égal à la justice et un traitement empreint d'équité et de respect aux autochtones et aux personnes faisant partie des minorités religieuses et culturelles. Le mandat général confié par la Ministre à la Commission consistait essentiellement à élaborer « de nouvelles méthodes et de nouveaux concepts de droit correspondant à l'évolution des besoins de la société canadienne moderne et des individus qui la composent[3]. »

À notre avis, la demande de la Ministre rendait nécessaire la division du travail en deux volets : d'abord, étudier la justice pratiquée à l'endroit des autochtones ; ensuite, étudier celle pratiquée à l'endroit des minorités religieuses et culturelles. Voici donc le premier des deux rapports faisant suite à la demande de la Ministre.

Ceux qui connaissent bien le travail de la Commission et son orientation en matière de réforme de la justice pénale pourraient croire qu'avec le présent rapport, la Commission change de cap. Tout au long de nos travaux, nous avons préconisé une démarche uniforme, cohérente et globale pour la réforme du droit. Et voilà que la Ministre nous prie d'étudier en profondeur la situation d'un groupe précis et les difficultés particulières qu'il éprouve dans ses rapports avec la justice pénale. Elle nous demande de proposer des solutions qui corrigeront les iniquités issues d'une histoire ponctuée de préjudices et de souffrances causés par le système, et que l'on pourra adopter en priorité. En réalité, bon nombre des recommandations que nous formulons ici pourraient être appliquées à l'ensemble du système, même si notre but premier est de remédier à la situation particulièrement déplorable des peuples autochtones. D'autres, par contre, concernent spécifiquement ces derniers. Sans revenir sur notre engagement aux principes de l'uniformité et

---

1. L.R.C. (1985), ch. L-7.

2. L.R.C. (1985), ch. C-46.

3. *Loi sur la Commission de réforme du droit*, précitée, note 1, par. 11*d*).

de la cohérence, nous croyons qu'un traitement distinct se justifie du point de vue constitutionnel au regard des articles 25 et 35 de la *Charte canadienne des droits et libertés*[4], qui confèrent aux peuples autochtones un statut constitutionnel unique du fait de leurs droits ancestraux, si ce n'est en vertu des dispositions de la Charte relatives aux programmes de promotion sociale, sous la rubrique des droits à l'égalité.

Nous ne croyons pas que le présent rapport constitue une dérogation à l'approche que nous avons suivie dans nos travaux en droit pénal. Il s'inscrit plutôt dans la mission fondamentale de la Commission, soit celle de créer un système de justice pénale fondé sur la dignité humaine, la liberté et la justice.

Dans le présent rapport, nous avons employé à dessein le mot « autochtone » pour désigner les personnes visées par notre mandat. Tout au long de nos consultations, nous nous sommes rendu compte que les termes « indien » et « membre des premières nations » ne rendaient pas justice à la diversité des peuples auxquels renvoie, au Canada, l'expression « peuples autochtones ». De plus, les appellations incorporant le mot « indien » ne donnent pas entière satisfaction, car de nombreux autochtones le tiennent pour péjoratif. Enfin, notre choix terminologique est conforme à l'article 35 de la *Loi constitutionnelle de 1982*[5] qui parle « des Indiens, des Inuit et des Métis » dans la définition qu'on y donne des peuples autochtones du Canada.

II. Les limites de la présente étude

Un projet aussi vaste et complexe que le nôtre se heurte à d'inévitables limites. Plusieurs facteurs — délais à respecter, organisation à mettre en place et ressources à engager — viennent circonscrire la nature des recherches et, du même coup, le résultat final. Ainsi, dans d'autres circonstances, nous aurions adopté une stratégie de consultation tout à fait différente, par exemple en allant sonder sur place l'opinion des diverses collectivités autochtones. Au lieu de cela, nous avons dû nous contenter de rencontres sur des sujets précis avec un nombre restreint de représentants autochtones dans l'est et dans l'ouest du pays.

Malgré ses limites, ce rapport constitue pour nous la première étape d'un processus beaucoup plus vaste. Bien qu'il renferme de nombreux éléments susceptibles d'être mis en application dès maintenant, notre rapport tente également d'établir un plan d'action pour les années à venir afin qu'on puisse trouver une solution aux problèmes soulevés.

---

4. Partie I de la *Loi constitutionnelle de 1982* [annexe B de la *Loi de 1982 sur le Canada* (1982, R.-U., ch. 11)].

5. Annexe B de la *Loi de 1982 sur le Canada* (1982, R.-U., ch. 11).

III. Le processus de consultation

Dans un premier temps, nous avons fait un envoi postal massif à tous les organismes et experts intéressés par la question. Nous avons pris contact, par lettre ou autrement, avec divers ministères et organismes publics, ainsi qu'avec toutes les commissions d'enquête provinciales dont les travaux étaient en cours.

Nous nous sommes d'emblée rendu compte qu'il nous faudrait à tout le moins sonder les représentants des collectivités concernées et les experts du domaine, de même que les ministères et organismes publics dotés d'attributions touchant directement les peuples autochtones et le système judiciaire. En tout, nous avons organisé trois séances de consultation avec des représentants autochtones. Nous avons sondé les personnes qui étaient en mesure de fournir à la Commission le point de vue particulier des autochtones sur le fonctionnement du système actuel. Nous avons également commandé une série d'études de fond dont on trouvera la liste à l'annexe A.

IV. Le contexte de la réforme du droit

Les représentants autochtones que nous avons consultés ont exprimé de graves réserves à l'égard de la présente étude. Dans l'accent qui y est mis sur le *Code criminel* et la législation connexe, ils ont décelé la volonté, inacceptable à leurs yeux, d'appliquer un « cataplasme » sur le système actuel. À leur avis, il est devenu inutile de faire une fois de plus l'inventaire des lacunes du *Code criminel* ou celles de la pratique du droit pénal. Selon eux, la réflexion doit céder le pas à l'action. Ils estiment également qu'il est futile de vouloir changer le visage du système de justice pénale à une époque où des changements sociaux plus vastes, plus fondamentaux, s'imposent. La modification du *Code criminel* ne fera rien pour améliorer les conditions socio-économiques affligeantes des peuples autochtones, pas plus qu'elle ne satisfera à leurs revendications territoriales séculaires.

Il n'en reste pas moins que le *Code criminel* et l'ensemble de la législation pénale présentent des lacunes qu'il faut absolument combler et que la Commission a consacré une bonne partie des vingt dernières années à mettre en lumière.

Les changements fondamentaux que nous préconisons ne se feront pas du jour au lendemain. Dans l'intervalle, il ne faudra pas cesser de dénoncer les injustices et de les pourchasser jusque dans leurs derniers retranchements. Les peuples autochtones continuent de souffrir ; ils en ont assez d'être qualifiés de « victimes d'une tragédie nationale » et exigent réparation dès maintenant. Nos lois et nos méthodes doivent s'adapter à la situation : nous ne pouvons plus nous permettre d'attendre l'arrivée de quelque nouvel âge.

Nous proposons deux voies de réforme. La première comporte des améliorations à court terme mais risque, force est de l'admettre, de ne rien régler de fondamental. L'autre voie, par contre, s'éloigne sensiblement de la réalité actuelle. Sans doute cette approche parallèle laissera-t-elle perplexes certains lecteurs, du moins a priori. Nos solutions à court terme, comme le fait d'accroître la proportion d'autochtones au sein des effectifs de la justice pénale, pourraient sembler contraires aux changements fondamentaux qu'implique la création d'appareils judiciaires autochtones.

La notion de pluralisme juridique, soit la coexistence de plusieurs systèmes destinés à faire respecter la loi, est au cœur de notre démarche. Nous prévoyons que les collectivités autochtones opteront pour la création de plusieurs systèmes judiciaires, chacun à leur image et allant d'un système correspondant plus ou moins au modèle actuel jusqu'à un système profondément transformé, en passant par divers modèles assortis de traits typiquement autochtones (méthodes différentes de résolution des litiges, rôle des aînés et des « gardiens de la paix » (*peacekeepers*), etc.).

Pour chacune des voies de réforme envisagées, nous espérons susciter un climat propice à la création de systèmes respectés par les autochtones et par les autres Canadiens.

CHAPITRE DEUX

Le point de vue des autochtones sur la justice pénale

On dénombre plusieurs centaines de collectivités autochtones, et chacune d'elles a une expérience bien particulière de la justice pénale canadienne. Cette grande diversité nous oblige à dresser, dans les pages qui suivent, un portrait très sommaire des perceptions et aspirations de ces collectivités. Nous avons néanmoins été frappés par la remarquable uniformité des opinions formulées par les porte-parole autochtones.

I. Les perceptions des autochtones

Les autochtones estiment que la justice pénale est un système étranger à leur mode de vie, qui leur est imposé par la société blanche, dominante. Ballottés de part et d'autre du système, les délinquants, victimes et témoins appartenant à une collectivité autochtone sont submergés dans un océan de « Visages pâles ». Il n'est donc guère surprenant qu'ils tiennent le système pour profondément insensible à leurs traditions et à leurs valeurs : nombreux sont ceux qui le qualifient d'irrémédiablement raciste.

L'abus de pouvoir et l'exercice immodéré des pouvoirs discrétionnaires sont souvent cités comme les principales lacunes du système. Il arrive fréquemment que la police soit perçue par les autochtones comme une présence militaire, étrangère, qui envahit leur territoire pour y faire des ravages et le dépeupler. Loin d'être une source de stabilité et de sécurité, les forces de l'ordre y sont redoutées, même quand leur présence est requise pour rétablir un minimum de paix sociale.

Pour les autochtones qui habitent en région éloignée ou dans les réserves, l'appareil judiciaire semble surgir de nulle part, ce qui vient accentuer leur sentiment d'isolement et les empêche de comprendre les rouages du système.

Le processus judiciaire est carrément inintelligible pour qui ne parle ni le français ni l'anglais, surtout lorsque les services d'interprétation sont négligeables, voire inexistants. Même les autochtones qui parlent le français ou l'anglais ont du mal à comprendre la langue des tribunaux et des avocats. Mais l'incompréhension va bien au-delà des barrières linguistiques. Les autochtones se plaignent du paternalisme et du mutisme dans lesquels s'enferment les principaux acteurs du système (policiers, avocats, juges, personnel des services correctionnels) lorsqu'il s'agit de leur expliquer ce que l'on attend d'eux ou quel sort on leur réserve. Même ceux qui sont prêts à reconnaître certaines vertus au système actuel concluent à l'échec total.

Les maigres efforts entrepris pour faire participer les collectivités à l'administration de la justice sont jugés symboliques, et on est peu optimiste pour l'avenir. Aux yeux des aînés, les jeunes sont les grandes victimes du système : l'appareil judiciaire les coupe de leur milieu naturel, en même temps qu'il les prive de leurs traditions spirituelles et culturelles. Les aînés racontent les expériences vécues par ces enfants que l'on a retirés de leur collectivité et que le contact du processus judiciaire et correctionnel a durcis au point que les mesures de réinsertion les plus créatives sont restées inopérantes.

Toute discussion engagée sur les démarches propres à corriger le système ou à l'orienter dans la bonne direction aboutit inévitablement à l'épuisement et à la frustration, réactions faciles à comprendre dans le contexte. Pour les autochtones, le système dresse une série interminable d'obstacles et d'embûches sans leur offrir le moindre espoir d'exposer leurs griefs ou d'obtenir réparation, d'où leur incommensurable sentiment d'injustice. Ils se défient de l'idée que les avocats ou la magistrature soient à même de leur faire justice ou de trouver une solution juste aux conflits où ils sont en cause. À vrai dire, la plupart n'attendent plus rien du système de justice pénale.

II. Les aspirations des autochtones

Les autochtones aspirent à une justice sensible à leurs coutumes, à leurs traditions et à leurs croyances. Voilà qui découle naturellement de leurs aspirations à l'autodétermination et à la souveraineté. Ils souhaitent une justice pénale conçue et dirigée par des autochtones, avec des effectifs autochtones à tous les échelons.

Si les interprétations que l'on donne au contenu souhaité d'un système judiciaire autochtone sont nombreuses, tout le monde s'entend néanmoins sur le fait que le système doit être fidèle aux traditions et aux valeurs culturelles autochtones, compte tenu des réalités de la société moderne. Ainsi, un système judiciaire autochtone serait respectueux des aînés et des dirigeants de la collectivité, tiendrait compte des exigences de la spiritualité et ne manquerait pas de souligner l'étroitesse des rapports entre l'être humain et la nature.

Dans leur vision holistique et intégrationniste de la justice, les autochtones donnent préséance aux intérêts de la collectivité. Leur justice se fonde sur la collectivité et privilégie la médiation et la conciliation, tout en invitant ceux qui transgressent les règles sociales à reconnaître leurs torts. Tout en cherchant à réconcilier le délinquant et la victime, un système judiciaire authentiquement autochtone viserait un objectif plus large, celui de réinsérer le délinquant dans la collectivité.

On voit donc que la vision autochtone de la justice remet en question les préceptes de la common law et du droit civil. Le droit écrit perd son importance. Dans un système judiciaire autochtone, les lois ne seraient ni uniformes ni homogènes : elles varieraient d'une collectivité à l'autre, selon les us et coutumes de chacune. Le droit coutumier serait le ciment qui favoriserait l'harmonie au sein des collectivités.

La justice autochtone serait nécessairement pluraliste, bien que coiffée de certains traits communs. Nous ne savons pas avec certitude à quoi ressemblerait un tel système. Cette absence de précision est frustrante ; beaucoup de détails essentiels manquent, et les autochtones hésitent à en fournir, non parce qu'ils sont incapables de le faire (certaines collectivités disposent d'ailleurs d'un modèle bien au point et bien structuré), mais parce qu'ils estiment ne pas avoir à le faire. Ils aspirent à l'autodétermination à l'échelle locale. Leur position se résume à ceci : « Donnez-nous les clés. Laissez-nous prendre notre système en main. Nous ne pouvons pas faire bien pis que vous. »

CHAPITRE TROIS

Les notions d'égalité d'accès à la justice, de traitement équitable et de respect

---

Points saillants

La justice pénale doit assurer à tous un même niveau minimal de services. En outre, elle doit traiter les autochtones avec équité et respect. Cela suppose la reconnaissance et le respect des différences culturelles propres aux autochtones, ainsi que leur intégration au système de justice pénale là où la chose est indiquée.

L'un des objectifs de la présente étude consiste à trouver des moyens de réaliser sur le plan formel l'égalité d'accès à la justice. Il suffit pour cela que, dans la façon dont ils sont traités, les autochtones ne soient pas défavorisés par rapport aux autres citoyens. Ils doivent être en mesure, au même titre que les autres, d'obtenir les conseils d'un avocat ou de faire en sorte que la police réponde à leurs plaintes. Le système de justice pénale doit veiller à ce qu'ils ne soient pas plus susceptibles que d'autres d'être mis sous arrêt, d'être inculpés, d'être condamnés ou de se voir refuser une libération conditionnelle. Personne n'oserait remettre en question ces modestes objectifs.

Cela dit, la notion d'« accès à la justice » est large. Elle englobe évidemment la possibilité de recevoir des services suffisants mais, ce qui importe plus encore, elle repose sur le concept de *justice*. Notre mandat va plus loin que la simple égalité formelle et embrasse les notions d'*équité* et de *respect*. Le droit pénal substantiel et processuel impose a priori les mêmes exigences à tous les citoyens ; or, les notions d'équité et de respect débouchent sur la reconnaissance des spécificités culturelles. L'expression « traitement équitable » nous amène à nous interroger sur ce qu'est fondamentalement l'équité. Le mot « respect » suppose quant à lui la reconnaissance d'autres valeurs méritant d'être protégées. Notre mission consiste à trouver les moyens non seulement de faire à ces spécificités la place qui leur revient, mais aussi d'« assurer » un traitement empreint d'équité et de respect ; la tâche n'est donc pas facile.

Le point de vue traditionnel du droit pénal substantiel tient pour suffisante l'égalité formelle : tant et aussi longtemps que chacun reçoit le même traitement, chacun est traité sur un pied d'égalité. C'est précisément ce qu'on entend lorsqu'on dit que la justice est aveugle, car on ne tient pas compte des différences individuelles. Or, nous croyons que notre mandat nous oblige à nous éloigner de ce principe. Il nous paraît donc utile de voir, dans un premier temps, dans quelle mesure ce principe a façonné le droit pénal.

Le droit pénal s'applique à tous, exactement de la même façon. Par conséquent, la diversité culturelle n'entre pas en jeu : chacun est jugé à la même aune, quelles que soient ses croyances personnelles[6]. Ce principe vaut aussi pour l'application de la loi par les représentants du procureur général[7]. Le même point de vue s'applique souvent à l'égard de la procédure pénale. Le procès devant jury, par exemple, vise en partie à permettre à l'accusé d'être jugé par des personnes susceptibles de comprendre ses motifs, et peut-être même de partager avec lui certaines convictions et attentes. Pourtant, la loi exige tout simplement que les jurés soient choisis au hasard dans la collectivité où l'accusé subit son procès. Il se peut donc qu'aucun juré n'appartienne à la même race ou au même groupe ethnique que l'accusé, même si cette race ou ce groupe ethnique est bien représenté dans la collectivité. Or, à moins d'être en mesure de prouver une exclusion délibérée, l'accusé n'aura pas sujet de se plaindre d'une telle situation.

La notion d'égalité formelle joue également un rôle important dans la détermination de la peine. Lorsqu'il prononce une sentence, le juge tient effectivement compte de la situation particulière de l'accusé[8], tout en étant tenu de traiter « sur un pied d'égalité » les délinquants, ce qui signifie, en l'occurrence, qu'il doit les traiter plus ou moins de la même façon. Une amende a moins d'effet sur le riche que sur le pauvre : cela ne justifie pas pour autant l'emprisonnement du riche[9].

L'idée de traiter tout le monde sur le même pied semble impliquer que les valeurs et les éléments externes n'influent pas sur l'application objective des règles. Nous croyons qu'un tel point de vue est erroné : toute décision vient renforcer une valeur. Mais s'il s'agit d'une valeur défendue par la classe dominante d'une société, il devient d'autant plus facile pour les possédants, non pas de considérer la décision comme positive, mais de la tenir pour neutre.

L'application du même traitement à tous ne débouche pas nécessairement sur l'égalité. Considérons, par exemple, la détermination de la peine : le juge fait intervenir divers facteurs lorsqu'il détermine la peine que mérite le délinquant. Même lorsqu'on les applique uniformément, toutefois, ces facteurs portent en eux le reflet de certaines convictions et produisent forcément des résultats inégaux. Le fait que le délinquant puisse perdre son

---

6. Voir *Re Church of Scientology and The Queen (No. 6)* (1987), 31 C.C.C. (3ᵉ) 449, 450 (C.A. Ont.) : [TRADUCTION] « Le droit pénal canadien impose effectivement des limites à la pratique religieuse, même lorsqu'elle est fondée sur des croyances sincères ou authentiques. »

7. Voir *R.* c. *Catagas* (1977), 38 C.C.C. (2ᵉ) 296 (C.A. Man.).

8. Afin de « déterminer la sentence en fonction de l'accusé plutôt qu'en fonction de l'infraction. » : *R.* c. *Gardiner*, [1982] 2 R.C.S. 368, 414.

9. Voir, par ex., *Johnson* c. *The Queen* (1971), 5 C.C.C. (2ᵉ) 541 (C.A. N.-É.).

emploi s'il est incarcéré peut légitimement être pris en considération dans la détermination de la peine. Ses antécédents et ses perspectives d'avenir jouent également un rôle : le délinquant peut avoir été un bon étudiant, ou encore être sur le point d'embrasser une belle carrière. Pourtant, la prise en considération de ces facteurs signifie que les pauvres, les chômeurs et les personnes appartenant à un groupe où la stabilité d'emploi ou la poursuite d'études universitaires est notoirement improbable sont susceptibles d'être traités plus durement[10]. Arrêtons-nous, de même, aux sentences qui prévoient l'incarcération advenant le défaut de payer une amende : la menace de l'incarcération ne constitue qu'un moyen d'obliger le délinquant à acquitter l'amende. Cependant, la sentence suppose [TRADUCTION] « que le condamné dispose de plus d'argent que de temps. Et cette hypothèse laisse entendre en retour que la personne participe activement à l'économie fondée sur l'échange monétaire[11]. » Dans le cas des groupes pour lesquels cette hypothèse se révèle mal fondée — quantité d'autochtones, par exemple —, on aboutit à une surreprésentation en milieu carcéral.

Quoi qu'il en soit, malgré la position traditionnelle du droit pénal, on en est venu à admettre que la simple égalité formelle ne suffit pas toujours. Les administrations publiques et les tribunaux canadiens ont reconnu que le droit d'avoir recours à un avocat, contrairement à celui de retenir une chambre d'hôtel luxueuse, par exemple, ne peut être réservé aux seules personnes qui peuvent se le permettre. C'est pourquoi des mesures ont été prises pour garantir que ce droit est effectivement accessible à tous, abstraction faite des moyens dont chacun dispose. Les dispositions de la Charte relatives à l'égalité ont également eu une incidence considérable : la Cour suprême a établi que la discrimination peut résulter « d'une politique ou d'une pratique qui est neutre à première vue, mais qui a un effet négatif disproportionné sur un individu ou un groupe d'individus[12]. » La Cour a également souligné qu'un « traitement identique [peut] souvent engendrer de graves inégalités, [et que] [...] favoriser l'égalité au sens de l'art. 15 vise un but plus précis que la simple élimination de distinctions[13]. » Par conséquent, ce n'est pas introduire une notion entièrement nouvelle dans le système de justice pénale que de proposer la reconnaissance d'un objectif qui dépasse la simple égalité formelle.

Avant de déterminer si divers groupes jouissent d'un accès égal à la justice et sont traités avec équité et respect, nous devons nous demander si le droit pénal substantiel et processuel accorde à tous les citoyens le même niveau minimal de services. Si l'on peut dire que l'objectif est généralement atteint, les exceptions restent nombreuses. En effet,

---

10. Les décisions touchant le cautionnement et la libération, conditionnelle ou non, subissent aussi l'influence de ces facteurs ou de facteurs analogues.

11. Paul HAVEMANN, Lori FOSTER, Keith COUSE et autres, *Law and Order for Canada's Indigenous People*, Régina, Prairie Justice Research, 1985, p. 173.

12. *Compagnie des chemins de fer nationaux du Canada* c. *Canada (Commission canadienne des droits de la personne)*, [1987] 1 R.C.S. 1114, 1137.

13. *Andrews* c. *Law Society of British Columbia*, [1989] 1 R.C.S. 143, 171 (j. McIntyre).

des études ont montré que le système de justice pénale n'est pas dénué de racisme[14] ; or, même en l'absence de tout racisme, l'objectif peut ne pas être atteint. Il faut donc s'attaquer à ces inégalités.

Pourtant, il ne suffit pas simplement de chercher à remédier aux inégalités. Notre droit substantiel et nos règles de procédure doivent faire en sorte que les différences pertinentes ne soient ni ignorées ni considérées comme sans importance[15]. Notre droit doit reconnaître que ces différences sont parfois essentielles et que l'égalité véritable ne se résume pas à la simple égalité formelle.

Le système de justice pénale doit fournir à tous le même niveau minimal de services, ce qui, en pratique, n'est pas toujours le cas. Les services (rapports avec la police, accès à l'aide juridique, vulgarisation du processus judiciaire, etc.) ne sont pas dispensés de la même façon à tous les groupes, en particulier aux autochtones. Et là où l'égalité formelle n'existe pas, il faut l'imposer.

De plus, le système de justice pénale doit traiter les autochtones avec équité et avec respect. Voilà qui suppose la reconnaissance et le respect des spécificités culturelles, ainsi que leur intégration au système de justice pénale là où la chose est indiquée. Il faut donc que les policiers, les poursuivants, les avocats de la défense, les juges, le législateur et tous les autres protagonistes du système de justice pénale tiennent compte des différences qui existent entre les groupes sociaux. De fait, la structure de l'appareil judiciaire lui-même doit être modifiée de manière à favoriser la prise en considération de ces différences. La justice ne peut plus rester aveugle : elle doit s'ouvrir aux inégalités sociales et veiller à ce que celles-ci ne soient pas perpétuées par l'appareil judiciaire.

RECOMMANDATION

1. Le système de justice pénale doit fournir à tous le même niveau minimal de services, et doit traiter les autochtones avec équité et respect. Pour cela, il faudrait reconnaître et respecter les spécificités culturelles des peuples autochtones et, là où cela est indiqué, les intégrer au système de justice pénale.

---

14. Voir, par ex., NOUVELLE-ÉCOSSE, ROYAL COMMISSION ON THE DONALD MARSHALL, JR., PROSECUTION, *Findings and Recommendations*, vol. 1, Halifax, la Commission, 1989, p. 162 (président : T. A. Hickman) (ci-après rapport de la commission d'enquête sur l'affaire Marshall) ; ALBERTA, *Justice on Trial: Report of the Task Force on the Criminal Justice System and Its Impact on the Indian and Métis People of Alberta*, vol. 1, Edmonton, the Task Force, 1991, p. 12-3 (président : R. A. Cawsey) (ci-après *Justice on Trial*).

15. Rappelons l'observation du juge en chef Lilles reproduite dans *Justice on Trial, op. cit.*, note 14, p. 5-5 : [TRADUCTION] « La notion d'égalité devant les tribunaux est fondée sur le principe voulant que la loi s'applique également à tous et soit comprise de tous, et que tous ceux qui y sont assujettis y adhèrent. Il s'agit là, en réalité, d'une homogénéité culturelle hypothétique, qui vise à maintenir l'ordre social existant. En langage non juridique, cette hypothèse est manifestement fausse. »

CHAPITRE QUATRE

Des systèmes de justice autochtones

Points saillants

Les collectivités autochtones que les représentants légitimes des autochtones auront désignées comme disposées et aptes à établir un système de justice qui leur est propre devraient être investies du pouvoir de le faire. Les gouvernements fédéral et provinciaux devraient engager des négociations pour transférer ce pouvoir aux collectivités autochtones visées.

Ovide Mercredi a exprimé sans détour un point de vue que partagent la plupart des représentants autochtones que nous avons consultés dans le cadre de la présente étude :

[TRADUCTION]
La plupart des Canadiens ont l'impression que le système de justice pénale est presque parfait, mais qu'on pourrait l'améliorer en y apportant de légers changements qui tiendraient compte des préoccupations et des droits des autochtones. Or, le véritable problème tient plutôt à ce que certains ont appelé l'impérialisme culturel, en vertu duquel un groupe distinct de personnes prend une décision pour l'ensemble [. . .] Si on regarde la situation dans le contexte de la loi, de la police, des tribunaux et du système correctionnel, on se pose la question suivante : « Peut-on améliorer le système ? » Eh bien ! je vous répondrai très franchement qu'on ne le peut pas. L'expérience nous apprend que, même si vous rendez votre système plus représentatif, vous continuerez d'imposer vos lois, de les faire appliquer par vos forces de police, de les faire interpréter par vos tribunaux et d'emprisonner ceux qui y contreviennent dans vos établissements. Votre système ne parlerait pas notre langue. Nous n'y retrouverions pas nos lois. Nos traditions, nos coutumes, nos valeurs seraient sans effet à l'intérieur de ce système. Voilà ce que j'entends par impérialisme culturel. Par conséquent, un système plus représentatif, où on compte plus de juges autochtones, plus d'avocats autochtones, plus de greffiers autochtones, plus de gardiens de prison autochtones, plus de directeurs de prison autochtones, n'est pas la solution. À mon avis, nous devons nous libérer de ce carcan impérialiste, si cela est possible, et trouver des solutions de rechange au système actuel [. . .][16]

---

16. Ovide MERCREDI, Observations recueillies à l'occasion des consultations de la Commission de réforme du droit du Canada à Edmonton (Alb.), mars 1991.

Des solutions créatives ont de bien meilleures chances d'obtenir l'appui et le respect des autochtones, tout en assurant l'égalité d'accès et le traitement équitable. Le moment est venu de favoriser l'émergence de systèmes judiciaires administrés par les autochtones, et il existe plusieurs modèles possibles[17].

Nous reconnaissons que la volonté d'établir des systèmes de justice entièrement séparés s'inscrit dans le cadre de revendications politiques liées principalement à l'autodétermination, et nous ne voyons pas l'utilité d'entrer ici dans ce débat. L'établissement de systèmes de justice autochtones présente des avantages en soi, indépendamment de toute considération d'ordre politique.

On prétend souvent que la criminalité chez les autochtones résulte de la marginalisation de ces peuples, par suite de la colonisation[18]. D'après cette théorie, au fur et à mesure que les autochtones ont vu la maîtrise de leur destin leur échapper, les suicides et la criminalité ont grimpé, en même temps que le tissu social s'est désagrégé. La réforme de la justice pénale ne suffira pas à régler ces problèmes. Comme le souligne LaPrairie, [TRADUCTION] « on ne réglera pas les problèmes en rejetant la responsabilité sur le système de justice pénale plutôt qu'en s'attaquant au cœur même des disparités économiques et sociales qui sévissent dans les réserves[19]. »

Il n'en reste pas moins que la justice pénale elle-même a contribué à la marginalisation. Dans les sociétés autochtones traditionnelles, un chef ne restait un chef que tant que la collectivité continuait de lui témoigner du respect[20]. Le respect des aînés était [TRADUCTION] « le ciment qui liait les gens entre eux, dans l'obéissance relativement paisible aux règles acceptées par la collectivité[21]. » Cependant, nous dit-on, [TRADUCTION] « la

---

17. On trouvera une description de l'ensemble des modèles possibles de systèmes pour les autochtones du Canada dans *Justice on Trial, op. cit.*, note 14, pp. 11-2 à 11-5.

18. Voir, par ex., Mary HYDE et Carol LAPRAIRIE, *Amerindian Police Crime Prevention*, Document de travail nº 1987-21, Ottawa, Solliciteur général Canada, 1987, où la criminalité chez les autochtones est définie comme un sous-produit de la désorganisation du tissu social amené par la colonisation. Dans le même esprit, voir Michael JACKSON, « Locking Up Natives in Canada » (1989), 23 *U.B.C. L. Rev.* 215, 218-219 ; Lawrence J. BARKWELL, David N. CHARTRAND, David N. GRAY et autres, « Devalued People: The Status of the Métis in the Justice System » (1989), 9:1 *Can. J. of Native Studies* 121 ; P. HAVEMANN et autres, *op. cit.*, note 11; NOUVELLE-ÉCOSSE, ROYAL COMMISSION ON THE DONALD MARSHALL, JR., PROSECUTION, *The Mi'kmaq and Criminal Justice in Nova Scotia: A Research Study*, par Scott CLARK, vol. 3, Halifax, la Commission, 1989, notamment la deuxième conclusion principale, p. 69 (président : T. A. Hickman) (ci-après rapport de la commission d'enquête sur l'affaire Marshall); et *Northern Frontier, Northern Homeland: The Report of the MacKenzie Valley Pipeline Inquiry*, vol. 1, Ottawa, Approvisionnements et Services Canada, 1977, p. 152 (commissaire : Thomas R. Berger).

19. Carol LAPRAIRIE, *If Tribal Courts Are the Solution, What Is the Problem?* (document de consultation du ministère du Procureur général, Province de Nouvelle-Écosse, janvier 1990), p. viii [non publié].

20. Michael COYLE, « Traditional Indian Justice in Ontario: A Role for the Present? » (1986), 24 *Osgoode Hall L.J.* 605, 614.

21. Rupert Ross, « Cultural Blindness and the Justice System in Remote Native Communities » (discours prononcé à la « Sharing Common Ground » Conference on Aboriginal Policing Services, Edmonton, mai 1990), p. 13. Les personnes que nous avons consultées ont formulé des remarques analogues à la lumière de leur propre expérience.

présence même de nos tribunaux a privé les autochtones d'une tribune où ils pouvaient manifester leur sagesse et mériter le respect[22]. » Les intervenants du système de justice pénale remettent de plus en plus en question cette hégémonie culturelle.

Grosso modo, nous croyons que le droit pénal substantiel et processuel devrait imposer les mêmes exigences à tous les citoyens, quelles que soient leurs croyances personnelles. Par contre, nous estimons que la situation historique tout à fait particulière des autochtones justifie une dérogation à ce principe général. Nous sommes d'avis que, en règle générale, tous ceux qui arrivent au Canada ou qui s'y trouvent déjà devraient se soumettre au droit canadien, et qu'il revient au droit pénal de définir les limites de ce que la société est prête à tolérer. Toutefois, les autochtones n'ont pas immigré au Canada, ce serait plutôt le contraire. Ils jouissent d'une reconnaissance constitutionnelle et de droits ancestraux qui les distinguent des autres Canadiens.

[TRADUCTION]
Les Algonquins ont habité la vallée de l'Outaouais au moins aussi longtemps que les Français ont habité la France ou les Anglais, l'Angleterre. Avant la création de ce qu'on appelle le Canada, avant que Jacques Cartier ait remonté le Saint-Laurent avec son petit navire, les Algonquins ont vécu dans la vallée de l'Outaouais, ont occupé ce territoire, l'ont exploité et l'ont défendu[23].

Au statut constitutionnel distinct, il convient d'ajouter les particularités culturelles. Le système juridique contradictoire est étranger à bon nombre d'ethnies autochtones. Ce trait culturel les rendrait moins susceptibles de s'en remettre aux garanties offertes par notre système judiciaire, comme la présomption d'innocence :

[TRADUCTION]
Chez les Mohawks, l'un des crimes les plus graves est le mensonge, dont la définition recouvre également le fait de ne pas reconnaître un acte dont on est justement accusé [. . .] il est probable que l'infraction reprochée est moins grave, à leurs yeux, que de mentir sur le fait d'y avoir participé ; c'est précisément ce qu'un plaidoyer de non-culpabilité représente pour eux[24].

---

22. R. Ross, *ibid.* [TRADUCTION] « L'important n'est pas le système que nous adoptons, mais le fait que les collectivités autochtones puissent retrouver la maîtrise de leur destin qu'ils ont perdue, par suite des bouleversements dont ils ont été victimes depuis la venue des Européens en Amérique. » Déclaration du juge Coutu, juge-coordonnateur de la cour itinérante du district de l'Abitibi, dans NOUVELLE-ÉCOSSE, ROYAL COMMISSION ON THE DONALD MARSHALL, JR., PROSECUTION, *Consultative Conference on Discrimination against Natives and Blacks in the Criminal Justice System and the Role of the Attorney General*, vol. 7, Halifax, la Commission, 1989, p. 27 (ci-après rapport de la commission d'enquête sur l'affaire Marshall).

23. Chef Greg SARAZIN, « 220 Years of Broken Promises », dans Boyce RICHARDSON (dir.), *Drumbeat: Anger and Renewal in Indian Country*, Toronto, Summerhill, 1989, p. 169.

24. Rupert Ross, « Leaving Our White Eyes Behind: The Sentencing of Native Accused », [1989] 3 *C.N.L.R.* 1, 9. En outre, [TRADUCTION] « l'autochtone respectueux des traditions a tendance à éviter les conflits, les disputes et les affrontements. Même s'il s'est déclaré non coupable, l'autochtone pourrait bien ne pas fournir à la cour, *ni même à son avocat*, le moindre élément de preuve susceptible de nuire aux témoins de la partie adverse » : INDIGENOUS BAR ASSOCIATION, *The Criminal Code and Aboriginal People* (document préparé pour la Commission de réforme du droit du Canada, 1991), p. 21 [non publié] (ci-après IBA). De même, les autochtones font parfois de mauvais témoins, autant pour la défense que pour la poursuite, parce que [TRADUCTION] « à leurs yeux, il est immoral de tenir, au sujet de quelqu'un et *en sa présence*, des propos hostiles, critiques et implicitement venimeux. » R. Ross, *id.*, p. 6.

On observe les effets des différences culturelles à divers stades. Au moment de la rédaction d'un rapport préalable à la sentence ou de l'étude de sa demande de libération conditionnelle, le délinquant autochtone a souvent une piètre performance :

[TRADUCTION]
Ce qui peut nous échapper, c'est que le délinquant adopte une telle attitude parce que nos *techniques* de réinsertion, de nature « curative », lui paraissent non seulement différentes, mais encore incongrues au regard de ses traditions. Son refus peut provenir non de son indifférence ou de son amoralisme, mais de son *adhésion* à des principes moraux que nous ignorons[25].

Certaines collectivités autochtones, nous dit-on, aimeraient qu'on leur fournisse l'occasion de réinsérer les délinquants chez elles. Elles prétendent que, tel qu'il est constitué, notre système de justice gêne ce processus et que nos tribunaux ne peuvent se substituer à la collectivité : [TRADUCTION] « étant donné qu'on ne peut éprouver de la honte que devant un personnage respecté et admiré, la réinsertion ne peut être assurée par une cour itinérante[26]. » Pour ces collectivités, l'incarcération d'un délinquant retardera d'autant sa réinsertion sociale. Elle risque aussi de l'isoler davantage de la collectivité et de le rendre plus rebelle[27] ; de fait, elle peut même lui fournir l'occasion d'éviter des solutions plus déplaisantes[28].

Certains observateurs pourraient avoir du mal à concilier les vœux des autochtones avec les conditions de vie misérables qui sévissent dans les réserves les plus touchées par la dépression, le découragement et la criminalité. Au bout du compte, toutefois, il s'agit là d'un exercice tout à fait stérile. À notre avis, là où les circonstances s'y prêtent, nous devrions adopter de nouvelles démarches.

Après examen, nous avons conclu que le système actuel ne convient pas aux peuples autochtones et qu'il ajoute à leurs difficultés. Les problèmes que pose pour eux le système de justice pénale sont, pour la plupart, manifestes et remontent loin dans le passé. Les autochtones estiment que le système est truffé d'obstacles qui prennent leur source dans l'éloignement, autant géographique que conceptuel et culturel. L'éloignement culturel ressort également des différentes attitudes que suscitent l'action législative et le contexte juridique. Les peuples autochtones continuent de croire à la supériorité de leurs méthodes traditionnelles pour résoudre les conflits et maintenir l'ordre social. Ce sont d'ailleurs ces méthodes anciennes qui, ironiquement, jettent les bases des nouvelles méthodes et nouveaux concepts de droit que la Ministre nous a chargés d'élaborer.

---

25. R. Ross, *op. cit.*, note 21, p. 10.

26. Mémoire de la bande de Sandy Lake au ministère ontarien du Procureur général, cité dans R. Ross, *op. cit.*, note 21, p. 12.

27. Mémoire du gouvernement tribal d'Alexander présenté dans le cadre du rapport *Justice on Trial, op. cit.*, note 14, p. 6-43.

28. Voir Michael JACKSON, *In Search of the Pathways to Justice: Alternative Dispute Resolution in Aboriginal Communities* (document préparé pour la Commission de réforme du droit du Canada, 1991), pp. 82-83 [non publié].

RECOMMANDATION

2. Les collectivités autochtones que les représentants légitimes des autochtones auront désignées comme disposées et aptes à établir un système de justice qui leur est propre devraient être investies du pouvoir de le faire. Les gouvernements fédéral et provinciaux devraient engager des négociations pour transférer ce pouvoir aux collectivités autochtones visées.

I.   Mise en œuvre

Il va de soi qu'il faudra résoudre certains problèmes fondamentaux avant de mettre en application cette recommandation. Étant donné la grande diversité des collectivités autochtones, il faudra négocier avec chacune d'elles les mesures spécifiques qui s'imposent. Les parties régleront elles-mêmes les questions litigieuses à la faveur du processus de négociation. Puisqu'aucun système judiciaire autochtone n'arrivera à combler les besoins et les vœux de toutes les collectivités, il n'existe pas de réponse unique aux questions importantes qui se posent ; voilà encore une raison suffisante pour faire de la négociation la base même de nos propositions. Après tout, cette démarche est celle qu'il faudrait privilégier quand on aborde la presque totalité des grandes questions intéressant les autochtones.

Il paraît clair que les réserves et les villages inuit sont des collectivités autochtones bien identifiables et que bon nombre, sinon la plupart, des villages métis devraient être considérés, eux aussi, comme des collectivités autochtones, même si des non-autochtones y vivent. Mais qu'en est-il des autochtones habitant les centres urbains ? Forment-ils une collectivité[29] ? Dans l'affirmative, cette collectivité présente-t-elle suffisamment de cohésion pour pouvoir assumer la responsabilité d'aspects importants du système judiciaire ? Nous sommes d'avis que ces décisions devraient être prises au départ par les autochtones. Passons maintenant à d'autres questions importantes et de nature semblable.

À prime abord, il peut sembler radical de proposer la création de systèmes de justice distincts dans les collectivités autochtones. En réalité, les autochtones assument déjà, en plusieurs endroits au Canada, la responsabilité d'aspects importants du système judiciaire et ont institué des méthodes parallèles permettant d'établir l'ordre social et l'harmonie au sein de leur collectivité. Examinée à la lumière de cette réalité, notre recommandation peut être considérée comme un prolongement logique des progrès déjà réalisés.

---

29.   Le mot « collectivité » a été défini ailleurs comme [TRADUCTION] « un groupe d'autochtones partageant une certaine solidarité, une identité et des traditions communes, une forme donnée d'organisation et la détermination à se protéger lui-même en tant qu'entité distincte. Le mot définit donc les groupes tant locaux que régionaux. » DIRECTION GÉNÉRALE DES AFFAIRES AUTOCHTONES DE L'ONTARIO, *Guidelines for the Negotiation of Aboriginal Self-Government*, document déposé à l'Assemblée législative de l'Ontario, 14 décembre 1989.

On peut aussi considérer que le système judiciaire actuel s'apprête à incorporer diverses innovations proposées par les autochtones. Cela est particulièrement manifeste là où l'on a recours à d'autres méthodes de résolution des conflits[30]. Quelques exemples devraient nous aider à éclaircir ce point.

Le South Island Tribal Council, sur l'île de Vancouver, s'est remarquablement bien intégré au système local de justice pénale. Un Conseil des aînés a été formé, et ses membres interviennent à divers stades du processus pénal. Les aînés participent à la déjudiciarisation, à la surveillance des mises en liberté sous cautionnement, à la préparation des rapports préalables à la sentence, ainsi qu'aux plaidoiries sur la détermination de la peine. Ils supervisent également la garde en milieu ouvert et la probation, et agissent comme conseillers et directeurs spirituels dans les établissements correctionnels[31]. Des projets comme ceux-là font maintenant partie intégrante, à toutes fins utiles, de la justice pénale. Dans chaque cas, les autochtones agissent à titre consultatif, tandis que le pouvoir réel relève de quelqu'un d'autre. Ailleurs, on a appliqué ou formulé d'autres recommandations qui confèrent aux autochtones un pouvoir réel plus étendu.

La réserve de Kahnawake s'est dotée d'un effectif de gardiens de la paix pour veiller au maintien de l'ordre public, encore que leur statut juridique exact reste flou[32]. En outre, les juges de paix nommés en vertu de la *Loi sur les Indiens*[33] se réunissent deux fois par semaine pour entendre et juger les causes en matière d'infractions punissables sur déclaration de culpabilité par procédure sommaire. Il s'agit d'un champ de compétence relativement mineur, mais qui donne à la collectivité un pouvoir direct sur certains aspects de la justice locale.

Il y a peu de temps, le gouvernement ontarien annonçait la création d'un programme de justice destiné aux autochtones d'âge adulte accusés d'infraction criminelle. Dans le cadre de ce programme, les candidats choisis par les travailleurs sociaux autochtones affectés aux tribunaux, le coordonnateur du Native Community Council et le procureur de la Couronne auront la possibilité de comparaître devant le Conseil et de s'y faire entendre suivant la procédure traditionnelle. Le Conseil, composé d'aînés et d'autres membres respectés de la collectivité, prendrait la décision qui s'impose.

---

30. En termes de justice pénale, les autres méthodes de résolution des conflits englobent des notions comme la déjudiciarisation et la réconciliation victime-délinquant. Voir, *infra*, notre analyse au sujet de la détermination de la peine et, surtout, l'étude de M. JACKSON, *op. cit.*, note 28. Voir aussi le rapport de la commission d'enquête sur l'affaire Marshall, *op. cit.*, note 14, où l'on cite le ministère des Affaires indiennes et du Nord Canada, p. 167 : [TRADUCTION] « les nombreuses autres méthodes de résolution des conflits [...] sont celles-là mêmes qui font partie du droit coutumier. »

31. IBA, *op. cit.*, note 24, pp. 38-39. Une autre expérience bien connue en ce qui concerne le pouvoir accru de la collectivité est le programme de justice destiné aux jeunes sur l'île Christian, dans le nord de l'Ontario. Grâce à ce programme, le taux de délinquance a considérablement chuté. Voir Rick H. HEMMINGSON, « Jurisdiction of Future Tribal Courts in Canada: Learning from the American Experience », [1988] 2 *C.N.L.R.* 1, 50 ; M. JACKSON, *loc. cit.*, note 18 ; et M. COYLE, *loc. cit.*, note 20.

32. Voir *R. c. Norton*, C.S.P. Longueuil, n° 2286-81, 27 septembre 1982, j. Fortier, où l'on a décidé que les gardiens de la paix étaient des agents de la paix au sens de l'art. 2 du *Code criminel*. Toutefois, leur statut n'a été défini ni par une cour supérieure ni par le législateur. Un exemple encore plus éloquent de corps policier autonome est en voie chez les Cris de la baie James dans le cadre de la convention du même nom. Les policiers cris posséderont une autonomie juridique quasi totale dans quelques années.

33. L.R.C. (1985), ch. I-5.

De même, la commission d'enquête sur l'affaire Marshall a proposé la création d'une cour criminelle autochtone qui serait placée sous l'autorité de la collectivité[34]. Le gouvernement de la Nouvelle-Écosse envisage aussi la réalisation d'autres projets-pilotes, notamment un tribunal établi dans la collectivité, ainsi qu'un tribunal de la jeunesse et des comités consultatifs à l'échelle de la collectivité[35].

Des projets comme ceux-là ne présentent un intérêt que s'ils répondent aux aspirations des collectivités. Certaines d'entre elles voudront établir un système qui correspond étroitement à leurs notions de justice. Les sociétés Gitksan et Wet'suwet'en, par exemple, laissent entendre qu'elles ne peuvent s'accommoder ni d'une structure judiciaire hiérarchisée ni de l'attribution de pouvoirs spéciaux aux corps policiers. Elles préfèrent voir comment les deux « cultures » juridiques pourraient coexister dans la dignité, plutôt que de s'évertuer à intégrer de force dans un système d'importants éléments empruntés à l'autre[36]. Conformément à l'esprit de notre mission qui consiste à élaborer de nouvelles méthodes et de nouveaux concepts de droit correspondant à l'évolution des besoins de la société canadienne, nous sommes d'avis que, là où les collectivités autochtones le souhaitent, les gouvernements fédéral et provinciaux devraient collaborer à la création de systèmes de justice autochtones, fondés sur les modèles traditionnels.

Nous croyons que maintes collectivités voudront instaurer, du moins dans un premier temps, un système de justice calqué sur le modèle actuel. D'autres pourraient proposer des modèles plus originaux. Il serait difficile de donner une idée précise de ces derniers parce qu'ils pourront varier d'une collectivité à l'autre en fonction des traditions qui leur sont propres[37]. Il se pourrait que des notions fondamentales, comme la distinction entre droit civil et droit pénal, ne soient pas reconnues[38]. Les collectivités pourraient vouloir protéger les droits et assurer l'équité par des moyens différents de ceux que nous employons[39].

---

34. Rapport de la commission d'enquête sur l'affaire Marshall, *op. cit.*, note 14, recommandation 20, p. 168. Ce projet comprend la nomination d'un juge de paix en vertu de la *Loi sur les Indiens*, divers programmes de déjudiciarisation et de médiation, des projets de travaux communautaires comme solutions de rechange aux amendes et à l'incarcération, la prestation, dans les réserves, de services aux personnes libérées, la participation de la collectivité à la détermination de la peine et l'intervention de travailleurs sociaux affectés aux tribunaux.

35. C. LaPrairie, *op. cit.*, note 19. Voir aussi *Justice on Trial*, *op. cit.*, note 14, ch. 11, p. 11-2, où l'on décrit sept modèles possibles de système judiciaire, qui vont d'un modèle très semblable au système actuel à un modèle conférant aux autochtones le droit de créer leur propre système judiciaire et de l'organiser comme ils l'entendent.

36. *Unlocking Aboriginal Justice*, cité dans M. Jackson, *op. cit.*, note 28, p. 92.

37. [Traduction] « On ne peut pas exiger la connaissance de règles lorsque le cadre juridique ne s'exprime pas sous forme de règles. » James W. Zion, « Searching for Indian Common Law », dans Bradford W. Morse et Gordon R. Woodman (dir.), *Indigenous Law and the State*, Providence, Foris Publications, 1988, p. 120 à la p. 136. Voir aussi M. Coyle, *loc. cit.*, note 20, 615.

38. Voir M. Jackson, *op. cit.*, note 28, p. 77 : [Traduction] « chez les Salish de la côte ouest, une rupture de l'harmonie familiale ou sociale exige réparation, mais sans qu'il soit nécessaire de qualifier le conflit comme relevant du droit pénal ou du droit familial. » Voir aussi *Justice on Trial*, *op. cit.*, note 14, ch. 9, « An Aboriginal Perspective on Justice ».

39. Ce faisant, ces collectivités pourraient créer de nouvelles lois et règles de procédure dont le système canadien aurait avantage à s'inspirer. Voir, par ex., *The Code of Offenses and Procedures of Justice for the Mohawk Territory at Akwesasne* (proposition adressée au Conseil des chefs de la nation mohawk par le Conseil des Mohawks d'Akwesasne, Conseil de la tribu mohawk de Saint-Régis, août 1989) [non publié] ; il s'agit d'une initiative qui mérite d'être examinée attentivement.

Il importe toutefois de ne pas exagérer ces différences. Ce ne sont pas toutes les collectivités qui voudront instaurer leur propre système judiciaire. Les nouveaux systèmes seront, en gros, parallèles à ceux qui existent déjà. De plus, même dans les modèles autochtones traditionnels, les différences peuvent paraître plus grandes qu'elles ne le sont en réalité. Les comportements que notre justice pénale cherche à réprimer ne sont généralement pas mieux reçus chez les autochtones. Les systèmes fondés sur les modèles autochtones traditionnels auront sans doute des objectifs globaux analogues à ceux de notre système (dissuasion et réinsertion, par exemple)[40]. La justice autochtone, comprise de cette façon, devrait trouver sa place à l'intérieur de la société canadienne.

Enfin, n'oublions pas que la création d'un système de justice autochtone n'implique pas la mise sur pied de structures monolithiques et coûteuses. N'allons pas imaginer que le système de justice autochtone aura la même ampleur que le système judiciaire canadien. Les divers systèmes auront une taille proportionnelle à celle de chaque collectivité et refléteront ses besoins et ses priorités.

II. Les inconvénients

La création de systèmes de justice autochtones suscite d'importantes interrogations, mais aucune n'est insoluble.

On ne sait pas avec certitude si le gouvernement fédéral a le pouvoir constitutionnel d'autoriser la création de systèmes de justice autochtones. La question est examinée à fond dans une étude que nous avons commandée[41]. Les auteures y affirment clairement que les soi-disant obstacles constitutionnels ne sont pas insurmontables. Ce point de vue est appuyé implicitement par l'entérinement de systèmes autochtones de la part des gouvernements ontarien et néo-écossais, et par l'esprit du rapport de la commission d'enquête sur l'affaire Marshall et des rapports Cawsey et Osnaburgh/Windigo, qui recommandent tous la création de tels systèmes, à l'instar de l'Association du Barreau canadien[42]. Suivant l'opinion la plus répandue parmi ceux qui ont examiné la question de près, les enjeux juridiques, bien qu'importants, [TRADUCTION] « ne devraient pas l'emporter sur les motifs sociaux, d'ordre pratique, qui justifient la création d'un système judiciaire autonome, géré

---

40. M. COYLE, *loc. cit.*, note 20, 627, et IBA, *op. cit.*, note 24, p. 7.

41. Patricia A. MONTURE et Mary Ellen TURPEL (dir.), *Aboriginal Peoples and Canadian Criminal Law: Rethinking Justice* (document préparé pour la Commission de réforme du droit du Canada, 1991) [non publié].

42. La Section du droit des autochtones de l'Association du Barreau canadien, dont la conclusion est reproduite par le Cawsey Task Force, affirme que la création de systèmes de justice autochtones parallèles repose sur des fondements constitutionnels solides. Voir *Justice on Trial*, *op. cit.*, note 14, p. 11-5, voir aussi *infra*, note 43.

par les autochtones, si c'est là le vœu exprimé par les premières nations[43]. » Après avoir examiné ces points de vue, ainsi que d'autres documents sur le sujet, nous estimons que, suivant les particularités du système sur lequel on s'entendra, cette proposition peut fort bien être mise en œuvre sans qu'il soit nécessaire de modifier le cadre constitutionnel actuel.

L'une des difficultés fondamentales que soulève la création de systèmes de justice autochtones vient de la nécessité d'équilibrer, d'une part, les droits et intérêts de l'accusé et, d'autre part, les droits et intérêts de la collectivité qui décide d'instaurer un système distinct. En pareil cas, les droits individuels peuvent-ils et doivent-ils s'effacer devant l'affirmation des droits collectifs ? Il faudra trouver un moyen de concilier les droits individuels légitimement invoqués et les droits collectifs ainsi affirmés.

Certains peuvent voir dans la Charte un obstacle à cet égard, et ceux qui seront chargés de négocier les accords devront rester sensibles aux exigences constitutionnelles. Certains peuples autochtones, nous dit-on, ne reconnaissent pas le droit au silence ou rejettent l'idée que la procédure contradictoire soit le bon moyen de résoudre un conflit. Une réserve soutient même qu'il n'y a pas de place dans son système judiciaire pour les avocats[44].

Vu le risque de conflit entre plusieurs conceptions différentes des droits, les systèmes de justice autochtones devront être édifiés avec grand soin et recueillir l'appui presque entier de la collectivité. Les justiciables d'un nouveau système doivent avoir vraiment souhaité les changements réalisés. Le problème consiste à trouver un moyen d'accommoder les écarts souhaités par rapport à la Charte. On pourra difficilement éluder la question de savoir dans quelle mesure les droits protégés par la Charte sont négociables. Le gouvernement fédéral, en tant que partie aux négociations, aurait intérêt à s'assurer de sa position constitutionnelle et pourrait même chercher à la clarifier en s'adressant à la Cour suprême du Canada. De même les représentants autochtones désireux de convaincre les négociateurs fédéraux de la justesse de leur position pourraient, eux aussi, vouloir obtenir des clarifications. Aussi les autochtones devraient-ils, à ce chapitre, avoir accès aux tribunaux au même titre que le gouvernement.

Certains observateurs soutiennent qu'aucune démarche particulière n'est nécessaire[45]. Les droits des autochtones sont protégés par l'article 25 de la *Loi constitutionnelle de 1982*, aux termes duquel les droits et libertés garantis par la Charte n'ont pas pour effet de porter atteinte aux droits des autochtones, ainsi que par l'article 35 qui confirme les droits existants et issus de traités des autochtones ; les droits des autochtones peuvent en effet avoir

---

43. OSNABURGH/WINDIGO TRIBAL COUNCIL JUSTICE REVIEW COMMITTEE, *Tay Bway Win: Truth, Justice and First Nations* (rapport préparé à l'intention du Procureur général et du Solliciteur général de l'Ontario, 1990), p. 38 [non publié], (ci-après Rapport Osnaburgh/Windigo). Voir aussi comment ce rapport aborde quatre grandes conceptions erronées, mais fort répandues, à propos des droits des autochtones et de leur statut dans la société canadienne (*id.*, pp. 38-41).

44. L'accusé peut demander à l'avocat de relater les faits devant le tribunal, mais le contre-interrogatoire n'est pas permis. Grand Chef Michael MITCHELL, « An Unbroken Assertion of Sovereignty », dans *Drumbeat*, *op. cit.*, note 23, p. 125 ; l'auteur fait allusion à Akwesasne.

45. Voir, par ex., P. A. MONTURE et M. E. TURPEL (dir.), *op. cit.*, note 41.

pré-existé toute action législative[46]. Les mêmes observateurs prétendent qu'un système juridique traditionnel est concevable dans le cadre des droits existants des autochtones, et que les droits garantis par la Charte, dans la mesure où ils entrent en jeu, doivent céder le pas aux droits des autochtones[47].

Un autre moyen de pourvoir à la création de systèmes de justice autochtones consiste à invoquer le pouvoir dérogatoire de l'article 33 de la Charte, encore que le recours à ce pouvoir prête à controverse et présente des difficultés sur le plan politique ; il s'agit donc d'une solution de dernier recours.

D'autre part, il serait théoriquement possible pour chaque membre de la collectivité de renoncer aux droits que lui garantit la Charte. Cette solution semble peu pratique, mais si la compétence peut être attribuée au système autochtone par le consentement de l'accusé, ne serait-ce qu'en partie, l'obtention du consentement dans chaque cas, sous la forme d'une renonciation aux droits garantis par la Charte, demeure possible. Reste toutefois la question de savoir si une personne peut renoncer, en bloc, à tous les droits individuels que lui confère la Charte[48] ; cette question nécessitera sans doute l'intervention des tribunaux.

On peut penser que les négociations nécessaires à la mise en œuvre de la proposition permettront d'en arriver à une entente sur un seuil de respect minimum des droits conférés par la Charte. Tout dépend de la bonne volonté des parties, mais cela ne devrait sans doute pas présenter beaucoup de difficultés pour les nombreuses collectivités qui, selon nous, tiennent seulement à prendre davantage en charge certains aspects de la justice pénale ou qui choisiront d'établir un système parallèle au système actuel.

Par ailleurs, on aurait tort de penser que la Charte est réfractaire à l'idée d'établir des systèmes de justice autochtones : rien n'exige que l'« avocat » à l'assistance duquel chacun a droit soit membre d'un barreau ; le droit à un procès équitable ne signifie pas que celui-ci doit obligatoirement être instruit par un juge revêtu d'une toge ; les procès devant jury sont largement facultatifs, notamment lorsque l'infraction reprochée est punissable d'une peine d'emprisonnement de moins de cinq ans ; et ainsi de suite.

---

46. *Guerin* c. *La Reine*, [1984] 2 R.C.S. 335. Voir l'analyse de cette question dans P. A. MONTURE et M. E. TURPEL (dir.), *op. cit.*, note 41.

47. Cet argument est d'autant plus convaincant que les garanties juridiques figurant aux art. 7 à 15 de la Charte peuvent être écartées par l'effet de l'art. 33, alors que les droits des autochtones ne le peuvent pas. Une question différente, mais connexe, met en cause l'art. 96 de la *Loi constitutionnelle de 1867*, 30 & 31 Vict., R.-U., ch. 3 : est-il possible de contourner, sans modifier la Constitution, les exigences de l'art. 96 pour établir un système de justice autochtone ?

48. Pour une analyse générale de la renonciation aux droits garantis par la Charte, voir *Korponay* c. *Procureur général du Canada*, [1982] 1 R.C.S. 41 ; *R.* c. *Clarkson*, [1986] 1 R.C.S. 383 ; *R.* c. *Turpin*, [1989] 1 R.C.S. 1296 ; *R.* c. *Askov*, [1990] 2 R.C.S. 1199.

Certains se demanderont s'il est possible de satisfaire aisément aux exigences imposées par la complexité juridictionnelle de cette proposition. En réalité, le pluralisme juridique — pensons au droit civil québécois — et le partage des compétences législatives sont des caractéristiques fondamentales du droit canadien. La même infraction obéit à des règles différentes selon qu'elle est commise par un jeune contrevenant[49] ou par un adulte. Dans le même ordre d'idées, les infractions aux règles militaires relèvent d'une juridiction distincte dotée de règles de procédure différentes. Notre système de justice militaire montre aussi que la compétence peut aussi être partagée en fonction de la nature ou de la gravité de l'infraction commise[50].

Les règles d'attribution de la compétence peuvent s'articuler autour du délinquant, de l'infraction ou de l'endroit où celle-ci a été commise. Ainsi, la saisine d'un système de justice autochtone pourrait être automatique ou encore être facultative — lorsque le délinquant est un autochtone. Si elle est facultative, on peut penser à différentes façons pratiques de déterminer quel système jugera le délinquant : la décision pourrait appartenir à un conseil d'aînés, au poursuivant, à la victime, ou au délinquant lui-même, ou encore être prise conjointement par deux d'entre eux. L'attribution de la compétence pourrait aussi être établie comme suit : toute infraction commise dans une réserve ou un territoire désigné (ou encore par un autochtone dans une réserve) ressortirait au système de justice autochtone. Par conséquent, même si nous n'avons pas élaboré de règles juridictionnelles précises — il serait d'ailleurs inopportun que nous le fassions —, nous croyons sans l'ombre d'un doute à la possibilité de trouver une formule viable par la voie des négociations envisagées dans notre recommandation[51].

Les rapports entre les systèmes de justice autochtones et le système général de justice pénale que nous connaissons soulèvent d'autres questions. Par exemple, les accusés ou les condamnés auront-ils accès aux brefs de prérogative ? La personne reconnue coupable pourra-t-elle en appeler de sa condamnation ou de sa sentence, et devant quelle juridiction ? Voilà des problèmes qui ne sont pas faciles à résoudre et qui exigeront un examen attentif des enjeux.

Il ne faudrait pas oublier que ce sont surtout les collectivités autochtones qui exigent la création de tels systèmes. C'est sans succès que l'on tente, depuis des années, de régler la situation par l'application du principe de l'égalité de tous devant la loi et du principe voulant que tout le monde soit traité sur le même pied. Devant ce constat d'échec, continuer à réclamer une justice unique et uniforme semble revenir à s'accrocher à un simulacre d'égalité formelle, au détriment de l'égalité de fond.

---

49. Dans ce cas, c'est la *Loi sur les jeunes contrevenants*, L.R.C. (1985), ch. Y-1, qui trouve son application.

50. Certains agissements ne sont incriminés que par la *Loi sur la défense nationale*, L.R.C. (1985), ch. N-5.

51. Il ne faudrait pas pour autant passer sous silence les difficultés pratiques qui entourent le règlement des questions touchant le partage de la compétence juridictionnelle. Si le pluralisme s'accentue, la diversité des règles d'attribution pourrait être une source de confusion. Ainsi, un Cri comparaissant devant une cour torontoise pourrait disposer d'un éventail de solutions différent de celui qui s'offrirait à un Mohawk dans la même situation.

C'est pourquoi nous proposons l'établissement de systèmes de justice autochtones au moyen d'un processus de négociation et d'entente. Même si nous prévoyons des écarts importants dans la démarche adoptée par les diverses collectivités, nous croyons que les participants aux négociations auraient intérêt à considérer les points suivants :

a) l'importance du droit coutumier ;

b) les méthodes traditionnelles de résolution des conflits, assorties de solutions de rechange axées sur la médiation, l'arbitrage et la conciliation ;

c) la participation des aînés et des conseils des aînés ;

d) le recours à des « conciliateurs » (peacemakers) ;

e) l'établissement de cours tribales composées de juges autochtones et d'employés autochtones occupant d'autres postes clés[52] ;

f) l'établissement de corps policiers autonomes, régis par des commissions de police autochtones et d'autres mécanismes assurant le respect de l'obligation de rendre compte ;

g) la création d'établissements correctionnels, de services de probation et de services aux ex-détenus accessibles dans les collectivités et placés sous l'autorité de celles-ci ;

h) la création d'un Institut de justice autochtone.

On ne manquera pas non plus d'objecter que les systèmes autochtones ne tiendront pas le coup, qu'ils échoueront ; voilà un jugement nettement prématuré. Certes, la gageure est de taille, mais n'allons pas établir des normes de comparaison déraisonnables. C'est le désespoir suscité par le fonctionnement du système actuel qui a incité les autochtones à réclamer des changements. Même très imparfait, un système de justice autochtone pourrait répondre bien mieux que ne le fait le nôtre aux besoins de cette partie de la population. Comme Donald Marshall Jr. le sait trop bien, la police arrête parfois des innocents, les procureurs les poursuivent en justice et les tribunaux les condamnent. Nous n'en avons pas conclu pour autant que le système était irrémédiablement voué à l'échec ; nous tentons plutôt de l'améliorer. Il importe d'envisager la création de systèmes de justice autochtones dans le même esprit.

---

52. Cette solution fait des détracteurs lorsqu'elle renvoie au type de tribunaux établis surtout dans le sud-ouest américain. Le Rapport Osnaburgh/Windigo, op. cit., note 43, p. 37, décrit les cours tribales aux États-Unis comme un pâle reflet du système judiciaire américain et une mesure à éviter au Canada. Jonathan RUDIN et Dan RUSSELL, Native Alternative Dispute Resolution Systems: The Canadian Future in Light of the American Past, Toronto, Ontario Native Council on Justice, 1991, p. i, concluent, que de transposer tel quel au Canada le système américain des cours tribales ne vaudrait pas grand-chose (voir en particulier le chapitre 5). Voir aussi, de façon générale, l'analyse de M. JACKSON, loc. cit., note 18, 225-229.

CHAPITRE CINQ
Favoriser la compréhension et rapprocher les collectivités

Points saillants

Les autochtones devraient occuper des postes à tous les échelons du système de justice pénale et dans toutes ses branches, notamment à titre d'agents de police, d'avocats, de juges, d'agents de probation et d'agents des services correctionnels. Il faudrait recruter des autochtones, les former et favoriser leur avancement en recourant, au besoin, à l'action positive.

Il faudrait élargir et améliorer les programmes de sensibilisation aux différences culturelles dispensés à tous ceux qui jouent un rôle dans le système de justice pénale, notamment les policiers, les avocats, les juges, les agents de probation et les agents des services correctionnels.

Il faudrait démanteler les barrières linguistiques et culturelles érigées entre le système de justice pénale et les collectivités autochtones.

Il faudrait établir des liens permanents et efficaces entre, d'une part, la police, les services de poursuite, la magistrature et les services correctionnels et, d'autre part, les collectivités autochtones.

Il faudrait reconnaître dans la loi le droit des autochtones de s'exprimer dans leur langue maternelle devant tous les tribunaux. Il faudrait fournir les services d'interprètes qualifiés à tout autochtone qui a besoin d'assistance au cours d'une procédure judiciaire ou pendant l'enquête policière qui la précède.

Les gouvernements devraient établir des politiques claires au sujet de l'interprétation des droits des autochtones et des droits issus de traités.

I.   Les obstacles à la justice dans les collectivités autochtones

Nous sommes bien conscients que la mise en place de systèmes de justice autochtones ne pourrait être réalisée dans toutes les collectivités immédiatement. Du reste, certaines choisiront de ne pas en établir. De toute façon, advenant la mise en place de systèmes de justice distincts, les autochtones auront tout de même à composer avec le système actuel dans certaines situations. C'est pourquoi des mesures doivent être prises afin de rendre celui-ci plus équitable, même si cette solution peut paraître insuffisante aux yeux d'un grand nombre de collectivités. Ces mesures font l'objet du présent chapitre, ainsi que du suivant.

Nous avons eu l'avantage d'étudier les rapports de plusieurs commissions d'enquête provinciales qui se sont penchées sur les liens entre le système de justice pénale et les autochtones[53]. Nous nous heurtons toutefois à un obstacle que ces commissions d'enquête provinciales n'ont pas connu : nos recommandations ne portent pas seulement sur les pratiques locales, mais sur les lois de tout le pays. Si le mandat des commissions d'enquête provinciales s'est généralement limité à la situation d'un petit nombre de collectivités, notre rapport a forcément des visées beaucoup plus larges.

Il en résulte un danger que nos consultants ont porté à notre attention : une fois qu'on a défini un problème dans les rapports entre le droit pénal ou le système de justice pénale et les autochtones, on pourrait croire que ce problème est commun à toutes les collectivités autochtones. Or, à l'évidence, voilà une hypothèse à éviter, car les autochtones font face à toutes sortes de situations. Leurs expériences et leurs problèmes, tout comme les solutions, varient d'une collectivité à l'autre.

On peut dès à présent définir au moins trois grands types de situations : les collectivités autochtones éloignées, les collectivités autochtones situées à proximité des agglomérations non autochtones et les autochtones qui habitent une agglomération non autochtone. Les problèmes se posent différemment dans chacun de ces contextes[54].

L'isolement engendre certains problèmes, notamment l'insuffisance des services policiers, la difficulté d'avoir accès à un avocat, de même que l'élargissement, loin de la collectivité, des personnes arrêtées. Les collectivités éloignées risquent plus que les autres de souffrir de la lenteur du processus judiciaire. Les rapports Cawsey[55] et Osnaburgh/Windigo[56] ont tous deux signalé que les tribunaux, en particulier les cours

---

53.   Le présent rapport a toutefois été rédigé et approuvé avant la publication du rapport de la commission d'enquête sur l'administration de la justice à l'égard des populations autochtones du Manitoba. MANITOBA, ENQUÊTE PUBLIQUE SUR L'ADMINISTRATION DE LA JUSTICE ET LES POPULATIONS AUTOCHTONES, *Report of the Aboriginal Justice Inquiry of Manitoba*, vol. 1 et 2, Winnipeg, Queen's Printer, 1991 (commissaires : A. C. Hamilton et C. M. Sinclair).

54.   Il paraît opportun d'établir des distinctions plus significatives entre les divers types de collectivités. Dans une étude, on a classé les collectivités autochtones en quatre groupes et analysé dans chacun la criminalité qui y sévissait et les besoins en services policiers. Voir Carol Pitcher LAPRAIRIE, « Community Types, Crime, and Police Services on Canadian Indian Reserves » (1988), 25:4 *J. Research in Crime and Delinquency* 375.

55.   *Justice on Trial, op. cit.,* note 14.

56.   *Op. cit.,* note 43.

itinérantes, voient souvent leurs séances annulées en raison du mauvais temps. De plus, le processus d'instruction est souvent retardé en raison de la non-comparution des prévenus ou des témoins lorsqu'un procès a lieu loin de la collectivité. Enfin, n'oublions pas que la nécessité de trouver des interprètes peut aussi entraîner des retards[57].

Les retards sont particulièrement inopportuns dans les collectivités géographiquement isolées. D'abord, un procès tardif pourrait en fait gêner une affaire résolue par d'autres moyens. Ensuite, le retard pourrait empêcher que l'affaire soit réglée de manière satisfaisante dans le cadre du système actuel[58]. D'autre part, les difficultés pratiques que pose la simple présence du délinquant en liberté dans la collectivité en attendant son procès peuvent prendre des proportions insoupçonnées quand cette collectivité est petite et relativement isolée. Des conditions de mise en liberté provisoire déjà inadéquates sont encore plus difficiles à faire respecter sur une longue période ; le délinquant et la victime risquent alors de se retrouver nez à nez, et les répercussions risquent d'être fâcheuses[59].

En revanche, certaines solutions, comme la surveillance locale des personnes en liberté provisoire ou des personnes bénéficiant d'une libération conditionnelle, ou encore une meilleure sensibilisation aux différences culturelles, pourraient être plus facilement mises en œuvre dans les collectivités éloignées. La réinsertion des délinquants peut aussi être plus aisée dans les collectivités isolées.

Par ailleurs, on nous a signalé que, même si elles ne sont pas géographiquement isolées, les collectivités autochtones peuvent être « culturellement éloignées » de la société qui les entoure. Certes, on a vu des collectivités situées à proximité des centres urbains conserver leur caractère distinct. Souvent, elles disposent de ressources importantes pour améliorer le système actuel ou en instaurer un qui leur est propre.

Les autochtones établis dans une agglomération non autochtone peuvent aussi faire face à de graves difficultés. Non seulement ils éprouvent les problèmes liés à leur incompréhension du système judiciaire, mais encore ils ne peuvent bénéficier de l'appui sur lequel ils pourraient compter dans une collectivité autochtone.

Ces différences pourraient avoir une incidence sur bon nombre de recommandations, et nous avons essayé d'en tenir compte systématiquement. Certaines recommandations ne valent que pour les collectivités isolées ; d'autres touchent l'ensemble des collectivités autochtones ; d'autres enfin devraient bénéficier à tous les autochtones, où qu'ils se trouvent. Nous espérons que nos recommandations auront chaque fois une portée claire.

---

57. Pour autant que nous sachions, personne ne s'est encore prévalu des dispositions de la Charte pour saisir un tribunal de ces questions, mais il paraît clair, à la lumière de la décision *Askov*, précitée, note 48, que l'insuffisance de ressources pour la tenue d'un procès dans une collectivité autochtone ou à proximité de celle-ci ne justifie pas de tels retards.

58. R. Ross, *loc. cit.*, note 24, 4, évoque le cas d'une adolescente autochtone victime de viol qui refusait de témoigner au procès de son agresseur plus d'un an après le fait : [TRADUCTION] « À ses yeux, il était tout simplement trop tard pour le faire traduire en justice. Le passé était le passé. »

59. Dans certaines régions et pour certaines infractions, nous dit-on, on ordonne au prévenu de quitter la collectivité lorsqu'on le relâche en attendant son procès ; même si cette solution s'avère préférable à l'incarcération, elle n'est pas nécessairement satisfaisante.

II. Le recrutement et la formation à l'intérieur du système de justice pénale

Quantité de rapports et d'études ont montré l'ignorance généralisée dont fait preuve le personnel du système judiciaire à l'endroit des autochtones ; à cause de cette lacune, le système est moins susceptible de traiter les autochtones avec équité et respect. Il y a deux façons principales de s'attaquer à ce problème : recruter davantage d'autochtones à l'intérieur du système judiciaire et sensibiliser les intervenants aux différences culturelles.

A. Accroître la représentation autochtone dans l'ensemble du système

Le recrutement systématique d'autochtones leur permettrait sans doute de s'apprivoiser au système judiciaire et pourrait même leur donner un certain sentiment d'« appartenance ». D'autre part, le système judiciaire pourrait s'ouvrir davantage à la culture autochtone : les agents et les juges autochtones seraient moins exposés aux malentendus de nature culturelle dans leurs rapports avec les citoyens de même origine qu'eux, et auraient une influence sur leurs collègues non autochtones.

On a toutefois soulevé des objections à une représentation accrue. D'abord, il n'est pas sûr que les fonctionnaires autochtones seraient nécessairement plus ouverts à leur culture d'origine : [TRADUCTION] « On peut s'attendre à des attitudes très fermes de la part de ceux qui ont dû faire preuve d'acharnement pour se sortir d'un milieu défavorisé[60]. » De même, les autochtones pourraient être [TRADUCTION] « amenés, dans l'exercice de pouvoirs discrétionnaires, à adopter les procédés qui caractérisent actuellement l'administration du droit pénal », et ainsi être considérés [TRADUCTION] « comme ''vendus'' aux façons d'agir des Blancs[61]. » Certaines des personnes que nous avons consultées ont donné à entendre que le fait d'augmenter la participation des autochtones dans le système actuel ne servirait qu'à détourner l'attention, les ressources et le personnel, masquant ainsi la solution qu'est l'établissement de systèmes de justice proprement autochtones.

Nous convenons que le recrutement d'autochtones en plus grand nombre n'est pas une panacée, mais il ne s'agit pas non plus d'une solution dévastatrice comme certains l'ont prétendu. À tout prendre, nous favorisons l'élaboration de programmes destinés à augmenter la participation des autochtones dans tous les aspects du système de justice pénale, notamment à titre d'agents de police, d'avocats, de juges, d'agents de probation et d'agents des services correctionnels. En outre, les corps policiers et les services correctionnels[62] devraient recruter des autochtones, au besoin dans le cadre d'un programme d'action positive. Et une politique d'action positive devrait aussi être élaborée à l'égard de la

---

60. Peter H. RUSSELL, *The Judiciary in Canada: The Third Branch of Government*, Toronto, McGraw-Hill Ryerson, 1987, p. 165.

61. IBA, *op. cit.*, note 24, pp. 13 et 32. Le document conclut que [TRADUCTION] « malgré ces problèmes, il vaut certes mieux recruter des autochtones pour agir comme policiers dans ces collectivités. »

62. Voir L. J. BARKWELL et autres, *loc. cit.*, note 18, 139, où l'on décrit les programmes communautaires du Manitoba, à l'intérieur desquels on a créé des emplois pour un plus grand nombre d'autochtones.

formation et des décisions touchant l'avancement. Tant que l'on s'acharnera à appliquer pour l'avancement des critères jugés inacceptables pour le recrutement[63], les autochtones ne pourront accéder à des fonctions de niveau supérieur et abandonneront tôt ou tard.

Les autochtones sont sous-représentés dans l'exercice du droit[64]. Les programmes de recrutement visant à attirer davantage d'autochtones dans les facultés de droit devraient bénéficier d'un appui financier plus important qu'à l'heure actuelle. De plus, on devrait nommer des juges autochtones à tous les niveaux de juridiction, après avoir consulté les collectivités autochtones sur le choix des candidats. Pour autant que nous sachions, on ne compte aucun autochtone parmi les juges nommés par le fédéral et, du côté des tribunaux provinciaux, leur nombre est honteusement bas.

La présence de travailleurs sociaux autochtones auprès des tribunaux est déjà monnaie courante dans bien des collectivités éloignées et centres urbains du Canada. Leur présence contribue à réduire le fossé entre les délinquants autochtones et le système judiciaire. Ils offrent une gamme étendue de services : ils informent les prévenus, les fonctionnaires de la justice et les employés des tribunaux et leur expliquent la nature des procédures ; ils facilitent l'intervention d'autres organismes ; ils fournissent une aide en matière de traduction et d'interprétation extrajudiciaires ; ils offrent leur concours pour retenir les services d'avocats, arrêter les modalités de la mise en liberté provisoire et rédiger les rapports préalables à la sentence ; ils sont les porte-parole des autochtones non représentés ; ils aident au contrôle du respect des ordonnances de probation et à la surveillance des libérations conditionnelles. Idéalement, les travailleurs sociaux auprès des tribunaux devraient exercer davantage de fonctions[65] et offrir leurs services dans un plus grand nombre de régions ; malheureusement, les compressions budgétaires ont diminué leur nombre[66]. À notre avis, il faudrait élargir les programmes concernant les travailleurs sociaux autochtones auprès des tribunaux, et confier à ceux-ci la tâche d'être en contact avec les prévenus autochtones à toutes les étapes des enquêtes et des procédures, notamment lorsqu'il est impossible d'avoir accès aux services d'un avocat dans l'immédiat et de façon suivie.

---

63. Cela semble être le cas au sein de la GRC, par exemple. Voir Robert H. D. HEAD, *Policing for Aboriginal Canadians: The R.C.M.P. Role* (rapport préparé pour la GRC, 1989) [non publié].

64. La Société du barreau du Haut-Canada signale que les avocats autochtones ne constituent que 0,8 % du nombre d'avocats en Ontario, alors que les autochtones forment 1,5 % de la population adulte de cette province. Voir le « Rapport du Comité spécial sur l'équité dans la formation juridique et dans l'exercice du droit » (15 février 1991), La Société du barreau du Haut-Canada, Délibérations du Conseil 1, 36-37.

65. Par ex., ils pourraient participer aux interrogatoires policiers et aux consultations avec les avocats, expliquer au tribunal les us et coutumes autochtones, formuler des stratégies et des avis à l'intention du tribunal.

66. Voir M. JACKSON, *loc. cit.*, note 18, 256. Les programmes ont été abandonnés dans quatre provinces : Île-du-Prince-Édouard, Nouvelle-Écosse, Nouveau-Brunswick et Saskatchewan. Dans la foulée des recommandations contenues dans le rapport de la commission d'enquête sur l'affaire Marshall, *op. cit.*, note 14, on a engagé des discussions en vue du rétablissement de ce programme en Nouvelle-Écosse.

RECOMMANDATIONS

3. (1) Des programmes devraient être élaborés afin d'augmenter la participation des autochtones dans tous les aspects du système de justice pénale, notamment à titre d'agents de police, d'avocats, de juges, d'agents de probation et d'agents des services correctionnels. Plus précisément, les mesures suivantes devraient être prises :

> ***a*) les corps policiers et les services correctionnels devraient recruter des autochtones, au besoin dans le cadre d'un programme d'action positive, et une politique d'action positive devrait être élaborée à l'égard de la formation et des décisions touchant l'avancement ;**

> ***b*) les programmes de recrutement visant à attirer davantage d'autochtones dans les facultés de droit devraient bénéficier d'un appui financier plus important qu'à l'heure actuelle ;**

> ***c*) des juges autochtones devraient être nommés à tous les niveaux de juridiction, en consultation avec les collectivités autochtones sur le choix des candidats.**

(2) Les programmes concernant les travailleurs sociaux autochtones auprès des tribunaux devraient être étendus, et les fonctions de ceux-ci devraient comprendre la tâche d'être en contact avec les prévenus autochtones à toutes les étapes des enquêtes et des procédures, notamment lorsqu'il est impossible d'avoir accès aux services d'un avocat dans l'immédiat et de façon suivie.

B.   La sensibilisation aux différences culturelles

Dès 1975, à l'occasion de la Conférence nationale sur les autochtones et le régime de justice pénale[67], on plaidait en faveur d'une sensibilisation accrue aux différences culturelles. Malgré cela, quinze ans plus tard, le Cawsey Task Force observait qu'en général, les fonctionnaires judiciaires en savait toujours très peu sur la culture des autochtones albertains[68]. L'absence d'ouverture à la culture autochtone se manifeste insidieusement : nous faisons tous des suppositions sur la base de notre expérience du comportement des autres, et nous les jugeons en fonction de ces suppositions. Si les « autres » n'appartiennent pas à la même culture, cependant, nos suppositions peuvent être mal fondées. Comme le faisait remarquer un procureur de la poursuite, [TRADUCTION] « je croyais avoir affaire à des réponses évasives, à un manque de sincérité et peut-être même à des mensonges,

---

67. *Les autochtones et la justice : Rapports de la Conférence nationale et de la Conférence fédérale-provinciale sur les autochtones et le régime de justice pénale*, Edmonton, du 3 au 5 février 1975, Ottawa, Solliciteur général Canada, 1975. Aucune suite n'a été donnée aux recommandations soumises à l'époque, ce qui a donné lieu à des critiques et à des commentaires dans les milieux universitaires : voir Curt T. GRIFFITHS et Simon N. VERDUN-JONES, *Canadian Criminal Justice*, Toronto, Butterworths, 1989, p. 573, pour une étude bibliographique sélective.

68. *Justice on Trial, op. cit.*, note 14, p. 5-1. Voir aussi le Rapport Osnaburgh/Windigo, *op. cit.*, note 43, p. 59.

alors que j'aurais dû y voir du respect et de la sincérité[69]. » Ces erreurs, lorsqu'elles sont le fait de la police, d'avocats, de juges ou de fonctionnaires des services correctionnels, peuvent avoir des conséquences désastreuses.

On dispense à l'heure actuelle une certaine initiation aux différences culturelles. Dans le cadre de leur formation, les agents de la GRC suivent des cours sur la culture autochtone[70], et divers programmes éducatifs portant sur la justice ont été mis sur pied[71]. À elle seule, toutefois, cette formation pourrait bien ne pas suffire. Car si elle permet de mieux comprendre les coutumes et les façons d'agir des autochtones, elle n'a généralement pas pour but de modifier les convictions profondes. Il y aurait donc lieu d'explorer la possibilité d'élaborer des programmes de formation visant précisément ces préjugés (il s'agit en fait de programmes de sensibilisation au racisme ou de lutte contre le racisme ; nous reviendrons sur cette question à la section I du chapitre VIII, sous la rubrique « Un plan d'action pour l'avenir »). Quoi qu'il en soit, les changements ne s'opèrent pas du jour au lendemain ; il faut institutionnaliser les programmes et les faire entrer dans les mœurs.

RECOMMANDATION

3. (3) Les programmes de sensibilisation aux différences culturelles devraient être améliorés et étendus à tous ceux qui jouent un rôle dans le système de justice pénale, notamment les policiers, les avocats, les juges, les agents de probation et les agents des services correctionnels. Cette formation devrait être obligatoire et permanente pour les personnes obligées, de par leurs fonctions, d'entrer souvent en contact avec des autochtones. Les groupes locaux d'autochtones devraient participer de près à la conception des programmes et à leur mise en œuvre.

---

69. R. Ross, *loc. cit.*, note 24, 2. De même, il existe un danger de percevoir le refus ou l'incapacité des autochtones de recourir à *nos* techniques de réinsertion comme un signe manifeste de leur refus ou de leur incapacité de vouloir recourir à quelque technique que ce soit. Voir aussi R. Ross, *op. cit.*, note 21, p. 10.

70. On a fait des recommandations visant à améliorer ces cours : voir R. H. D. HEAD, *op. cit.*, note 63, pp. 88-89, qui recommande de consacrer plus de temps aux droits des autochtones et d'assurer une initiation aux différences culturelles aux responsables de l'élaboration des politiques. Voir aussi *Justice on Trial*, *op. cit.*, note 14, pp. 2-36 à 2-40, et l'analyse que contient MANITOBA MÉTIS FEDERATION, *Submission to the Aboriginal Justice Inquiry*, 1989, p. 28 [non publié].

71. Voir, par ex., les actes du Western Workshop, en Alberta, sous les auspices conjointes du Western Judicial Education Centre et de l'Association canadienne des juges de cours provinciales, conjointement avec le Centre canadien de la magistrature, au Lac Louise (Alb.), du 12 au 18 mai 1990 [non publié]. Voir aussi les remarques du juge Diebolt, juge en chef adjoint de la cour provinciale, faites à l'occasion d'une conférence tenue sous les auspices de l'Affiliation of Multi-cultural Societies and Service Agencies of British Columbia, à Vancouver, du 3 au 5 juin 1991, où le magistrat décrit la formation multiculturelle et les cours de sensibilisation dispensés aux juges de la cour provinciale de la Colombie-Britannique.

Les programmes devront être offerts par l'entremise de tout un ensemble d'organismes : centres de formation de la magistrature, barreaux provinciaux, établissements correctionnels et ainsi de suite. En outre, les programmes des facultés de droit devraient comprendre des cours sur la culture autochtone. Certaines facultés de droit ont pris des mesures dans ce sens, mais pas toutes[72]. De même, les services d'aide juridique devraient permettre à des avocats de se spécialiser dans la représentation des autochtones. En ayant régulièrement affaire à des autochtones, ces avocats pourraient apprendre à connaître les problèmes juridiques particuliers qui peuvent surgir[73].

RECOMMANDATIONS

3. (4) Les programmes des facultés de droit devraient comprendre des cours sur la culture autochtone.

(5) Les services d'aide juridique devraient permettre à des avocats de se spécialiser dans la représentation des autochtones.

III. Surmonter les barrières linguistiques et culturelles

En principe, les problèmes auxquels font face les autochtones en matière de traduction ne devraient même pas exister sous le régime du droit actuel. L'article 14 de la Charte garantit en effet des services d'interprétation à quiconque ne comprend pas la langue employée au cours d'une procédure, garantie qui existait de toute façon en common law[74]. Comme c'est le cas dans bien des domaines, il s'agit ici d'assurer le plein exercice des droits dont jouissent les autochtones.

Parmi les problèmes d'ordre linguistique qui intéressent les autochtones et qui ont été portés à notre connaissance, citons les suivants : les juges ont tendance à refuser les services d'un interprète si l'accusé se débrouille en anglais ; souvent, les interprètes ne sont pas impartiaux, car ils connaissent bien l'accusé ; la formation des interprètes présente des lacunes ; maintes notions juridiques sont sans équivalent dans les langues

---

72. « Rapport du Comité spécial sur l'équité dans la formation juridique et dans l'exercice du droit », *loc. cit.*, note 64, 35 : « [o]n a aussi évoqué le fait que les programmes d'étude des écoles de droit de la Société du barreau font peu de cas de la réalité propre aux minorités. » D'autres préconisent l'incorporation de la culture et de l'histoire des autochtones dans le programme d'études général ; cette suggestion paraît judicieuse, bien qu'elle déborde le cadre de la présente étude.

73. Le rapport de la commission d'enquête sur l'affaire Marshall, *op. cit.*, note 14, contient une recommandation au même effet (rec. 26).

74. Voir *Société des Acadiens* c. *Association of Parents*, [1986] 1 R.C.S. 549.

autochtones[75] ; même lorsqu'une assistance est offerte, elle n'est ni recherchée ni bien comprise par les avocats ou par les autres intervenants[76].

Les autochtones maîtrisant l'anglais ou le français peuvent eux aussi être désavantagés. La commission d'enquête sur l'affaire Marshall, par exemple, a observé que Donald Marshall, fils, dans ses témoignages, paraissait plus à l'aise en langue micmac qu'en anglais, langue qu'il parle couramment[77]. De légères nuances peuvent faire toute la différence entre une déclaration inculpatoire et une déclaration disculpatoire devant la police, entre un témoignage digne de foi et une déclaration invraisemblable, entre la condamnation et l'acquittement, entre une peine sévère et une peine légère.

L'appareil judiciaire dispose d'un moyen privilégié pour témoigner du respect aux autochtones : offrir l'aide nécessaire à ceux qui parlent d'autres langues. [TRADUCTION] « Il n'est pas étonnant que les premières nations tiennent l'appareil judiciaire pour une institution qui leur est étrangère, quand on fait aussi peu d'efforts pour en expliquer les rouages dans la langue de la majorité des occupants du territoire[78]. » Les solutions proposées ailleurs, comme une sensibilisation accrue aux différences culturelles et un recrutement plus intensif d'autochtones au sein de l'appareil judiciaire, peuvent parfois régler une partie de ces problèmes. Quoi qu'il en soit, des recommandations précises s'imposent sur le plan linguistique.

RECOMMANDATION

4. (1) Le droit des autochtones de s'exprimer dans leur propre langue dans toute procédure judiciaire devrait être reconnu par la loi. Les services d'interprètes qualifiés devraient être offerts aux frais de l'État à tout autochtone qui en a besoin dans le cadre d'une procédure judiciaire.

---

75. On a signalé divers problèmes au sujet de la traduction du mot fondamental « coupable », et on a pensé traduire la demande de plaidoyer par « l'avez-vous commis ? » et « vous le reproche-t-on ? ». Voir le rapport de la commission d'enquête sur l'affaire Marshall, *op. cit.*, note 18, pp. 47-48 ; *R. c. Koonungnak* (1963), 45 W.W.R. (N.S.) 282 (C. terr. T.N.-O.) ; R. Ross, *loc. cit.*, note 24, 9-10.

76. Sur l'ensemble de ces questions, voir *Justice on Trial, op. cit.*, note 14, pp. 4-14 à 4-18 ; rapport de la commission d'enquête sur l'affaire Marshall, *op. cit.*, note 14, pp. 171-173; P. A. MONTURE et M. E. TURPEL (dir.), *op. cit.*, note 41, pp. 11-12 ; John BAYLY, « Unilingual Aboriginal Jurors in a Euro-Canadian Criminal Justice System: Some Preliminary Views of the Northwest Territories Experience », dans COMMISSION ON FOLK LAW AND LEGAL PLURALISM, *Proceedings of the VIth International Symposium, Ottawa, August 14-18, 1990*, vol. 1, Ottawa, la Commission, 1990, p. 305 (président : Harald W. Finkler).

77. Rapport de la commission d'enquête sur l'affaire Marshall, *op. cit.*, note 14, pp. 171-172.

78. Rapport Osnaburgh/Windigo, *op. cit.*, note 43, pp. 58-59.

En principe, seule « la partie ou le témoin » peut se prévaloir du droit d'obtenir les services d'un interprète en vertu de l'article 14 de la Charte, et ce, seulement au stade du procès. Certains prétendent qu'un droit semblable existe au stade de l'enquête[79], mais la question n'est pas encore tranchée. À notre avis, la loi devrait prévoir que des services d'interprétation doivent être mis à la disposition de tout suspect qui a besoin d'assistance au cours des étapes préalables au procès d'une enquête menée par la police, y compris l'interrogatoire. Toute enquête faisant appel aux services d'un interprète devrait idéalement être enregistrée, de manière qu'on puisse contrôler ultérieurement la justesse de la traduction.

D'après le Cawsey Task Force, on se serait plaint de ce que des accusés ont été obligés de payer eux-mêmes les services d'un interprète. Il ne fait aucun doute qu'une ordonnance pareille, de la part d'un tribunal, aurait pour effet d'« affaiblir la garantie constitutionnelle elle-même[80] », et nous osons croire qu'il s'agit là d'un cas isolé. Néanmoins, à supposer que la question suscite le moindre doute, le *Code criminel* et la *Loi sur la preuve au Canada* devraient préciser que l'État prend à sa charge le coût des services d'interprétation fournis à un accusé, à toutes les étapes du processus pénal.

En outre, la Charte n'exige pas expressément que l'accusé et les témoins soient informés des droits que leur garantit l'article 14. Or, les personnes qui ne parlent ni le français, ni l'anglais ont peu de chances d'être au courant de cette garantie constitutionnelle ; d'autre part, certains accusés hésiteront à soulever la question, en particulier ceux qui maîtrisent assez bien l'une des deux langues officielles. Ajoutons que les contacts entre l'accusé et le tribunal — et même entre l'accusé et son avocat — sont parfois si brefs qu'ils ne permettent pas d'apprécier les compétences linguistiques de l'accusé.

RECOMMANDATIONS

4. (2) La loi devrait prévoir que des services d'interprétation doivent être mis à la disposition de tout suspect qui a besoin d'assistance au cours des étapes préalables au procès d'une enquête menée par la police, y compris l'interrogatoire.

(3) Le *Code criminel* et la *Loi sur la preuve au Canada* devraient préciser que l'État prend à sa charge le coût des services d'interprétation fournis à un accusé, à quelque étape du processus pénal.

(4) Des avis rédigés dans les langues couramment utilisées dans la collectivité et expliquant le droit à l'assistance d'un interprète garanti par l'article 14 de la Charte devraient être affichés en des endroits bien en vue dans chaque palais de justice ou, de préférence, à l'extérieur de chaque salle d'audience. Ces avis devraient préciser :

---

79. Voir les par. 10*a*) et *b*) de la Charte, et *R. c. Evans* (C.S.S., non publié, 18 avril 1991).

80. André MOREL, « Les garanties en matière de procédure et de peines », dans Gérald-A. BEAUDOIN et Edward RATUSHNY (dir.), *Charte canadienne des droits et libertés*, 2ᵉ éd., Montréal, Wilson & Lafleur, 1989, p. 555, à la page 596 n. 177 ; voir aussi *Justice on Trial, op. cit.*, note 14.

a) les conditions d'admissibilité aux services d'un interprète ;

b) le fait que l'accusé ou le témoin maîtrisant assez bien l'anglais ou le français peut néanmoins avoir droit aux services d'un interprète ;

c) le fait que l'accusé ou le témoin ne sera pas tenu de défrayer les services d'interprétation ordonnés par le tribunal.

(5) L'avocat de service devrait avoir pour instruction de prêter une attention particulière aux compétences linguistiques de tout accusé autochtone.

Au besoin, l'avocat retiendra les services d'un interprète dans ses entretiens avec l'accusé et demandera au tribunal d'en fournir à l'accusé au cours de la procédure. Il faudra éventuellement établir, à l'intérieur des programmes d'aide juridique, des mécanismes permettant d'obtenir sans délai des services d'interprétation en vue d'un entretien, et de retarder l'inscription au rôle jusqu'à ce qu'un entretien ait pu avoir lieu entre l'accusé et son avocat en présence d'un interprète.

RECOMMANDATION

4. (6) À moins que l'avocat ne lui ait fait savoir que la chose est inutile, le juge devrait s'assurer, dès la première comparution, que l'accusé ou le témoin autochtone parle et comprend la langue dans laquelle se déroulera la procédure.

Les besoins de l'accusé ou du témoin en matière linguistique doivent être consignés au dossier du tribunal, de façon que, une fois ordonnée par le tribunal, la présence d'un interprète soit assurée au moment des audiences ultérieures.

On doit aussi tenir compte des besoins des membres de la collectivité qui ne sont ni accusés ni témoins, mais dont la présence est requise dans le cadre d'une procédure. Les audiences des tribunaux visent à promouvoir publiquement les valeurs et à condamner les comportements déviants, mais les citoyens des collectivités autochtones ignorent souvent les enjeux des procès, car ceux-ci ne sont ni tenus ni traduits dans une langue connue de la majorité d'entre eux[81].

RECOMMANDATION

4. (7) La possibilité de fournir des services d'interprétation simultanée aux autochtones qui assistent aux procès se déroulant dans une réserve ou à proximité devrait être examinée du point de vue de l'opportunité, de la faisabilité et du coût.

Le dernier problème concerne la compétence des interprètes. Tout porte à croire que la qualité de la traduction est généralement médiocre. Comme il est difficile de traduire certaines notions juridiques en langue autochtone, il importe d'assurer une formation

---

81. Rapport Osnaburgh/Windigo, *op. cit.*, note 43, p. 58.

particulière aux interprètes. En fait, les interprètes sont souvent convoqués d'office et selon leur disponibilité, qu'ils comprennent ou non les dialectes locaux[82]. Les personnes que nous avons consultées nous apprennent que, dans certains cas, on retiendra, en qualité d'interprète, la première personne disponible, même si elle est apparentée à l'accusé et qu'elle ne puisse justifier d'aucune formation. L'importance de la compétence des interprètes a déjà été signalée ailleurs[83].

La jurisprudence exige que les interprètes soient compétents et impartiaux[84], mais tout porte à croire que cette exigence est rarement suivie dans les affaires mettant en cause des autochtones.

RECOMMANDATION

4. (8) Un système devrait être établi afin de former des interprètes professionnels qualifiés et indépendants pour les causes criminelles. En règle générale, seuls ces interprètes seraient habilités à servir dans les causes criminelles.

IV. Mieux intégrer les collectivités dans le système judiciaire

Les collectivités autochtones ne comprendront le système judiciaire, ne le respecteront et n'auront le sentiment d'avoir prise sur lui que si elles participent à tous les stades importants du processus :

[TRADUCTION]
Il faut que les tribunaux sachent ce que chaque collectivité tient pour une infraction grave, quelle peine elle envisage et comment il faudrait traiter l'affaire. Les tribunaux ne fonctionnent pas dans le vide : leurs décisions, leurs délibérations et les répercussions qui en découlent touchent non seulement les délinquants, mais aussi les victimes et la collectivité en général. Les juges et les procureurs de la poursuite doivent connaître la population et la collectivité au nom desquelles ils agissent. Eux aussi ont des comptes à rendre aux citoyens[85].

La plupart du temps, c'est la collectivité qui comprend le mieux les problèmes et la façon de les régler.

---

82. *Ibid.*

83. Voir J. BAYLY, *loc. cit.*, note 76, 305, où l'on fait état de la pénurie d'interprètes qualifiés dans les Territoires du Nord-Ouest.

84. *Unterreiner* c. *La Reine* (1980), 51 C.C.C. (2e) 373 (C. comté Ont.).

85. GIFT LAKE COUNCIL, mémoire présenté au Task Force on the Criminal Justice System and Its Impact on the Indian and Métis People of Alberta, cité dans *Justice on Trial, op. cit.*, note 14, p. 5-2.

Toute réforme qui se veut efficace doit intéresser les collectivités au système de justice pénale. À notre avis, leur participation prendrait diverses formes : elles pourraient formuler des conseils sur les orientations générales, jouer un plus grand rôle dans les affaires individuelles, et parfois même se substituer à l'appareil judiciaire. Quels en seraient les avantages ? Le nombre d'autochtones accusés d'infraction diminuerait, les décisions seraient sans doute mieux reçues dans les collectivités, et celles-ci auraient moins l'impression de se voir imposer un système étranger à leurs us et coutumes. Bien entendu, la participation d'une collectivité n'est possible que dans la mesure où elle dispose des ressources humaines voulues et choisit de s'engager dans cette voie.

Un bon moyen de faire accepter l'appareil judiciaire par les collectivités autochtones consiste à favoriser le recours aux méthodes traditionnelles pour résoudre les conflits.

RECOMMANDATION

5. (1) Les « conciliateurs » (*peacemakers*) devraient se voir conférer un rôle officiel de médiation des conflits à l'intérieur du système de justice.

Le conciliateur[86], sorte de médiateur traditionnel, se recrute auprès de la famille, des aînés et des chefs élus de la collectivité. Son rôle est multiple : enseignement et renforcement des valeurs et des traditions, consultation, choix d'un foyer d'accueil pour les enfants, et résolution des conflits[87]. Le Dakota Ojibway Tribal Council a recommandé que les conciliateurs remplissent les fonctions suivantes dans le cadre d'un système judiciaire purement autochtone :

a) décider s'ils s'occuperont de telle affaire ou en déféreront au ministère public ;

b) nommer des personnes au sein de la collectivité qui s'occuperont de situations, d'infractions ou de problèmes particuliers ;

c) nommer des personnes qui veilleront au maintien de l'ordre social au sein de la collectivité ;

d) organiser des cérémonies, des fêtes ou d'autres manifestations pour assurer la cohésion au sein de la collectivité ;

e) résoudre les conflits entre les personnes ou entre les familles, et prêter assistance aux personnes en difficulté. Les conciliateurs pourraient également prendre la parole à l'occasion d'événements sociaux pour rappeler aux membres de la collectivité leurs obligations, leurs principes et leurs valeurs, et pour les inviter à respecter la discipline[88].

---

86. Les « conciliateurs » (*peacemakers*) doivent être distingués des « gardiens de la paix » (*peacekeepers*) de Kahnawake, qui jouent essentiellement le rôle d'agents de la paix.

87. *Reflecting Indian Concerns and Values in the Joint Canada-Saskatchewan-FSIN Justice Studies of Certain Aspects of the Justice System as They Relate to Indians in Saskatchewan*, vol. 6, 1985, p. 29 [non publié].

88. DAKOTA OJIBWAY TRIBAL COUNCIL, *Submission to the Commission of Inquiry on the Administration of Justice for Aboriginal Peoples* (mémoire présenté à une assemblée publique tenue à Brandon, Manitoba, 27 avril 1989), pp. 8-9 [non publié].

Nous croyons aussi que la participation des collectivités aux divers aspects de l'appareil judiciaire peut se faire sous de nombreux rapports. Par exemple, l'intégration officielle des conciliateurs dans un programme de déjudiciarisation reconnu rapprocherait énormément l'appareil des méthodes traditionnelles de conciliation et de médiation en usage dans les collectivités autochtones et l'éloignerait du principe des débats contradictoires privilégié par nos tribunaux[89].

RECOMMANDATION

5. (2) Des mécanismes de liaison permanente devraient être établis entre les poursuivants locaux, d'une part, et les collectivités et dirigeants autochtones, d'autre part.

Grâce à ces mécanismes, les procureurs du ministère public et les dirigeants de la collectivité auraient l'occasion d'aborder plusieurs sujets intéressant celle-ci, notamment : les critères régissant le dépôt d'accusations, l'opportunité de déjudiciariser telle ou telle affaire, de même que la suffisance des ressources de la collectivité. Des rapports devraient être transmis régulièrement au procureur général, à ses adjoints et aux collectivités autochtones touchées.

Ainsi, l'article 518 du *Code criminel* définit la preuve admissible à l'enquête sur le cautionnement. En Australie, les tribunaux ont tenu compte des châtiments traditionnels autochtones au moment de statuer sur la demande de cautionnement[90]. Toutefois, le Code canadien ne contient aucune procédure permettant explicitement à une collectivité d'intervenir dans ce sens. Nous croyons pour notre part que les représentants de la collectivité à laquelle appartient le prévenu devraient être autorisés à déposer, au cours de l'enquête sur cautionnement, au sujet des solutions de rechange à l'incarcération en attendant le procès. Bien entendu, il importe de s'assurer que le porte-parole représente bien le point de vue de la collectivité mais, cela posé, nous ne voyons pas ce qui pourrait empêcher un groupe représentatif de présenter une preuve de cette nature[91]. De même, la loi devrait permettre expressément à des assesseurs non juristes (des aînés ou d'autres membres respectés de la collectivité) de siéger avec le juge et de donner leur avis sur la peine à imposer. Ces assesseurs devraient assister au procès ou à l'énoncé des faits au terme duquel le plaidoyer est enregistré. Ils auraient pour tâche de consulter les intéressés et de recommander au juge le dispositif indiqué. Des programmes semblables existent

---

89. Voir aussi Brad MORSE et Linda LOCK, *Native Offenders' Perceptions of the Criminal Justice System*, Ottawa, ministère de la Justice, 1988 ; AUSTRALIAN LAW REFORM COMMISSION, *The Recognition of Aboriginal Customary Laws: Summary Report*, rapport n° 31, Canberra, Australian Government Publishing Service, 1986 ; et M. JACKSON, *loc. cit.*, note 18, 242-255.

90. Dans *R. c. Jungarai* (1981), 9 N.T.R. 30 (C. suprême T.-N.) une personne accusée de meurtre avait été relâchée sous cautionnement, à la condition de se soumettre à un châtiment corporel traditionnel. Par cette ordonnance plutôt inhabituelle, on voulait notamment empêcher la famille de la victime de s'en prendre à la famille de l'accusé. Pour un bref résumé de cette affaire, voir M. JACKSON, *loc. cit.*, note 18, 270-271.

91. Force est d'admettre que cette proposition ne tournera pas toujours à l'avantage du prévenu lui-même, mais la collectivité dans son ensemble en fera son profit.

déjà[92] ou sont sur le point d'être créés[93] dans certaines collectivités. Les recommandations des assesseurs pourraient éventuellement s'éloigner des peines établies par la jurisprudence ou même contredire la jurisprudence générale des cours d'appel. Cela ne devrait surprendre personne ; et si nous faisons cette recommandation, c'est précisément parce qu'il arrive que les règles habituelles n'aient pas leur place dans les collectivités autochtones.

Nous recommandons aussi l'établissement d'un processus permanent de consultation entre les personnes et organismes qui fournissent des services aux autochtones, les fonctionnaires du Service correctionnel du Canada et la Commission nationale des libérations conditionnelles. Les consultations devraient s'engager avec un organisme représentatif de l'ensemble des groupes autochtones plutôt qu'avec des collectivités individuelles. Des rencontres plus fréquentes favoriseront la circulation de l'information, l'efficacité de l'élaboration et de la mise en œuvre des programmes, ainsi qu'une uniformité et une cohérence plus soutenues dans l'application des programmes correctionnels aux délinquants autochtones. À cet égard, les collectivités autochtones auraient certainement intérêt à participer à l'établissement de plans de sortie pour les délinquants autochtones et à la surveillance de ceux-ci dans la collectivité après leur libération. Elles sont les mieux placées pour juger de l'opportunité de replacer un délinquant dans son milieu, de la qualité de la surveillance après la libération conditionnelle et de son incidence sur les ressources locales.

RECOMMANDATIONS

5. (3) Les représentants de la collectivité à laquelle appartient le prévenu devraient être autorisés à déposer, au cours de l'enquête sur cautionnement, au sujet des solutions de rechange à l'incarcération en attendant le procès.

(4) La loi devrait permettre expressément à des assesseurs non juristes (des aînés ou d'autres membres respectés de la collectivité) de siéger avec le juge et de donner leur avis sur la peine à imposer.

(5) Un processus permanent de consultation devrait être établi entre les personnes et organismes qui fournissent des services aux autochtones, les fonctionnaires du Service correctionnel du Canada et la Commission nationale des libérations conditionnelles.

---

92. Le South Island Tribal Council (C.-B.) s'est doté d'un tel programme, tout comme la collectivité de l'île Christian, en Ontario. Voir R. H. HEMMINGSON, *loc. cit.*, note 31, 50 ; M. COYLE, *loc. cit.*, note 20. Des programmes semblables existent aussi en Australie : voir AUSTRALIAN LAW REFORM COMMISSION, *op. cit.*, note 89, par. 142, p. 68.

93. Le gouvernement ontarien a mis sur pied, dans deux collectivités autochtones du nord de la province, des programmes en application desquels des aînés participent à la détermination des peines à la Cour provinciale, assurent des services entourant la probation et participent à l'administration des mesures de justice traditionnelle, aux services de consultation, à la formation juridique et à l'initiation aux différences culturelles destinée aux non-autochtones. Voir « Natives Get $200,000 to Study Justice System », *Law Times* (23-29 avril 1990) 3.

(6) Les collectivités autochtones devraient participer à l'établissement de plans de sortie pour les délinquants autochtones et à la surveillance de ceux-ci dans la collectivité après leur libération.

Toutefois, il serait injuste de passer sous silence les questions que soulèvent toutes ces recommandations. Les ressources humaines ne sont pas inépuisables. Idéalement, les aînés joueraient les rôles de conseiller et de décideur, comme nous le proposons, car ces personnes sont les plus susceptibles de conférer au processus la légitimité nécessaire. Dans maintes collectivités, cependant, il n'y aura pas assez d'aînés pour remplir toutes ces fonctions[94] ; dans d'autres, on pourrait tout simplement ne pas souhaiter une participation aussi active. En outre, même si nous espérons que l'intervention des aînés conférera une certaine légitimité au système actuel, il n'est pas impossible que cette collaboration ait pour effet de discréditer les aînés qui s'y seront prêtés. Quoi qu'il en soit, nous recommandons que les collectivités autochtones aient la possibilité de se prévaloir de solutions de ce type. Certaines pourraient être incapables de tirer parti de toutes les formules, alors que d'autres pourraient les rejeter après les avoir jugées inefficaces. En tout état de cause, chaque collectivité devrait avoir la possibilité de participer plus activement à chacune des étapes du processus judiciaire.

V. Appliquer le droit coutumier et ses pratiques

Pendant des années, on a cru qu'il fallait assimiler les autochtones au lieu de les encourager à conserver leur culture. Aussi une bonne partie de leurs « traditions » sont-elles passées dans l'oubli, ou sont en voie de le faire. À la faveur du regain d'intérêt pour les traditions dans certaines collectivités, la connaissance de l'histoire a repris de l'importance. En réalité, le droit coutumier peut être aussi efficace que le droit écrit à titre de mécanisme de régulation sociale :

[TRADUCTION]
Il est malheureux que le terme « coutume » évoque quelque chose de plus ou moins inférieur à ce que recouvre le mot « droit ». On a l'impression que la « coutume » est étrangère, en quelque sorte, à la notion stricte de « loi », norme émanant de l'État à laquelle on n'échappe pas. Il s'agit là d'un point de vue ethnocentrique[95] [. . .]

Le droit coutumier pourrait influer sur la détermination des peines. Les tribunaux ne se sont pas toujours montrés cohérents dans leurs tentatives de réconcilier le droit coutumier autochtone et le droit pénal. Dans *R.* c. *Fireman*[96], par exemple, la Cour

---

94. On nous a fait savoir que la gestion d'un programme de solutions de rechange à l'amende pourrait drainer les ressources d'une collectivité (voir IBA, *op. cit.*, note 24, pp. 48-49), et que le nombre d'aînés disponibles pour les centres d'accueil ou capables d'offrir des conseils aux prisonniers est insuffisant.

95. J. W. ZION, *loc. cit.*, note 37, 123-124.

96. (1971) 4 C.C.C. (2ᵉ) 82.

d'appel de l'Ontario s'est interrogée sur la peine à infliger à un accusé habitant une collectivité autochtone isolée. Au départ, la collectivité avait répudié Fireman mais, dès la fin de l'enquête préliminaire, elle paraissait disposée à le recevoir de nouveau. La Cour d'appel a conclu que ce n'était pas la durée de l'emprisonnement qui aurait un effet dissuasif sur l'accusé, mais bien sa condamnation et sa séparation d'avec les siens. En fait, la Cour a reconnu qu'une peine trop longue nuirait à la réinsertion de Fireman dans sa collectivité, ce qui neutraliserait l'effet de dissuasion.

Dans *R. c. Naqitarvik*, par contre, la Cour d'appel des Territoires du Nord-Ouest a accordé très peu d'importance aux méthodes traditionnelles autochtones pour régler les problèmes sociaux. La Cour a estimé que les services de consultation dispensés à l'accusé par le Inumarit Committee d'Arctic Bay, collectivité située sur le littoral nord de la Terre de Baffin, ne devaient pas être considérés comme [TRADUCTION] « provenant d'un organisme traditionnel de consultation et de décision [. . .] [ni comme] le vestige d'une culture ancienne ; il s'agissait plutôt des services habituels de consultation » prévus dans le cadre du système de justice pénale[97]. Apparemment, Arctic Bay n'était pas suffisamment attachée aux coutumes et pratiques traditionnelles pour justifier une dérogation aux règles habituelles en matière de détermination des peines : la présence de l'électricité, du téléphone et du tourne-disque rendait dérisoire le recours aux coutumes. L'arrêt *Naqitarvik* semble exiger que les institutions culturelles des autochtones soient restées figées dans le temps, et que l'on ait empêché l'évolution des cultures et des coutumes qui y sont rattachées.

Nous croyons plutôt que les méthodes modernes peuvent s'inspirer des usages traditionnels. Les juges doivent s'éveiller davantage aux pratiques coutumières des collectivités autochtones.

L'information sur le droit coutumier autochtone pourrait avoir une incidence sur une foule de décisions d'ordre procédural dans les limites du système actuel de justice pénale. Ainsi, elle pourrait influencer la décision du juge des faits appelé à se prononcer sur le comportement d'une « personne raisonnable », critère qui entre en jeu dans la détermination de l'élément moral en matière de témérité, de négligence criminelle et de provocation. Le droit coutumier autochtone pourrait également avoir une incidence sur divers moyens de défense prévus au *Code criminel*[98], comme l'existence d'une justification ou d'une excuse légale (paragraphe 429(2)), ou d'une apparence de droit (article 322 et paragraphe 429(2)), ou encore l'obéissance à une loi *de facto* (article 15). Il faudra en savoir plus long à ce sujet avant de pouvoir formuler des recommandations précises[99].

---

97. *R. c. Naqitarvik* (1986), 26 C.C.C. (3ᵉ) 193, 196.

98. L'Australian Law Reform Commission a proposé de reconnaître dans la loi un moyen de défense s'inspirant en partie du droit coutumier. Pareille défense n'exonérerait pas l'accusé, mais mitigerait sa responsabilité, à l'instar de la défense fondée sur la provocation : AUSTRALIAN LAW REFORM COMMISSION, *op. cit.*, note 89, p. 43.

99. Certains travaux ont été entrepris : voir, par ex., E. Jane DICKSON-GILMORE, « Resurrecting the Peace: Traditionalist Approaches to Separate Justice in the Kahnawake Mohawk Nation », dans COMMISSION ON FOLK LAW AND LEGAL PLURALISM, *op. cit.*, note 76, p. 259.

RECOMMANDATION

6. Le gouvernement fédéral devrait subventionner la recherche en matière de droit coutumier autochtone[100].

VI. Les droits issus de traités devant la juridiction criminelle

À mesure que les peuples autochtones ont perdu la maîtrise de leur destin, leurs sociétés se sont démembrées. L'introduction de notre système de justice d'inspiration britannique a sapé les bases de leurs modes traditionnels et informels de régulation sociale. Mais notre système s'est révélé un substitut inadéquat. Par conséquent, avec le temps, maintes collectivités autochtones ont été largement privées des outils nécessaires pour réprimer les comportements asociaux[101].

Le conflit entre les valeurs des autochtones et celles que véhicule notre système de justice ne porte pas réellement sur la définition des comportements jugés inacceptables. On a fait valoir que, [TRADUCTION] « dans l'ensemble, ''nos'' crimes sont tout aussi répréhensibles à leurs yeux[102]. » Les divergences portent plutôt sur les mesures à prendre contre ceux qui adoptent un comportement inacceptable.

Cela dit, il faut accorder une attention particulière à une question où les divergences sont manifestes : l'exercice des droits issus de traités devant la juridiction criminelle. Certaines des personnes que nous avons consultées n'apprécient guère que les tribunaux criminels constituent le lieu principal où les autochtones font valoir leurs droits issus de traités. Cette procédure, estiment-ils, est avilissante. Les droits issus de traités définissent les rapports entre les autochtones et le reste de la population canadienne. Toutefois, c'est surtout lorsqu'ils sont invoqués devant une juridiction pénale en réponse à une accusation criminelle que ces droits prennent leur sens. Résultat : les droits des autochtones n'ont d'existence que celle que leur reconnaît la juridiction pénale. Autre difficulté pratique : ce moyen de défense peut être invoqué par tout autochtone, si peu préparé soit-il, et la décision le concernant lie alors toutes les autres personnes visées par le même traité. Bien qu'il arrive à d'autres Canadiens de devoir faire appel aux tribunaux criminels pour faire

---

100. Dans la foulée de cette recommandation, voir *infra* la rec. 15(2), p. 99, où nous proposons la création d'un Institut de justice autochtone. Bien entendu, l'établissement de systèmes de justice autochtones ne consiste pas seulement à ressusciter les méthodes employées il y a des siècles ; il suppose néanmoins une certaine connaissance du droit coutumier.

101. On a souvent décrit cet état de choses comme l'un des sous-produits de la colonisation. Voir *supra* au ch. IV, à la p. 13 et *infra* au ch. VI, sous la rubrique VI, « La détermination de la peine », à la p. 72.

102. R. Ross, *loc. cit.*, note 24, 13. L'IBA, *op. cit.*, note 24, p. 41, signale que les craintes des autochtones, pour la plupart, [TRADUCTION] « portent sur des sujets qui concernent les procédés de la justice pénale plutôt que sur les textes d'incrimination du Code criminel et de la législation connexe. »

valoir leurs droits (par exemple, les limites de la liberté d'expression pourront être déterminées dans le cadre d'une affaire d'obscénité), la Cour suprême du Canada a compati à la situation difficile des autochtones : « le procès concernant la violation d'une interdiction pénale ne constitue pas le cadre idéal pour déterminer l'existence d'un droit ancestral[103]. »

À notre avis, la juridiction pénale n'est pas l'endroit le mieux choisi pour définir les droits ancestraux et les droits issus de traités. D'ailleurs, les tribunaux en général sont loin de constituer une tribune idéale pour donner de la chair aux droits issus de traités. Ceux-ci devraient, dans toute la mesure du possible, être définis par voie de négociations et, uniquement lorsque cela s'impose, par voie de litige. Cette démarche nous semble plus respectueuse des autochtones.

RECOMMANDATION

7. Les gouvernements devraient adopter des politiques officielles claires concernant les méthodes à privilégier pour définir les droits ancestraux et les droits issus de traités. Ces politiques devraient encourager le dialogue avec les collectivités autochtones, en vue de cerner les points de désaccord et d'en arriver à la conclusion d'ententes négociées avec les parties concernées. Lorsque l'intervention des tribunaux est nécessaire, le jugement déclaratoire ou le renvoi constitutionnel devrait être préféré à un procès pénal ; toutefois, si des poursuites sont entamées, la multiplication des procédures devrait être vigoureusement découragée au profit d'une seule procédure type[104].

Suivant cette recommandation, de nombreuses questions aujourd'hui tranchées individuellement à la lumière des circonstances de chaque affaire pourraient faire l'objet d'une décision globale. Ainsi, bien que les droits issus de traités aient préséance sur les lois provinciales en vertu de la *Loi sur les Indiens*[105], il arrive encore que des autochtones soient condamnés pour infraction à des lois provinciales[106]. La négociation permet de régler bien plus facilement les grandes questions à caractère général et d'éviter ainsi d'inutiles litiges.

---

103. *R.* c. *Sparrow*, [1990] 1 R.C.S. 1075, 1095.

104. C'est le parti adopté au Québec et en Ontario pour la contestation de la validité constitutionnelle des dispositions du *Code criminel* relatives à l'avortement, dans le cadre des poursuites intentées au Dr Henry Morgentaler.

105. Précitée, note 33, art. 88.

106. Les jugements ne s'accordent pas, par ex., lorsqu'il s'agit de savoir si un autochtone est coupable d'infraction quand il se sert d'une lampe pour chasser (comparer *Prince* c. *The Queen*, [1964] R.C.S. 81, et *Myran* c. *La Reine*, [1976] 2 R.C.S. 137) ou quand il transporte une arme chargée dans un véhicule (comparer *R.* c. *Anderson and Beardy*, [1983] 2 C.N.L.R. 117 (C. comté Man.) et *R.* c. *Polchies*, [1982] 4 C.N.L.R. 132 (C.P. N.-B.)).

CHAPITRE SIX

Transformer les rôles et réformer le processus

Points saillants

La police doit être plus présente dans les collectivités qu'elle sert et leur rendre compte de façon plus rigoureuse. On pourrait atteindre cet objectif en donnant une certaine permanence à la présence de la police au sein même des collectivités autochtones désireuses de faire appel à des services de police externes. D'autre part, les gouvernements fédéral et provinciaux devraient favoriser la création de corps policiers autochtones autonomes dans les collectivités qui le désirent.

Les policiers devraient conserver le pouvoir discrétionnaire de porter des accusations quand bon leur semble, mais ils devraient systématiquement demander conseil aux procureurs du ministère public, notamment quant à l'opportunité de porter ou non des accusations. Il y aurait lieu de faire savoir clairement aux poursuivants, par le biais de directives et de la formation qu'ils reçoivent, qu'ils doivent exercer leurs pouvoirs discrétionnaires indépendamment de l'influence ou des pressions exercées par la police, et que les conseils qu'ils donnent aux policiers doivent demeurer objectifs et impartiaux.

Des règles d'interrogatoire particulières devraient être élaborées pour régir la réception des déclarations des autochtones, notamment en ce qui concerne la présence d'un avocat au moment de l'interrogatoire.

Les barreaux provinciaux et les organismes d'aide juridique devraient mettre à la disposition des autochtones leur matériel éducatif et, en particulier, l'information sur la manière d'obtenir les services de l'aide juridique.

Chaque fois que la chose est possible et que la collectivité le souhaite, les séances d'un tribunal devraient avoir lieu dans la collectivité autochtone où l'infraction a été commise, ou à proximité.

Les règles de la procédure pénale, comme celles qui régissent la prestation du serment, la mise en liberté provisoire et la présence des intéressés devant le tribunal devraient être adaptées aux besoins, aux traditions et à la culture autochtones.

Les solutions de rechange à l'emprisonnement devraient être utilisées dans toute la mesure du possible et être considérées en priorité au moment de la détermination de la peine.

Une liste de facteurs qui, conjugués à d'autres circonstances, viendraient atténuer la peine lorsque le délinquant est un autochtone devrait être dressée.

Le non-paiement d'une amende devrait entraîner l'incarcération seulement si la personne refuse ou néglige sciemment de payer l'amende, et non lorsqu'elle est incapable de le faire.

Une étude portant sur la conception et la pertinence culturelle de tous les programmes utilisés dans le cadre de la déjudiciarisation, de la probation ou de la libération conditionnelle devrait être entreprise en collaboration avec les autochtones et les organismes qui les représentent. Les juges, les procureurs du ministère public et les avocats de la défense devraient recevoir une formation adéquate au sujet de l'existence et des buts de ces programmes.

Il y aurait lieu de formuler les critères d'admissibilité à la mise en liberté provisoire et de rédiger les rapports de probation en tenant bien compte des différences culturelles et en répondant aux besoins des délinquants et des collectivités autochtones.

Il y aurait lieu, dans un texte de loi, d'accorder à la spiritualité autochtone la même reconnaissance qu'aux autres religions, et les aînés devraient avoir le même statut et jouir de la même liberté de manœuvre que les aumôniers des pénitenciers.

La Commission nationale des libérations conditionnelles et le Service correctionnel du Canada devraient établir une politique et des directives nationales en matière de renonciation au droit à une audience et à la révision en matière de libération conditionnelle. L'information pertinente devrait être communiquée au personnel des services correctionnels et aux détenus.

Des établissements correctionnels locaux de dimensions réduites devraient être créés et placés sous la responsabilité des collectivités.

46

I. La police

Le rôle de la police est de faire respecter la loi. Concrètement, toutefois, ses responsabilités vont beaucoup plus loin. Elle assure aussi, en quelque sorte, un service social de base : [TRADUCTION] « Lorsqu'on fait appel à [un policier], on s'attend à ce qu'il règle la situation, à moins qu'il ne soit en mesure de recommander un organisme qui fera mieux l'affaire. Et le policier ne s'en lavera pas les mains en prétendant que cela ne le regarde pas[107]. » La multiplicité des services assurés par la police contribue à lui donner une assez bonne réputation dans le grand public.

Malheureusement, on ne peut pas en dire autant des rapports que la police entretient avec les autochtones[108]. Même si la situation n'est pas la même d'une collectivité à l'autre, on se plaint souvent — du moins nous en a-t-on fait la remarque à plusieurs reprises durant nos consultations — que la police n'est présente dans les collectivités autochtones que pour y pratiquer des arrestations. Sur le strict plan des interventions policières « curatives », les collectivités autochtones n'auraient pas trop sujet de se plaindre : en fait, certains attribuent même le taux d'inculpation élevé dans les réserves au fait que la présence policière y est, à certains égards, trop forte. Quoi qu'il en soit, dans la mesure où la police ne fournit pas aux collectivités autochtones le même type de services dont bénéficie le reste de la société, les autochtones ne jouissent pas d'un accès égal à la justice, pas plus qu'ils ne sont traités avec équité et respect.

Ajoutons que, même en ce qui concerne l'intervention policière curative, il existe un clivage important, sur le plan des valeurs et de la culture, entre le point de vue du policier et celui de l'autochtone. De simples malentendus d'ordre culturel font naître des soupçons mais, chose plus grave encore, peuvent déboucher sur l'intolérance et le racisme manifestes.

A. Changements de structure au sein des corps policiers

RECOMMANDATION

8. (1) La police devrait être plus présente dans les collectivités qu'elle sert et leur rendre compte de façon plus rigoureuse.

---

107. Lloyd L. WEINREB, *Denial of Justice*, New York, Free Press, 1977, p. 15. Voir aussi André NORMANDEAU et Barry LEIGHTON, *Une vision de l'avenir de la police au Canada : Police-défi 2000*, Ottawa, Solliciteur général Canada, 1990, pp. 43-44 (ci-après *Police-défi 2000*).

108. Voir Douglas SKOOG, Lance W. ROBERTS et Edward D. BOLDT, « Native Attitudes toward the Police » (1980), 22 *Rev. can. crim.* 354, où l'on établit un contraste entre l'attitude des Blancs, bienveillants envers la police manitobaine, et celle des autochtones, ambivalents à son endroit.

Il existe deux moyens principaux d'atteindre cet objectif : soit modifier les ententes qui touchent les corps policiers existants, soit remplacer ces derniers par des corps policiers autochtones, constitués en collaboration avec les collectivités, gérés par elles et relevant directement d'elles.

B.   La présence policière dans les collectivités

« [L]e modèle de police communautaire est la réponse la plus appropriée aux problèmes et aux défis de la prochaine décennie[109]. » La présence accrue de la police dans la collectivité n'est pas une panacée, mais constitue un pas dans la bonne direction[110]. Il s'agit d'accorder moins d'importance à l'intervention consécutive à une plainte, et de favoriser plutôt une sorte de « partenariat entre la police et la communauté pour résoudre la criminalité et les problèmes connexes[111]. » On cherche davantage à cerner les problèmes en consultant la collectivité et à s'attaquer à leurs causes sous-jacentes. La responsabilité du corps policier envers la collectivité se manifeste autant par des consultations informelles menées auprès du public, que par des mécanismes de nature juridique, tels les comités d'examen. La présence communautaire de la police permet aux collectivités autochtones de mieux cibler leurs priorités.

À l'heure actuelle, l'évaluation des besoins en détachements et des crédits budgétaires nécessaires se fait d'après les statistiques relatives à l'action policière curative[112]. De même, les critères établis pour l'appréciation du rendement des agents contribuent eux aussi à renforcer l'action curative. Le modèle de police communautaire, en revanche, comporte de nouvelles techniques d'appréciation, notamment des critères inédits servant à évaluer le rendement individuel des agents[113].

RECOMMANDATION

8. (2) Il y aurait lieu de donner, dans toute la mesure du possible, une certaine permanence à la présence de la police dans les collectivités autochtones qui désirent continuer à bénéficier d'un service de police externe[114].

---

109. *Police-défi 2000*, *op. cit.*, note 107, p. 41.

110. Voir *Policing in Relation to the Blood Tribe: Report of a Public Inquiry, Commissioner's Report: Findings and Recommendations*, vol. 1, Edmonton, Alberta Solicitor General, février 1991, p. 189 (commissaire : C. H. Rolf) (ci-après *Policing in Relation to the Blood Tribe*), où la police communautaire est vue comme une solution appropriée aux besoins culturels des membres de la tribu des Gens-du-Sang.

111. *Police-défi 2000*, *op. cit.*, note 107, p. 43.

112. *Justice on Trial*, *op. cit.*, note 14, p. 2-17. Il en résulte un cercle vicieux : la réduction de l'action curative débouche sur des effectifs réduits, ce qui rend plus difficile les activités de type communautaire. Comme on consacre moins de temps à ces activités, on en consacre davantage à l'action curative, ce qui exige une augmentation des effectifs. Voir aussi *Policing in Relation to the Blood Tribe*, *op. cit.*, note 110, p. 151.

113. *Police-défi 2000*, *op. cit.*, note 107, p. 49.

114. Voir SOLLICITEUR GÉNÉRAL CANADA, *Rapport annuel 1988-1989*, Ottawa, Solliciteur général Canada, 1989, p. 26, où l'on apprend que huit réserves, sur un total possible de 355, se sont déjà dotées d'une police communautaire, et que d'autres détachements sont prévus.

La présence accrue de la police dans la collectivité et une meilleure connaissance des attentes de celle-ci devraient atténuer l'impression que les policiers sont des étrangers chargés de faire respecter des lois imposées de l'extérieur.

Cela dit, le fait d'être consulté sur les priorités et d'avoir son mot à dire sur le rôle de la police n'équivaut pas à une prise en charge. Parfois, il sera difficile d'assurer la permanence de la police au sein de la collectivité, en particulier dans les régions isolées[115]. Aussi certaines collectivités voudront-elles instituer un corps policier autonome plutôt que d'accueillir un détachement communautaire relevant d'une autorité extérieure. Nous avons constaté que certaines collectivités préféreraient nettement recourir à des solutions autres que la police communautaire[116].

C. Les corps policiers autochtones

À l'heure actuelle, la présence des corps policiers dans les réserves est régie par une multitude d'ententes[117]. Bien qu'à première vue on soit porté à souhaiter une plus grande uniformité des services policiers, la diversité nous paraît justifiée dans ce contexte, étant donné que les aspirations, les besoins, les exigences varient d'une collectivité à l'autre.

RECOMMANDATION

8. (3) Les gouvernements fédéral et provinciaux devraient favoriser la création de corps policiers autochtones autonomes dans les collectivités qui le désirent. Il n'y aurait pas lieu d'exiger pour ces corps policiers ni une structure ni un rôle uniques. L'autonomie implique qu'il faut laisser à la collectivité le pouvoir de décider de la structure qu'elle lui donnera.

---

115. D'après AFFAIRES INDIENNES ET DU NORD CANADA, *Rapport du maintien de l'ordre dans les réserves indiennes : rapport du groupe d'étude*, Ottawa, AINC, 1990, p. 4 (ci-après *Maintien de l'ordre dans les réserves indiennes*), il y a 599 bandes indiennes, dont 135 environ se trouvent dans des régions éloignées ou isolées.

116. Voir aussi MANITOBA MÉTIS FEDERATION, *op. cit.*, note 70, pp. 27-33.

117. *Maintien de l'ordre dans les réserves indiennes*, *op. cit.*, note 115, où l'on décrit 12 programmes différents de services policiers propres aux autochtones. Il existe au moins 14 ententes financières, en vertu desquelles le financement est assuré soit exclusivement par une administration publique — fédérale, provinciale ou tribale —, soit au moyen de programmes à frais partagés. Voir R. H. D. HEAD, *op. cit.*, note 63, p. 150. La plupart des réserves sont servies par la GRC. Pour une description détaillée de ces programmes, voir R. H. D. HEAD, *op. cit.*, note 63, ou *Maintien de l'ordre dans les réserves indiennes*, *op. cit.*, note 115. Certaines se sont dotées de corps policiers autonomes : les pouvoirs conférés aux agents proviennent habituellement des lois provinciales sur la police. Les agents relèvent souvent d'une commission de police composée de délégués fédéraux, provinciaux et tribaux. Une exception importante : les gardiens de la paix de Kahnawake n'ont pas le statut d'agents de la paix aux termes d'une loi fédérale ou provinciale, et relèvent d'un comité de police dont les membres sont nommés par le conseil de la tribu.

Nombre de structures différentes cadreraient avec l'esprit de cette recommandation, notamment des organismes parallèles à ceux qui existent déjà, mais dont la charge reviendrait à la collectivité. Cependant, les fonctions qu'une collectivité donnée aimerait confier à sa police ne sont pas forcément identiques à celles souhaitées ailleurs[118]. La solution la plus indiquée pour résoudre les problèmes sociaux dans les réserves, et celle qui est la plus conforme à la conception traditionnelle de la justice chez les autochtones, consiste peut-être à recourir, non pas à un corps policier au sens où nous l'entendons, mais à un organisme qui remplirait une gamme de fonctions beaucoup plus étendue sur le plan social : services de consultation, d'orientation, de conciliation, de résolution des conflits. Même si aucun obstacle juridique n'empêche une collectivité de créer dès maintenant pareil organisme, il en existe sur le plan pratique, d'ordre financier surtout. Les gouvernements ne devraient toutefois pas oublier que ces organismes pourraient servir, jusqu'à un certain point, de solution de rechange aux services de police.

RECOMMANDATION

8. (4) Le financement d'un corps policier autonome ne devrait pas se limiter aux programmes en tous points semblables à ceux des organismes existants.

D. La « suraccusation »

Comme nous l'avons déjà signalé, les collectivités autochtones, qu'elles soient établies en région éloignée ou en milieu urbain, font souvent l'objet d'une étroite surveillance policière. Il peut donc arriver que des accusations soient portées sans motif valable, ou encore qu'elles soient portées même si l'agissement reproché répond à peine aux critères d'incrimination. Dans ces cas-là, le pouvoir discrétionnaire est mal utilisé ou ne l'est pas du tout. C'est ce qu'on peut appeler la « suraccusation ».

RECOMMANDATION

8. (5) Les policiers devraient conserver le pouvoir discrétionnaire de porter des accusations quand bon leur semble, mais ils devraient systématiquement demander conseil aux procureurs du ministère public, notamment quant à l'opportunité de porter ou non des accusations[119].

---

118. Robert Depew, *Native Policing in Canada: A Review of Current Issues*, Document de travail n° 1986-46, Ottawa, Solliciteur général Canada, 1986, p. 125.

119. Voir Commission de réforme du droit du Canada (ci-après CRD), *Poursuites pénales : les pouvoirs du procureur général et des procureurs de la Couronne*, Document de travail n° 62, Ottawa, la Commission, 1990, rec. 19, p. 75.

Pratiqué avec intelligence, ce contrôle permettrait de poser un second regard sur les accusations et devrait avoir un effet salutaire sur l'exercice du pouvoir discrétionnaire officiel.

En guise de complément, nous avons recommandé aux pages 37 et 38 que les procureurs du ministère public sollicitent des collectivités autochtones des orientations générales en matière de politique d'inculpation. En outre, nous proposons à la page 38 que les conciliateurs, les aînés ou d'autres membres de la collectivité soient consultés en vue de la déjudiciarisation de certaines affaires. À notre avis, l'effet conjugué de ces recommandations atténuera la tendance à la suraccusation.

E.   L'avis de comparution

Il arrive souvent, en particulier dans les régions éloignées, qu'un prévenu autochtone ne saisisse pas la gravité de l'avis de comparution que lui tend le policier au moment où il le remet en liberté. Il peut ne pas comprendre qu'il est tenu de se présenter devant le tribunal, ni les conséquences d'un défaut de sa part. Le problème se complique du fait que les dates de comparution sont fixées arbitrairement et peuvent coïncider avec la période de l'année au cours de laquelle les autochtones chassent ou font du trappage pour gagner leur vie. La non-comparution se traduit alors par des accusations supplémentaires qui ne font qu'aggraver l'affaire.

Les autochtones ne sont pas les seuls à se retrouver dans cette situation, mais leurs besoins et leurs difficultés sont particulièrement criants. À condition que le motif soit valable, la police ou la poursuite est en mesure de reporter à un moment mieux choisi la première comparution, ce qui éviterait au tribunal des pertes de temps et la délivrance de mandats d'arrestation inutiles. Par contre, un ajournement ne sera accordé que si l'on en fait la demande. Les autochtones, notamment ceux des régions éloignées qui ont du mal à retenir les services d'un avocat, ne penseront vraisemblablement pas à le faire.

Par conséquent, en vue d'éviter le problème de la non-comparution et de mettre les autochtones sur le même pied que le reste de la population, nous proposons ce qui suit :

RECOMMANDATIONS

8. (6) Les policiers devraient prendre tout le soin voulu, lorsqu'ils remettent un avis de comparution à un autochtone, pour s'assurer que cette personne comprend bien la gravité du défaut de comparaître devant le tribunal et pour lui indiquer la date de sa comparution. En particulier, l'agent devrait demander à la personne si un motif quelconque l'empêche de se présenter et, le cas échéant, faire preuve de souplesse concernant la date de comparution. Il convient toutefois de préciser qu'aucun accusé ne devrait être détenu inutilement aux seules fins de l'application de la présente recommandation.

(7) Les corps policiers devraient être encouragés à employer des formulaires traduits dans la langue de la collectivité lorsque la chose est possible et que la nature et l'étendue des contacts policiers avec la collectivité le justifient.

II. Les poursuivants

A. Le procureur général et le procureur du ministère public

Le procureur général est le ministre responsable de l'administration de la justice pénale. C'est lui qui dicte, tant par des moyens informels que par le biais de grandes orientations et de lignes directrices, l'esprit général des rapports qui s'établissent entre le service des poursuites et les collectivités autochtones. Ce service, qui relève pour l'essentiel du procureur général, est personnifié par le procureur du ministère public[120] affecté à la collectivité.

Le poursuivant représente le procureur général et, à toutes fins utiles, exerce presque tout l'ensemble des vastes pouvoirs discrétionnaires de ce dernier en matière de poursuite. Le procureur du ministère public occupe une place unique dans notre tradition judiciaire. Son rôle, qualifié parfois de « quasi judiciaire », [TRADUCTION] « exclut toute notion de victoire ou de défaite ; sa fonction en est une de service public qui, dans la vie civile, n'a pas d'égal sur le plan de la responsabilité individuelle[121]. » Au Canada, le procureur est indépendant de la police. Cette dichotomie est essentielle et doit être jalousement préservée, faute de quoi l'utilité de la fonction serait compromise et son importance, dépréciée[122].

---

120. L'ouvrage de base dans ce domaine demeure celui de John Ll. J. EDWARDS, *The Law Officers of the Crown*, Londres, Sweet & Maxwell, 1964. Voir aussi CRD, Document de travail n° 62, *op. cit.*, note 119.

121. *Boucher* c. *The Queen,* [1955] R.C.S. 16, 23 (j. Rand).

122. Malheureusement, un juge a conclu que ce danger devient parfois réalité dans le Grand Nord canadien : [TRADUCTION] « Chose étonnante, [les procureurs du ministère public fédéral au Yukon et dans les Territoires du Nord-Ouest] semblent hésitants à exercer leurs pouvoirs discrétionnaires de poursuite avec quelque fermeté, comme en témoignent l'acharnement avec lequel on a poursuivi des accusations relativement mineures et la réticence à abandonner ou à suspendre les accusations dans le cadre d'une procédure où il était clair que le principal témoin à charge n'avait pas produit la preuve souhaitée. [. . .] On peut penser que, à titre de poursuivants de carrière, ils sont peu enclins à s'opposer à la police ou à désavouer ses décisions [. . .] pour des motifs de promotion et d'avancement. Il s'ensuit que les procureurs de la Couronne sont portés à prendre leurs directives de la police et à n'exercer leurs pouvoirs discrétionnaires que rarement, dans les affaires les plus limpides. » Heino LILLES, « Some Problems in the Administration of Justice in Remote and Isolated Communities » (1990), 15 *Queen's L.J.* 327, 340.

Nous abordons dans le présent rapport diverses questions qui touchent directement le rôle et les responsabilités du poursuivant. Nous avons plaidé en faveur de liens plus étroits entre le service des poursuites et les collectivités autochtones. Nous avons souligné également la nécessité de recruter davantage d'autochtones au sein du ministère public, et de sensibiliser les poursuivants aux différences culturelles. Nous verrons qu'il est nécessaire d'assouplir l'exercice des pouvoirs discrétionnaires importants qui entrent en jeu dans des domaines comme la négociation du plaidoyer, afin de remédier aux effets d'un lourd héritage de méfiance et de malentendu. D'autres questions importantes se posent toujours à propos de l'engagement des poursuites, et c'est vers elles que nous allons maintenant nous tourner.

B.   Les policiers poursuivants

Parce que les ressources humaines sont généralement insuffisantes dans les régions éloignées, la même personne cumule souvent plusieurs fonctions (par exemple, un maire sera aussi juge de paix). Le compromis est parfois boiteux, ce qui peut entraîner de fâcheuses conséquences lorsque le processus judiciaire est en cause. Il en est ainsi lorsqu'un agent de la paix joue également le rôle de poursuivant dans des affaires prétendument mineures[123]. Même si l'on a confirmé la validité constitutionnelle[124] de cette solution, l'objectivité et l'impartialité professionnelles d'un véritable procureur n'y sont pas, et l'image de la justice en souffre. C'est pourquoi nous réitérons la recommandation que nous avons formulée dans notre document de travail n° 62, *Poursuites pénales : les pouvoirs du procureur général et des procureurs de la Couronne*, à savoir que toutes les poursuites pénales publiques devraient être exercées par un avocat qui relève du procureur général et sous la surveillance de celui-ci[125]. Pour ce qui concerne la situation particulière des autochtones, nous recommandons en outre que personne d'autre qu'un avocat relevant du procureur général et sous la responsabilité de celui-ci ne soit autorisé à poursuivre des infractions en matière de chasse, de trappage et de pêche.

RECOMMANDATIONS

9. (1) Toutes les poursuites pénales publiques devraient être exercées par un avocat qui relève du procureur général et sous la surveillance de celui-ci.

(2) Personne d'autre qu'un avocat relevant du procureur général et sous la responsabilité de celui-ci ne devrait être autorisé à poursuivre des infractions en matière de chasse, de trappage et de pêche.

---

123. Comme nous le signalons ailleurs, aucune affaire ne peut à proprement parler être tenue pour mineure en ce qui concerne les autochtones, étant donné la fréquence de l'incarcération résultant du défaut de payer une amende.

124. Voir *Re R. and Hart* (1986), 26 C.C.C. (3ᵉ) 438 (C.A. T.-N.) et *R. c. White* (1988), 41 C.C.C. (3ᵉ) 236 (C.A. T.-N.).

125. *Op. cit.*, note 119, rec. 15, p. 64.

C. Le pouvoir discrétionnaire de poursuite

Le ministère public dispose d'un vaste pouvoir discrétionnaire lorsque vient le moment de décider s'il faut ou non exercer des poursuites, une fois les accusations portées. Dans certains territoires, cette décision est prise en l'absence de critères clairement définis et accessibles au public. Nous estimons important, pour la confiance qu'on porte à l'endroit de l'administration de la justice, que le grand public connaisse les facteurs dont il devrait être tenu compte dans l'exercice de ce pouvoir. Une part importante de la criminalité chez les autochtones concerne des infractions mineures (souvent liées à la consommation d'alcool). Si, dans bien des cas, les poursuites sont clairement justifiées, il est tout aussi manifeste que les pouvoirs discrétionnaires pourraient mieux s'exercer dans d'autres.

Comme nous l'avons signalé ailleurs, le pouvoir discrétionnaire d'intenter des poursuites se trouve au cœur même de notre système de justice pénale[126]. Il nous paraît urgent que des lignes de conduite explicites soient élaborées et communiquées au public quant à l'exercice du pouvoir discrétionnaire de poursuite.

RECOMMANDATIONS

9. (3) Il y aurait lieu de faire savoir clairement aux poursuivants, par le biais des directives et de la formation qu'ils reçoivent, qu'ils doivent exercer leurs pouvoirs discrétionnaires indépendamment de l'influence ou des pressions exercées par la police, et que les conseils qu'ils donnent aux policiers doivent demeurer objectifs et impartiaux.

(4) Une politique clairement énoncée devrait être publiée et mise en œuvre concernant les facteurs d'intérêt public dont il devrait ou non être tenu compte dans la décision d'engager ou d'interrompre des poursuites[127].

---

126. *Id.*, p. 83.

127. Dans notre document de travail n° 62, *id.*, rec. 23, pp. 82-83, nous avions recommandé l'inclusion, dans des lignes directrices, des facteurs suivants, entre autres : (1) Le poursuivant public estime-t-il qu'il existe des éléments de preuve au vu desquels un jury équitable ayant reçu des directives appropriées pourrait déclarer le suspect coupable ? (2) Dans l'affirmative, la poursuite est-elle dans une mesure raisonnable susceptible d'entraîner une déclaration de culpabilité ? Le poursuivant aurait également l'obligation de tenir compte des éléments suivants : (3) Des considérations liées à l'intérêt public rendent-elles la poursuite opportune malgré les faibles chances d'une déclaration de culpabilité ? (4) Des considérations humanitaires ou liées à l'intérêt public s'opposent-elles à l'engagement de poursuites malgré les chances raisonnables d'une déclaration de culpabilité ? Les ressources existantes justifient-elles l'inculpation ?

Pour ce qui concerne les infractions commises dans une collectivité autochtone ou mettant en cause un ou plusieurs autochtones, les facteurs suivants devraient être pris en considération au moment de décider d'engager des poursuites ou d'y mettre fin :

a) l'effet probable des poursuites sur le maintien de la paix, de l'harmonie et de la sécurité dans la collectivité autochtone ;

b) l'existence ou l'efficacité de toute solution de rechange aux poursuites (y compris les méthodes traditionnelles des autochtones) compte tenu des buts poursuivis par les sanctions pénales ;

c) le point de vue et les préoccupations de la collectivité autochtone touchée, y compris son aptitude à opérer une réconciliation ou à composer autrement avec les problèmes de justice pénale, que ce soit par des moyens traditionnels ou par des moyens autres que des poursuites ;

d) le fait qu'une condamnation aurait des répercussions démesurément cruelles ou oppressives ;

e) la nécessité de maintenir la confiance de la collectivité autochtone à l'endroit du législateur, des tribunaux et de l'administration de la justice ;

f) le caractère plus ou moins fréquent de l'infraction reprochée au sein des collectivités autochtones et l'importance à attacher à la dissuasion en l'espèce ;

g) l'incidence des droits issus de traités, en matière de chasse et de pêche, par exemple.

D. La communication de la preuve

Le procureur du ministère public a un rôle essentiel à jouer si l'on veut garantir que le système de justice pénale est rigoureusement juste et équitable. Sa responsabilité à cet égard se manifeste dans son obligation de communiquer l'ensemble de sa preuve à l'accusé. L'affaire Marshall nous rappelle avec amertume les conséquences tragiques que peut avoir un manquement grave de la part du ministère public à ce chapitre[128].

À l'évidence, le droit de l'accusé de présenter une défense pleine et entière est tributaire de la communication intégrale, en temps voulu, de la preuve de la poursuite. Le maintien d'une pratique qui semble reposer largement sur les velléités des autorités locales est une entrave manifeste à l'égalité d'accès à la justice et au traitement équitable.

---

128. Rapport de la commission d'enquête sur l'affaire Marshall, *op. cit.*, note 14, p. 238.

RECOMMANDATION

9. (5) Le *Code criminel* devrait être modifié de manière à imposer l'obligation de communiquer intégralement et en temps voulu la preuve de la poursuite dans toutes les poursuites[129].

E. Le filtrage des accusations

Il est question ailleurs dans le présent rapport de la pratique de la négociation du plaidoyer et des problèmes particuliers qu'elle pose relativement aux autochtones. L'un des dangers inhérents à la négociation du plaidoyer tient à la pratique policière de la suraccusation. Mis en présence d'un barrage d'accusations, l'accusé mal informé risque d'accepter un compromis défavorable au lieu de courir le risque de subir un procès. Les poursuivants pourraient corriger sensiblement cet état de choses en procédant le plus tôt possible au filtrage des accusations et au contrôle serré des accusations multiples.

RECOMMANDATION

9. (6) Les procureurs généraux, aux paliers fédéral et provincial, devraient adopter une ligne de conduite faisant aux procureurs du ministère public l'obligation de filtrer les accusations dès que possible après qu'elles ont été portées.

III. Les avocats de la défense

Les autochtones aux prises avec le système de justice pénale font face à des difficultés particulières : un malentendu d'ordre culturel peut inciter un policier ou un poursuivant à porter des accusations ou à exercer des poursuites ; des conditions de cautionnement normales pour tout autre Canadien peuvent se révéler singulièrement difficiles pour un autochtone ; un autochtone peut avoir beaucoup de mal à comprendre le déroulement d'un procès ; les arguments que l'accusé a à faire valoir pour sa défense peuvent être propres à la culture autochtone ; le juge des faits peut ne pas être à même d'apprécier la crédibilité des témoins s'il ne connaît pas la culture autochtone ; une peine donnée peut avoir des répercussions particulièrement pénibles pour un accusé autochtone. Dans chacun des cas précités, les policiers, poursuivants, juges, jurés et agents de probation doivent tous faire preuve de sensibilité, sans quoi les conséquences risquent d'être désastreuses. Mais c'est souvent l'avocat de la défense qui est en mesure de remédier aux lacunes des autres intervenants.

---

129. Voir CRD, *La communication de la preuve par la poursuite*, Rapport n° 22, Ottawa, Approvisionnements et Services Canada, 1984.

Étant donné le caractère protecteur de sa fonction, l'avocat d'un autochtone est la personne la mieux placée pour s'assurer que son client sera traité non seulement sur le même pied que les autres, mais aussi avec équité et respect. Les avocats qui représentent les autochtones doivent donc être bien au fait des problèmes de justice particuliers à cette partie de la population et doivent être à même de les soulever de manière opportune.

A.   L'accès aux services d'un avocat

En principe, les autochtones peuvent obtenir les services d'un avocat au même titre que n'importe quel autre accusé : ceux qui n'en ont pas les moyens peuvent recourir à l'aide juridique. En pratique, toutefois, il semble y avoir des obstacles. Il arrive qu'aucun avocat n'exerce sa profession à proximité d'une collectivité autochtone isolée. Et même si la collectivité n'est pas isolée, l'accès à l'aide juridique peut présenter des difficultés. Ainsi, le manque d'information ou de compréhension peut empêcher les délinquants autochtones, en particulier les jeunes, de recourir à l'aide juridique[130].

Même si certains bureaux d'aide juridique ont rédigé de la documentation en plusieurs langues autochtones pour mieux renseigner les collectivités sur les services offerts, la documentation n'est pas toujours disponible ni accessible[131]. Pour bien souligner l'importance que revêt l'information dans ce contexte, nous recommandons ce qui suit :

RECOMMANDATION

10. (1) Les barreaux et les organismes d'aide juridique provinciaux devraient mettre à la disposition des autochtones du matériel éducatif sur le droit, notamment sur les modalités d'obtention des services de l'aide juridique. Au besoin, on devrait faire appel à la technologie vidéo ou faire en sorte que le matériel soit produit en langues autochtones.

---

130. Voilà qui expliquerait une conclusion à laquelle on en est arrivé dans une étude réalisée au Labrador en 1985 : bien que les jeunes délinquants aient su, au moment de leur arrestation, qu'ils avaient droit aux services d'un avocat, [TRADUCTION] « le plus souvent, ils enregistraient un plaidoyer de culpabilité avant même d'avoir consulté un avocat. » Le rapport consécutif à cette étude recommandait qu'on fasse connaître au public la *Loi sur les jeunes contrevenants* (précitée, note 49) : RES POLICY RESEARCH, *Needs of Native Young Offenders in Labrador in View of the Young Offenders Act: Final Report*, Ottawa, Ministère de la Justice, 1985, pp. 43-44.

131. Le rapport de la commission d'enquête sur l'affaire Marshall, *op. cit.*, note 14, p. 158, signale que les autochtones ont [TRADUCTION] « un accès limité à l'information juridique », et recommande qu'on fournisse aux collectivités autochtones et à la communauté noire de la documentation et des services d'éducation juridiques ; voir rec. 16, p. 158. Voir aussi ALBERTA, *The Report of the Task Force on Legal Aid*, Edmonton, the Task Force, 1988 et *Justice on Trial, op. cit.*, note 14, p. 3-4 sur le même sujet.

Ajoutons que les autochtones peuvent être victimes d'un traitement inéquitable en ce qui concerne l'admissibilité à l'aide juridique. Les infractions reliées à la chasse et à la pêche sont souvent exclues de l'aide juridique[132]. De même, au Yukon, un accusé n'a droit aux services d'un avocat que s'il est passible d'incarcération. Cette règle, même si elle s'applique également à tous, a des effets inéquitables sur les autochtones, étant donné qu'un pourcentage élevé d'entre eux sont incarcérés pour n'avoir pas acquitté l'amende infligée à la suite d'une infraction mineure qui, au départ, n'ouvrait pas droit à l'aide juridique[133].

RECOMMANDATION

10. (2) Les critères d'admissibilité à l'aide juridique devraient être revus de façon qu'ils n'aient aucun effet inéquitable sur les autochtones. Les gouvernements concernés devraient s'assurer que les fonds nécessaires sont disponibles pour financer les services juridiques dont tout autochtone peut avoir besoin.

Nous avons également entendu, de la part des autochtones, des plaintes quant à la qualité des services juridiques qu'ils obtiennent, qu'il s'agisse d'un avocat de pratique privée ou des services d'aide juridique[134] : les avocats connaissent mal la culture des autochtones et les problèmes auxquels ils se heurtent, commettent des erreurs d'appréciation en ce qui concerne les affaires qu'ils portent (ou ne portent pas) devant les tribunaux, sont trop expéditifs avec leurs clients et ne leur expliquent pas suffisamment les choses. Les recommandations que nous avons déjà formulées au sujet de la sensibilisation aux différences culturelles contribueraient sans doute à corriger ces problèmes dans une certaine mesure, mais il est clair qu'il faudra aller plus loin. À notre avis, il convient d'étudier davantage les mesures que pourraient prendre à cet égard les barreaux provinciaux et les organismes d'aide juridique, ou encore l'opportunité d'établir des normes nationales d'admissibilité aux services d'aide juridique.

B. L'interrogatoire et le rôle de l'avocat

Des problèmes particuliers ont été soulevés en ce qui concerne les accusés autochtones soumis à un interrogatoire de police. Dans *Justice on Trial*, on a signalé que certains autochtones sont si respectueux de l'autorité qu'ils ne se contentent pas de répondre aux questions posées, offrant même à l'interrogateur les réponses qu'il veut, à leur avis, entendre[135]. Le préjudice qui peut en résulter saute aux yeux, surtout si on allie cette tendance à la réticence des autochtones à critiquer un tiers en sa présence[136]. On peut douter de l'authenticité d'une déclaration faite en pareilles circonstances même si le droit actuel la tient pour volontaire et, du coup, admissible.

---

132. IBA, *op. cit.*, note 24, p. 44.

133. *Justice on Trial*, *op. cit.*, note 14, p. 3-16 signale un problème semblable en Alberta.

134. Voir aussi *id.*, ch. 3.

135. On a observé le même phénomène en Australie : voir AUSTRALIAN LAW REFORM COMMISSION, *op. cit.*, note 89.

136. Cette tendance a également été observée par R. Ross, *op. cit.*, note 21.

En Australie, les règles régissant la recevabilité de la déclaration faite par un autochtone ont été définies par les tribunaux, en particulier dans l'affaire *R. c. Anunga*[137]. Dans cet esprit, la Commission de réforme du droit australienne a fait la recommandation suivante : [TRADUCTION] « il y aurait lieu d'exiger qu'un ''ami du détenu'' soit présent lorsqu'un autochtone est mis sous garde ou est interrogé (sans être sous garde) relativement à une infraction grave[138] » ; la Commission ajoute que toute déclaration obtenue en violation de ces règles devrait être réputée irrecevable, sauf si certaines conditions ont été remplies[139]. Nous croyons qu'une approche analogue s'impose au Canada.

RECOMMANDATION

10. (3) Des règles d'interrogation particulières devraient être formulées pour la réception des déclarations des autochtones, notamment en ce qui a trait à la présence d'un avocat ou d'une autre personne au cours de l'interrogatoire.

Les règles comme celles qu'énonce la *Loi sur les jeunes contrevenants*[140] et les règles australiennes[141] sont des modèles à considérer. Elles pourraient du reste convenir tout aussi bien à d'autres groupes défavorisés.

Avant que cette recommandation puisse être mise en œuvre, divers détails importants devront avoir été réglés. Le rôle d'« ami du détenu », qui consisterait à expliquer à l'accusé ses droits durant un interrogatoire, pourrait incomber aux travailleurs sociaux autochtones auprès des tribunaux. Pourtant, une participation trop active de ces travailleurs aux enquêtes policières pourrait compromettre l'efficacité de leur contribution. En outre, comme les policiers peuvent ne pas toujours se rendre compte que la personne interrogée est un autochtone, la question est de savoir quand appliquer les règles. On peut aussi s'interroger sur la nature des règles elles-mêmes — doivent-elles être enchâssées dans la loi ou prendre la forme de directives ? — et sur les conséquences de leur violation.

IV. Les tribunaux

Pour la plupart des Canadiens, le caractère solennel et ésotérique du processus judiciaire pénal est source d'intimidation et de confusion. Il n'est donc pas étonnant que bien des autochtones craignent cet univers et s'y sentent étrangers. Les cours de justice sont presque

---

137. (1976) 11 A.L.R. 412 (C. suprême T.-N.) ; on trouvera un compte rendu de cette affaire dans *Justice on Trial, op. cit.*, note 14, p. 2-57.

138. *Op. cit.*, note 89, par. 115, p. 56.

139. Notamment, il faudrait que [TRADUCTION] « le suspect n'ait pas répondu par simple respect envers l'autorité ou en raison d'une trop grande suggestibilité » : *id.*, p. 57. Suivant les règles formulées à la suite de l'affaire *Anunga*, il y aurait lieu de poser les questions de manière à ne pas suggérer la réponse à laquelle on s'attend.

140. Précitée, note 49 ; voir, par ex., les art. 11 et 56 qui élargissent le droit aux services d'un avocat et à des explications quant à la gravité de la procédure et à l'importance de bénéficier des services d'un avocat.

141. Voir l'affaire *Anunga*, précitée, note 137, et *Justice on Trial, op. cit.*, note 14, pp. 2-56 à 2-59.

toujours situées à l'extérieur et parfois très loin des collectivités autochtones. Les juges, poursuivants, avocats de la défense et fonctionnaires des tribunaux sont rarement des autochtones. Dans maintes régions éloignées, il s'agit d'un tribunal itinérant qui se déplace en avion pour aller siéger dans les collectivités autochtones. Souvent, le juge, le procureur du ministère public et l'avocat de la défense descendent du même avion, ce qui pourrait laisser croire à une certaine collusion de leur part : tout serait décidé d'avance et la procédure ne servirait que les intérêts des avocats et des juges. Nous devons ouvrir le système aux autochtones si nous voulons que les principes de l'égalité d'accès à la justice et du traitement équitable et respectueux deviennent réalité.

A.   L'atmosphère des salles d'audience

La plupart des accusés sont vraisemblablement intimidés par le climat qui règne dans les salles d'audience. Et en un certain sens, c'est là un des objectifs poursuivis par le processus pénal : faire comprendre à l'accusé la gravité de la situation. Mais du fait que les autochtones perçoivent déjà le système comme complètement étranger, l'effet s'en trouve décuplé :

[TRADUCTION]
Beaucoup d'autochtones sont impressionnés par le climat qui règne dans les salles d'audience ; l'atmosphère y est encore plus angoissante du fait que le juge les regarde du haut de sa tribune. Ils aimeraient voir des objets représentatifs de leur culture exposés dans les salles d'audience où leur présence est requise, et un aménagement des pièces plus respectueux de leur culture[142].

Si les salles d'audience étaient moins solennelles et plus respectueuses de la culture des autochtones et de leur sensibilité, nous avons le sentiment qu'elles commanderaient le respect des autochtones.

RECOMMANDATION

11. (1) Les salles d'audience qui sont utilisées pour les collectivités autochtones devraient être aménagées de manière à respecter la culture et les traditions des autochtones.

---

142. *Justice on Trial, op. cit.*, note 14, p. 4-46.

B. Les juges de paix autochtones

Le processus pourrait également être rendu moins solennel si on nommait davantage de juges de paix autochtones dans les collectivités elles-mêmes[143]. Les juges de paix jouent un rôle de premier plan dans les collectivités autochtones[144] : ils sont responsables de la délivrance des mandats d'arrestation, de la mise en liberté provisoire et du jugement des affaires mineures. Bien que les juges de paix soient généralement nommés par les provinces, l'article 107 de la *Loi sur les Indiens* confère au fédéral un pouvoir de nomination peu utilisé et limité à quelques infractions mineures prévues au Code. Or, nous ne voyons pas l'intérêt de cette limitation.

RECOMMANDATION

11. (2) La législation fédérale devrait reconnaître aux juges de paix nommés par le fédéral toutes les compétences que confèrent aux juges de paix le *Code criminel* et la *Loi sur les Indiens*. Le fédéral devrait utiliser davantage son pouvoir de nomination pour nommer un plus grand nombre de juges de paix autochtones.

C. La prestation du serment

À l'heure actuelle, le témoin cité dans une procédure pénale dépose généralement après avoir juré sur la bible de dire la vérité. Or, les autochtones préféreraient prêter serment selon les rites de leur culture propre[145]. Le fait de mettre leurs croyances sur le même pied que celles des Canadiens de tradition judéo-chrétienne conférerait une expression à la fois concrète et symbolique au principe du respect envers les autochtones.

RECOMMANDATION

11. (3) Le droit des autochtones de prêter serment selon leurs rites traditionnels lorsqu'ils témoignent devant un tribunal devrait être reconnu.

---

143. Nous avons déjà proposé de nommer des autochtones à tous les échelons du système judiciaire ; voir *supra*, rec. 3(1)*c*), p. 30.

144. ONTARIO NATIVE COUNCIL ON JUSTICE, *The Native Justice of the Peace: An Under-employed Natural Resource for the Criminal Justice System*, Toronto, le Conseil, 1982, p. 10.

145. *Justice on Trial*, *op. cit.*, note 14, p. 4-46. Rappelons le contentieux entourant la prestation du serment des autochtones au cours des procès qui ont suivi les incidents d'Oka.

D. Le lieu des audiences

Le processus pénal exige généralement plusieurs comparutions devant le tribunal : enregistrement du plaidoyer, demande de mise en liberté provisoire, procès, etc. L'isolement de bon nombre de collectivités place les autochtones devant des difficultés particulières, étrangères à la plupart des Canadiens qui, eux, ont facilement accès aux tribunaux. Beaucoup de collectivités isolées font face à d'énormes difficultés de transport : absence complète de moyens de transport, coûts exorbitants, conditions météorologiques et routières rigoureuses, etc. Les difficultés d'accès aux tribunaux et la nécessité de chasser pour subsister donnent souvent lieu à des accusations pour défaut de comparaître et même à des plaidoyers de culpabilité injustifiés[146]. En outre, les autochtones des collectivités éloignées sont parfois arrêtés, puis remis en liberté provisoire loin de chez eux ; souvent, ils n'ont même pas les moyens de retourner dans leur collectivité[147]. Pour régler ces difficultés, plusieurs solutions sont possibles.

RECOMMANDATION

11. (4) Dans le cas d'accusés autochtones, les dates de comparution devraient être fixées de façon à éviter, dans la mesure du possible, les saisons de chasse et de trappage. La politique d'établissement du calendrier judiciaire devrait être mise au point par les juges en chef des tribunaux concernés, en collaboration avec les représentants de la collectivité.

En faisant preuve de souplesse, on se trouve simplement à accorder aux autochtones le traitement réservé aux autres Canadiens, qui peuvent reporter plus facilement une date de comparution inopportune. Il y aurait lieu également de simplifier le processus en vue d'éviter les comparutions inutiles. À plusieurs étapes de la procédure, la présence physique de l'accusé n'est pas vraiment indispensable. Dans cette optique, il faudrait envisager de recourir davantage aux moyens modernes de télécommunications : même les demandes de remise en liberté provisoire pourraient se faire par des moyens électroniques.

RECOMMANDATION

11. (5) La loi devrait permettre que les comparutions se fassent par des moyens électroniques.

Nous croyons toutefois que cette solution de rechange ne devrait être mise en place que lorsque les juges en chef auront formulé une politique où entrerait en ligne de compte, entre autres, le consentement de l'accusé. D'autre part, il faudrait s'attaquer directement aux problèmes liés au transport des autochtones.

---

146. Voir, par ex., le mémoire présenté par la Métis Association of Alberta au Cawsey Task Force, dont il est fait mention dans *Justice on Trial, op. cit.*, note 14, p. 4-26.

147. Voir le Rapport Osnaburgh/Windigo, *op. cit.*, note 43, p. 58.

RECOMMANDATIONS

11. **(6) L'accusé qui est relâché par un tribunal loin de l'endroit où il a été arrêté devrait, à la discrétion du tribunal, être retourné chez lui ou dans un lieu raisonnable qu'il aura lui-même désigné. Le *Code criminel* devrait obliger le juge à se renseigner à ce sujet. Les frais de transport devraient être à la charge de l'État.**

(7) Le Code devrait prévoir qu'une personne libérée inconditionnellement (c'est-à-dire sans que des accusations aient été portées) est en droit d'être transportée à l'endroit où elle a été arrêtée ou dans tout autre lieu raisonnable qu'elle aura désigné[148].

(8) Lorsqu'un tribunal ne tient pas ses audiences dans une collectivité autochtone ou à proximité de celle-ci, l'accusé et les témoins assignés à comparaître devraient bénéficier d'un service de transport entre leur domicile et l'endroit où se tiennent les audiences, ou encore être remboursés de leurs frais de déplacement[149].

L'endroit où le tribunal tient ses audiences a aussi de l'importance. Le Cawsey Task Force a conclu, pour sa part, que la solution raisonnable consiste à déplacer le tribunal là où se trouve la population. Il faudrait de façon générale élargir l'accès des collectivités autochtones aux services judiciaires. Par contre, cette solution ne devrait pas être imposée à l'encontre de la volonté des collectivités[150].

---

148. Une recommandation semblable a été faite par la Commission de réforme du droit de Nouvelle-Galles du Sud : voir NEW SOUTH WALES LAW REFORM COMMISSION, *Police Powers of Arrest and Detention*, Discussion Paper 16, Sydney, la Commission, 1987, proposition 50, p. 130.

149. Il faudrait régler certains détails d'ordre administratif ; ainsi, il ne serait peut-être pas souhaitable que l'accusé et les témoins à charge voyagent ensemble. Dans certains territoires, on a tenté de résoudre ces difficultés, avec un succès mitigé. On trouve le passage suivant dans le Rapport Osnaburgh/Windigo, *op. cit.*, note 43, p. 55 :

    [TRADUCTION]
    Vu la distance jusqu'au palais de justice, la Police provinciale de l'Ontario envoie un autobus à la réserve. Cependant, nous a-t-on dit, seuls les accusés dont le nom figure sur une liste remise au chauffeur sont autorisés à monter dans l'autobus, même si d'autres ont en main des documents prouvant qu'ils doivent se présenter devant le tribunal ce jour-là. Les témoins ne sont pas admis dans l'autobus et, à moins que des dispositions spéciales n'aient été prévues, ils doivent se débrouiller tout seuls. On nous a raconté que bien des accusations sont retirées ou rejetées parce que les témoins ne se présentent pas.

150. Dans le Rapport Osnaburgh/Windigo, *op. cit.*, note 43, p. 55, on fait remarquer que [TRADUCTION] « la communauté Osnaburgh ne souhaite pas la présence, sur son territoire, d'un tribunal qui dispense une justice qui, d'après elle, ne répond pas à ses besoins, dont la procédure se déroule dans une langue incomprise par bon nombre de ses membres et qui fait appel à des pratiques totalement étrangères à leur mode de vie. »

RECOMMANDATION

11. (9) Dans la mesure du possible et lorsque la collectivité le souhaite, les audiences des tribunaux devraient se dérouler dans la collectivité autochtone où a été commise l'infraction, ou à proximité.

On ne devrait pas déduire de ce qui précède que nous favorisons le système des tribunaux itinérants. Dans l'ensemble, nous préférerions voir disparaître les cours itinérantes qui se déplacent en avion. Force nous est toutefois d'admettre que, dans certains cas, ce pis-aller est la seule façon d'assurer la tenue d'audiences dans les collectivités autochtones. Là où l'on aura décidé de le conserver, le système des cours itinérantes devra être amélioré[151].

[TRADUCTION]
[...]Les juges, avocats et fonctionnaires judiciaires arrivent en trombe dans les collectivités qui font partie de leur itinéraire, obnubilés par l'avion à prendre ou par la route à faire pour rentrer chez eux. En conséquence, on expédie les procédures — ou on reporte systématiquement les causes — pour des motifs qui n'appartiennent qu'aux visiteurs. Les mauvaises conditions météorologiques sont souvent la cause d'ajournements. Dans certaines collectivités, cela signifie que les séances mensuelles deviennent bimestrielles, étant donné qu'on ne remplace pas, en général, la séance manquée. Les rôles s'allongent et les retards s'accumulent. Entre temps, les notions autochtones de pardon et de réparation ont eu le temps d'agir, d'où la redondance de la comparution reportée[152].

---

151. Rappelons les remarques du juge Coutu dans le rapport de la commission d'enquête sur l'affaire Marshall, *op. cit.*, note 22, p. 25 :

    [TRADUCTION]
    En règle générale, la population autochtone est insatisfaite de notre administration de la justice dans ses collectivités, et de plus en plus je partage son avis. Pour leur part, les juges sont insatisfaits du travail qu'ils font dans le Nord, car ils estiment que leur action n'a pas d'importance.

152. *Justice on Trial, op. cit.*, note 14, pp. 4-19 et 4-20. Les personnes que nous avons consultées nous ont laissé entendre que la négociation du plaidoyer a souvent lieu dans l'avion, avant que l'avocat ait consulté son client ; que le temps alloué aux consultations et à la préparation de l'affaire est dérisoirement restreint, ce qui altère inévitablement la qualité de la défense ; que l'arrivée du juge et des avocats dans le même avion suffirait à compromettre le caractère équitable d'un procès partout sauf dans le Grand Nord, où la chose est courante. Dans certaines régions, le procureur du ministère public et l'avocat de la défense arrivent une journée avant le juge afin de consulter les parties. Voir le Rapport Osnaburgh/Windigo, *op. cit.*, note 43, pp. 56-57. Cette façon d'agir constitue certes une amélioration, mais elle ne garantit pas nécessairement une préparation suffisante, pas plus qu'elle n'apaise les inquiétudes à propos des négociations sur le plaidoyer.

L'établissement d'un centre de services juridiques dans toutes les collectivités nordiques importantes[153] réglerait une partie du problème, mais n'aiderait en rien les collectivités isolées. Pour traiter sur un pied d'égalité les autochtones habitant les collectivités éloignées, il faudrait faire en sorte qu'ils aient accès aux tribunaux et aux avocats tout comme s'ils habitaient une collectivité où cela ne pose pas de problème. Les avocats de la défense devraient être disponibles non seulement un jour ou deux avant les auditions, mais aussi à intervalles réguliers. Les témoins, quant à eux, devraient être consultés pendant que les faits qu'ils ont à raconter restent frais à leur mémoire. On pourrait atteindre cet objectif en invitant les avocats (ceux de la défense comme ceux du ministère public) ou les techniciens judiciaires à visiter régulièrement la région. L'intérêt public commande que toutes les parties soient bien préparées. En outre, pour éviter les problèmes découlant de la surcharge du rôle quotidien des tribunaux, il serait sans doute nécessaire de nommer plus de juges. Il faudrait aussi davantage de ressources pour régler le problème de l'annulation des audiences en raison du mauvais temps.

RECOMMANDATION

11. (10) Puisque les tribunaux itinérants qui se déplacent en avion ne fournissent pas aux collectivités éloignées des services juridiques équivalents à ceux disponibles ailleurs, il faudrait donc, dans la mesure du possible, les éliminer progressivement. Là où on les maintiendra, il faudrait prendre les mesures nécessaires pour offrir les garanties suivantes :

a) **les services d'un avocat de la défense sont proposés à l'accusé à une date suffisamment antérieure à l'audition de l'affaire ;**

b) **les procureurs du ministère public consultent les collectivités touchées avec suffisamment d'avance pour veiller à ce que l'intérêt public soit protégé ;**

c) **on affecte des ressources suffisantes, notamment par le biais de nominations judiciaires additionnelles s'il y a lieu, de manière à ne pas précipiter les audiences et à pouvoir les tenir dans un délai raisonnable à compter de la perpétration de l'infraction.**

---

153. Comme on l'a proposé dans le rapport *Les autochtones et la justice*, *op. cit.*, note 67, p. 31.

V. La mise en liberté provisoire

Le concept de mise en liberté provisoire évoque le pouvoir de relâcher ou de détenir un prévenu en attendant le procès. Le peu de données dont nous disposons laisse supposer que les autochtones n'ont pas le beau rôle en vertu des dispositions actuelles à ce chapitre. D'après certaines projections, les autochtones seraient deux fois plus nombreux chez les personnes arrêtées qui se voient refuser un cautionnement[154]. Dans les pages suivantes, nous proposons des changements pour supprimer certaines iniquités à cet égard.

A. Le pouvoir de la police de relâcher un prévenu

L'article 499 du *Code criminel* permet à l'agent de la paix, une fois le mandat d'arrestation exécuté, de relâcher le prévenu si celui-ci remet sa promesse de comparaître ou contracte un engagement à cet égard, à la condition que le juge ayant délivré le mandat y ait apposé un visa à cet effet. Le juge ne peut viser le mandat que dans le cas d'infractions dites « mineures ». Parfois, il n'aura tout simplement pas envisagé de viser le mandat pour autoriser un agent de la paix à relâcher le prévenu. C'est ainsi que des prévenus autochtones ont été incarcérés en attendant leur procès, même si la police ne les considérait pas comme une menace pour la collectivité. La détention est particulièrement bouleversante pour les prévenus vivant en région éloignée et incarcérés très loin de chez eux.

RECOMMANDATION

12. (1) Le visa permettant à l'agent de la paix de relâcher un prévenu après lui avoir remis un avis de comparution devrait pouvoir être apposé sur un mandat d'arrestation à l'égard de n'importe quel crime. Le juge devrait être expressément requis par la loi de considérer l'opportunité d'apposer un visa sur tout mandat d'arrestation qu'il délivre[155].

Cette pratique promet de réduire le nombre de prévenus que l'on transporte des régions du Nord jusqu'aux centres de détention situés plus au sud. Elle diminuerait ainsi les coûts de détention et raccourcirait les délais de comparution du fait que les prévenus se trouveraient dans leur collectivité, sans compter qu'elle atténuerait la douleur et l'isolement dont souffrent les jeunes délinquants que l'on transporte et que l'on détient loin de chez eux, durant de longues périodes, pour des infractions plutôt mineures[156].

---

154. Voir Ontario Native Council on Justice, *op. cit.*, note 144, pp. 9-10 ; A. C. Birkenmayer et S. Jolly, *The Native Inmate in Ontario*, Toronto, Ministère des Services correctionnels, 1981.

155. Nous avons déjà formulé une recommandation dans ce sens dans CRD, *Les mesures assurant la comparution, la mise en liberté provisoire et la détention avant le procès*, Document de travail n° 57, Ottawa, la Commission, 1988, rec. 16(2)c), p. 60.

156. Voir Thérèse Lajeunesse, *Administration of Justice in Northern and Isolated Communities* (document de travail préparé pour le ministère de la Justice du Manitoba, 8 octobre 1986), p. 9 [non publié].

L'article 498 du Code soulève une question semblable. L'agent qui a procédé à l'arrestation n'a pas le pouvoir de relâcher le prévenu dans le cas de certains crimes : seul un fonctionnaire responsable peut libérer le prévenu à certaines conditions ou moyennant certaines garanties (comme la fourniture de cautions ou le dépôt d'une somme d'argent ou d'une autre valeur).

Dans notre document de travail n° 57, nous recommandions que tout agent de la paix puisse relâcher une personne arrêtée, quel que soit son crime, moyennant la remise d'un avis de comparution de portée plus étendue qui pourrait renfermer les conditions que le fonctionnaire responsable est seul, à l'heure actuelle, à pouvoir imposer[157]. Nous proposions aussi que l'agent de police soit tenu de relâcher le prévenu, à moins qu'il n'y ait spécifiquement matière à détention[158]. Ces recommandations nous paraissent comporter des avantages pour les suspects autochtones.

Le fait d'autoriser l'agent de la paix à relâcher le prévenu, quelle que soit l'infraction en cause, pourrait empêcher que le prévenu soit détenu inutilement parce qu'il doit être amené devant un fonctionnaire responsable dont le bureau se trouve loin du lieu de l'arrestation. En tout état de cause, cette recommandation ne portera fruit que si les agents de la paix usent de leur pouvoir discrétionnaire de manière à privilégier la remise en liberté plutôt que la détention.

RECOMMANDATION

12. (2) Tout agent de la paix devrait avoir le pouvoir discrétionnaire de libérer une personne qu'il a arrêtée, quel que soit le crime qui lui est reproché, après lui avoir remis un avis de comparution de portée plus étendue qui pourrait renfermer des conditions que le fonctionnaire responsable est seul, à l'heure actuelle, à pouvoir imposer. L'agent devrait être tenu de libérer la personne à moins qu'il n'existe des motifs précis de détention.

B. Les conditions de la remise en liberté

L'article 515 du Code permet au juge de paix de remettre en liberté le prévenu qui accepte de remettre soit une promesse, soit un engagement sans caution ni dépôt d'argent, soit un engagement avec caution mais sans dépôt d'argent, ou soit un engagement sans caution, mais avec dépôt d'argent. Chacune de ces procédures soulève des questions du point de vue de la réforme.

---

157. *Op. cit.*, note 155, rec. 1, 2 et 3, pp. 47-49.

158. *Id.*, rec. 7(1), p. 52.

(1) La promesse

Lorsqu'un prévenu est libéré sur remise d'une promesse, celle-ci comporte habituellement des conditions. Ces conditions peuvent s'appliquer à quiconque, mais certaines ont une incidence particulière sur les autochtones. On nous a laissé entendre que les juges imposent systématiquement de nombreuses conditions, sans vraiment se demander si elles sont nécessaires ou indiquées.

En milieu urbain, nous dit-on, les juges ordonnent souvent aux prévenus de se tenir loin de certains quartiers, lesquels correspondent souvent à ceux où habitent ou se réunissent la plupart des autochtones. Résultat : le prévenu est pour ainsi dire banni de son milieu, même si ce n'était pas là l'intention de la justice. De même, un prévenu en état de dépendance à l'égard de l'alcool — phénomène assez fréquent chez les prévenus autochtones — aura du mal à respecter une ordonnance d'abstinence. Les personnes que nous avons consultées ont signalé que les ordonnances de non-fréquentation présentent aussi des difficultés : dans les petites collectivités autochtones, il est pratiquement impossible de ne pas rencontrer certaines personnes ou d'éviter celles qui ont des antécédents criminels. En outre, l'autochtone qui vit de la chasse et du trappage sera bien plus incommodé que la plupart des autres citoyens si on lui impose des restrictions concernant l'usage d'armes à feu[159] ou l'obligation de voir régulièrement un agent de probation.

Loin de nous l'idée de proposer que les autochtones ne soient jamais assujettis à des conditions de ce type. Pourtant, les tribunaux doivent reconnaître les répercussions différentes que peuvent entraîner pareilles conditions : elles ne devraient pas être imposées systématiquement, mais seulement là où elles sont indiquées et sont en rapport avec le délinquant et l'infraction. L'alinéa 515(4)*f*) parle de « conditions raisonnables ». Or, n'est pas raisonnable une condition que le prévenu est manifestement incapable de respecter. Quoi qu'il en soit, il serait utile que le Code définisse mieux les critères servant à déterminer ce qui constitue une condition raisonnable.

RECOMMANDATIONS

12. (3) Les dispositions relatives à la mise en liberté provisoire devraient faire au juge de paix appelé à apprécier le caractère raisonnable d'une condition de mise en liberté l'obligation expresse de considérer les facteurs suivants :

a) **la profession du prévenu, son lieu de résidence et ses origines culturelles ;**

b) **l'emplacement géographique et l'importance de la collectivité à laquelle appartient le prévenu ;**

c) **les exigences particulières liées aux aspirations traditionnelles des autochtones.**

---

159. Les tribunaux ont conclu que l'interdiction de posséder une arme à feu constitue une peine cruelle et inusitée pour les autochtones : voir *R. c. Chief* (1989), 51 C.C.C. (3ᵉ) 265 (C.A. Yukon) ; *R. c. McGillivary* (1991), 12 W.C.B. (2ᵉ) 192 (C.A. Sask.). *Contra* : voir *infra*, note 208.

(4) L'interdiction de consommer de l'alcool ne devrait être imposée comme condition que si l'alcool a joué un rôle dans l'infraction reprochée au prévenu[160].

(2) L'engagement

L'engagement consiste pour le prévenu à promettre de payer une certaine somme d'argent au cas où il ne se présenterait pas à son procès ou ne respecterait pas certaines conditions non financières. Le prévenu qui ne respecte pas un engagement financier (ou même les conditions d'une promesse) sans excuse raisonnable peut être reconnu coupable d'avoir enfreint les conditions de sa mise en liberté. Voilà qui impose un dilemme au système. D'une part, les conditions imposées pourraient constituer le moyen le plus efficace d'assurer la protection du public ou d'empêcher la perpétration d'un autre crime. D'autre part, il pourrait en résulter une double punition pour le prévenu : il voit sa mise en liberté révoquée et se trouve sous le coup d'une nouvelle accusation criminelle. La même conduite serait donc sanctionnée deux fois. La double punition menace quiconque est mis en liberté sous cautionnement, mais, encore une fois, elle est particulièrement douloureuse pour les autochtones vu l'effet inégal produit par nombre des conditions habituelles.

Nous sommes d'avis que la violation des conditions non financières de remise en liberté ne devrait entraîner aucune responsabilité pénale ; cette règle devrait du reste être d'application générale et universelle en procédure pénale. La conduite qui constitue elle-même un crime pourrait faire l'objet d'une accusation distincte, et l'infraction de non-comparution devant le tribunal devrait être maintenue. Cela dit, la révocation de la mise en liberté constitue une peine suffisante si l'accusé enfreint une condition qui lui a été imposée. Sanctionner à nouveau la conduite de l'accusé ouvrirait la voie à la double punition[161].

RECOMMANDATION

12. (5) La violation des conditions non financières de la mise en liberté ne devrait pas engager la responsabilité pénale.

(3) La caution

Suivant le droit actuel, le prévenu remis en liberté peut être tenu de fournir une caution, c'est-à-dire d'amener une personne à garantir qu'il remplira ses obligations, à défaut de quoi la caution s'engage à verser une somme d'argent déterminée.

---

160. L'obligation de s'inscrire à un programme de désintoxication ne devrait pas être imposée au prévenu sans son consentement. Dans certaines régions, nous dit-on, les places en nombre limité qu'offrent les programmes de ce genre sont occupées par des prévenus qui s'y sont inscrits uniquement sous la contrainte d'une ordonnance judiciaire et qui en tirent peu d'avantages réels.

161. On trouvera une recommandation au même effet dans NEW ZEALAND CRIMINAL LAW REFORM COMMITTEE, *Report on Bail*, Wellington, le Comité, 1982, par. 140, p. 48.

Pour ce qui concerne les autochtones, deux questions se posent. D'abord, du point de vue du prévenu, le pouvoir d'exiger la fourniture d'une caution est-il trop étendu ? Ensuite, du point de vue de la caution éventuelle, la loi est-elle trop rigoureuse ? Les personnes que nous avons consultées ont laissé entendre, par exemple, que les autochtones ont beaucoup de mal à trouver une caution. Ce problème s'explique en partie par leur situation économique, mais se complique du fait que les résidents des réserves ne peuvent pas être propriétaires, à titre individuel, de leur terrain et ne peuvent donc pas donner leur maison en garantie, par exemple.

Le New Zealand Criminal Law Reform Committee a proposé un certain nombre de réformes d'ordre pratique à ce sujet[162]. D'abord, elle a recommandé que l'obligation de fournir caution soit officiellement assujettie à la règle générale voulant qu'aucune condition ne soit imposée à moins que le tribunal ne l'estime nécessaire pour empêcher la fuite du prévenu, la perpétration d'une nouvelle infraction ou une entrave à la justice. En outre, il faudrait tenir compte de tous les facteurs pertinents comme la réputation, les antécédents criminels et les ressources financières au moment de déterminer l'opportunité d'exiger une caution ou l'aptitude d'une personne à servir de caution. Enfin, le Comité néo-zélandais a conclu qu'une caution ne devrait pas être écartée pour la seule raison qu'elle n'a pas, pour le moment, de moyens suffisants pour remplir les obligations découlant du cautionnement, ce qui reviendrait à exclure les personnes aux ressources limitées. Les « ressources financières » ne devraient constituer qu'un facteur parmi d'autres lorsqu'il s'agit d'apprécier l'admissibilité d'une personne à titre de caution : il faudrait considérer d'abord et avant tout sa réputation et son sens des responsabilités.

Ces propositions ont la même pertinence au Canada. Si l'on fait preuve de souplesse au sujet de l'admissibilité d'une caution, il ne sera peut-être pas nécessaire d'exiger au départ la mise en gage d'un bien. Le fait que la caution est liée de près ou apparentée au prévenu et qu'elle jouit d'une bonne réputation, pourrait avoir une incidence sur son aptitude à remplir son rôle et sur la somme qu'elle garantit.

RECOMMANDATIONS

12. (6) Les dispositions relatives à la mise en liberté provisoire devraient être modifiées de manière à préciser que le juge doit tenir compte des facteurs suivants au moment d'apprécier l'admissibilité d'une personne à titre de caution :

a) **les ressources financières de la personne ou celles qu'on peut raisonnablement lui attribuer ;**

b) **sa réputation et la nature de toute condamnation antérieure ;**

c) **ses liens (de parenté, de voisinage ou autres) avec le prévenu ;**

d) **tout autre facteur pertinent.**

---

162. Le Comité néo-zélandais a étudié la possibilité d'abolir la fourniture de cautions, mais a rejeté cette solution qui, selon elle, aurait pour effet d'augmenter le nombre de détenus. On s'est en effet dit d'avis que, dans bien des cas, les tribunaux jugeraient trop élevé le risque de relâcher un prévenu, à moins que des tiers n'aient un intérêt quelconque dans sa conduite. Nous souscrivons à cette position. Voir *id.*, p. 52.

(7) **Le juge de paix ne devrait être autorisé à exiger que la caution dépose une somme d'argent ou une autre garantie que s'il est convaincu que la situation exceptionnelle de la caution (le fait de résider dans un autre ressort, par exemple) exige une telle ordonnance.**

Le Comité néo-zélandais a également recommandé que la responsabilité de la caution soit limitée et nous souscrivons à cette position. À notre avis, même si la caution doit officiellement s'engager à surveiller la conduite du prévenu, la défaillance de celui-ci ne devrait pas entraîner automatiquement l'exécution du cautionnement. L'existence même de cette forme d'obligation morale présente un intérêt pour le droit, même en l'absence d'une sanction juridique correspondante.

RECOMMANDATION

12. (8) La caution devrait avoir l'obligation de prendre tous les moyens raisonnables pour que le prévenu se présente devant le tribunal. En revanche, elle ne devrait pas encourir l'exécution du cautionnement parce que le prévenu n'a pas rempli les autres conditions de sa mise en liberté.

Il existe un problème connexe qui n'est pas forcément propre aux autochtones : un prévenu à qui on aurait accordé une mise en liberté provisoire pourrait rester incarcéré parce qu'il est incapable de trouver une caution acceptable. Dans ces conditions, il y aurait lieu d'exiger que les conditions de la mise en liberté soient réévaluées lorsqu'elles n'ont pas été remplies dans un court laps de temps, afin d'empêcher que le prévenu reste en détention simplement parce qu'il est pauvre et incapable de respecter des conditions qui pouvaient sembler raisonnables au départ. C'est pourquoi nous recommandons ce qui suit, à l'instar du Comité néo-zélandais.

RECOMMANDATION

12. (9) Lorsqu'un juge de paix ordonne à un prévenu de fournir caution et que cette condition n'est pas remplie dans les vingt-quatre heures, l'opportunité de cette condition devrait être reconsidérée.

(4) Le dépôt d'argent comptant

Le versement d'un dépôt en argent comptant peut constituer un obstacle particulier pour les autochtones et ce, pour les mêmes raisons d'ordre économique qui font qu'une caution est très souvent difficile à trouver. Le droit actuel en matière de dépôt en argent comptant compromet le traitement égal des autochtones.

Au Royaume-Uni, le Home Office Working Party a rejeté le mécanisme du dépôt en argent comptant et demandé son abolition pour deux raisons principales : la discrimination contre les démunis et la difficulté, pour ne pas dire l'impossibilité, de trouver de l'argent[163]. Le Comité néo-zélandais a pour sa part recommandé de conserver un pouvoir limité à cet égard : le tribunal n'aurait le pouvoir d'exiger un dépôt en argent comptant ou une autre garantie que s'il a des motifs raisonnables de croire que, sans cette mesure, le prévenu risque de fuir le pays[164]. La Commission de réforme du droit de Hong Kong a recommandé que le versement d'un dépôt en argent comptant soit retenu comme solution de rechange, mais que son utilisation soit découragée. Le projet de code de Hong Kong précise que le dépôt en espèces ne devrait être exigé que lorsqu'il est nécessaire pour assurer la présence du prévenu[165].

RECOMMANDATION

12. (10) La possibilité d'exiger un dépôt en argent comptant du prévenu devrait être abolie ou assujettie à des restrictions plus importantes ; par exemple, le dépôt en argent comptant pourrait être exigé seulement si le juge de paix a des motifs raisonnables de croire que cela est nécessaire pour empêcher le prévenu de fuir le pays.

VI. La détermination de la peine

C'est au stade de la détermination de la peine que le système judiciaire produit le plus d'impact sur les autochtones. Maintes études réalisées au cours des dernières années ont fait état du taux élevé d'incarcération chez les délinquants autochtones. Dans les provinces de l'Ouest et dans le Nord, les statistiques sont particulièrement éloquentes[166]. Ce qui est encore plus troublant, c'est que le pourcentage de détenus autochtones a grimpé avec les années. Voilà une situation carrément inadmissible dans une société qui se prétend libre et démocratique.

---

163. ROYAUME-UNI, HOME OFFICE WORKING PARTY, *Bail Procedures in Magistrates' Courts*, Londres, HMSO, 1974, pp. 32-33.

164. NEW ZEALAND CRIMINAL LAW REFORM COMMITTEE, *op. cit.*, note 161, p. 46.

165. LAW REFORM COMMISSION OF HONG KONG, *Report on Bail in Criminal Proceedings*, Topic 16, Hong Kong, Gov. Printer, 1989, p. 83.

166. Près d'un détenu sur trois dans les pénitenciers des Prairies est d'origine autochtone. Les autochtones représentent près de 10 % de la population carcérale dans les établissements fédéraux, même s'ils forment moins de 2 % de la population canadienne dans son ensemble. Les femmes autochtones représentent plus de 70 % de la population carcérale dans les Territoires du Nord-Ouest, au Manitoba et en Saskatchewan. Le taux de criminalité chez les jeunes autochtones est trois fois supérieur à la proportion qu'ils représentent par rapport à l'ensemble de la population. Voir M. JACKSON, *loc. cit.*, note 18, et aussi *Questions correctionnelles concernant les autochtones*, Document de travail n° 7, Ottawa, Solliciteur général Canada, 1988.

On a proposé toutes sortes d'explications à ce propos. La plus générale, qui a aussi la plus grande portée, renvoie à la notion de colonisation[167]. On a aussi évoqué les tendances à la discrimination du personnel judiciaire. D'autres explications mettent l'accent sur la fréquence de l'incarcération pour non-paiement d'une amende ou la criminalisation de la consommation d'alcool[168]. De toute évidence, les motifs de la surreprésentation des autochtones, tout comme les solutions au problème, sont complexes et ne se prêtent pas facilement au catalogage.

A. Les solutions de rechange à l'incarcération

Les réponses au problème de la surreprésentation privilégiées dans la doctrine sont les « solutions de rechange à l'incarcération ». Même si les analyses les plus récentes continuent de favoriser la créativité dans l'élaboration de solutions de rechange bien conçues et bien financées et le recours aux peines communautaires, il faut admettre que bon nombre des expériences menées dans ce domaine au cours des dernières années ont été vertement critiquées[169].

En théorie, il existe, au stade de la détermination de la peine, plusieurs solutions de rechange à l'emprisonnement, comme la mise en liberté sous condition, le sursis de peine, l'ordonnance de service communautaire, l'indemnisation, la réparation et les programmes de travaux compensatoires[170]. De plus, les mesures que sont la déjudiciarisation, les

---

167. Cette analyse des causes de la surreprésentation tend à se confondre avec les théories des causes de la criminalité. Ainsi, dans M. JACKSON, *loc. cit.*, note 18, 217-218, on peut lire que [TRADUCTION] « leur surreprésentation dans le système de justice pénale illustre la corrélation bien connue entre la misère économique et la criminalité ». Les vues de Jackson à ce sujet sont complexes. Il ajoute que la pauvreté ne suffit pas à expliquer le problème, et il insiste sur ce [TRADUCTION] « processus de dépossession et de marginalisation » qu'on appelle aussi « colonisation ». Cette théorie de la colonisation a été reprise dans le Rapport Osnaburgh/Windigo, *op. cit.*, note 43 (voir en particulier les pages 4 à 9) et constitue le fondement de l'analyse qu'on trouve dans P. HAVEMANN et autres, *op. cit.*, note 11. Elle recueille aussi une acceptation implicite dans le rapport de la commission d'enquête sur l'affaire Marshall, *op. cit.*, note 14.

168. Ces explications sont résumées dans John HAGAN, « Locking Up the Indians: A Case for Law Reform » (1976), 55 *Canadian Forum* 16. Voir aussi Carol P. LAPRAIRIE, « The Role of Sentencing in the Over-representation of Aboriginal People in Correctional Institutions » (1990), 32 *Rev. can. crim.* 429 ; dans un texte soigneusement rédigé et très fouillé, l'auteure propose trois explications possibles : (1) les autochtones et les autres Canadiens ne sont pas traités sur un pied d'égalité en ce qui concerne les services policiers, les accusations, les poursuites, les peines et la libération conditionnelle ; (2) les autochtones commettent davantage de crimes attribuables à des facteurs non raciaux, comme la pauvreté ou la consommation d'alcool ; et (3) les autochtones commettent des crimes qui sont plus faciles à détecter que ceux commis par les autres Canadiens.

169. Voir, par ex., Norval MORRIS et Michael TONRY, *Between Prison and Probation: Intermediate Punishments in a Rational Sentencing System*, New York, Oxford University Press, 1990.

170. Il convient de rappeler ici qu'il faut établir une distinction importante entre les solutions de rechange à l'incarcération et les divers types de peines intermédiaires (camps forestiers, probation en étroite surveillance, incarcération-choc, assignation à résidence avec surveillance électronique) avec lesquelles elles sont souvent confondues.

programmes de réconciliation victime-délinquant et la médiation sont également des solutions de rechange à l'incarcération, dans la mesure où elles permettent de contourner le processus habituel de jugement et de détermination de la peine. Il y a longtemps que la Commission de réforme du droit préconise ces solutions, mais elles sont encore très peu utilisées[171].

RECOMMANDATION

13. (1) Les solutions de rechange à l'incarcération devraient être utilisées dans toute la mesure du possible. Les dispositions du *Code criminel* qui prévoient ces solutions de rechange devraient préciser qu'elles doivent être considérées en priorité au moment de la détermination de la peine. Le juge qui condamne un autochtone à l'emprisonnement pour une infraction se prêtant à l'une ou l'autre de ces solutions devrait être tenu de préciser les raisons pour lesquelles il a opté pour l'incarcération.

Jackson, dans l'étude que nous lui avons commandée et qui s'intitule *In Search of the Pathways to Justice*[172], défend et décrit avec justesse les méthodes créatives employées par les autochtones pour résoudre les conflits. À notre avis, plusieurs raisons militent en faveur de l'élaboration de programmes propres aux autochtones. D'abord, ces programmes laissent entrevoir une réduction du nombre de détenus autochtones. Avec un minimum d'ajustements, ces programmes pourraient être conçus à l'image du droit coutumier, ce qui les rendrait plus acceptables aux yeux de la population touchée. Enfin, du fait qu'ils s'articulent autour de la participation de la collectivité, ils favoriseraient la paix sociale et le sentiment, pour la collectivité, de se prendre en main. L'élaboration de tels programmes est conforme aux valeurs traditionnelles des autochtones, dans la mesure où elle vise à réconcilier le délinquant et la collectivité dans son ensemble, et à rétablir l'harmonie[173].

RECOMMANDATION

13. (2) Les programmes offrant des solutions de rechange à l'incarcération devraient, dans toute la mesure du possible, comporter un caractère universel. À cette fin, des ressources humaines et financières suffisantes devraient être réunies, et des études complètes de faisabilité devraient être entreprises dès maintenant.

---

171. « Une raison pour laquelle le pourcentage d'autochtones incarcérés est disproportionnée [*sic*] est qu'un trop grand nombre d'entre eux sont inutilement condamnés à une peine d'emprisonnement. » *Des responsabilités à assumer : Rapport du Comité permanent de la justice et du solliciteur général sur la détermination de la peine, la mise en liberté sous condition et d'autres aspects du système correctionnel*, Ottawa, Approvisionnements et Services Canada, 1988, p. 237 (président : David Daubney) (ci-après *Des responsabilités à assumer*).

172. *Op. cit.*, note 28.

173. Le Rapport Osnaburgh/Windigo, *op. cit.*, note 43, p. 37, observe que le recours à des solutions de rechange, pour la résolution des conflits, par exemple, [TRADUCTION] « s'insère dans le mouvement général visant à instituer de tels systèmes dans l'ensemble de la société [...] »

Deux préoccupations reviennent souvent dans les pages suivantes : les ressources à engager et leur importance. Les lois d'habilitation doivent être adoptées, certes, mais elles auront peu d'effet si les ressources manquent et qu'on ait négligé la planification. Pour donner les résultats escomptés, les programmes doivent reposer sur des recherches et s'adapter aux collectivités individuelles.

RECOMMANDATION

13. (3) Les recherches devraient s'accompagner d'un suivi des programmes et d'analyses de politiques qui permettront d'ajuster le tir à la faveur de l'expérience.

Nous estimons qu'une bonne partie de cette recherche pourrait être confiée à un organisme autochtone (comme l'Institut de justice autochtone dont nous recommandons la création ailleurs dans le présent rapport).

(1) La réconciliation victime-délinquant

La réconciliation victime-délinquant ne fait pas partie au sens strict du processus de détermination de la peine, mais n'en est pas moins considérée comme une solution de rechange à l'incarcération. Les programmes de réconciliation victime-délinquant peuvent avoir pour conséquence de soustraire complètement les délinquants au système de justice pénale[174]. La déjudiciarisation est sans doute le mécanisme idéal pour faire participer les collectivités au règlement de certaines affaires (en particulier les infractions mineures où l'alcool aurait pu jouer un rôle). D'autres programmes de réconciliation interviennent ultérieurement, avant le prononcé de la sentence ; ils facilitent le jeu de la médiation et de la réparation[175] entre le délinquant et la victime. Ces programmes contribuent à rétablir

---

174. La déjudiciarisation ne se limite pas aux premiers stades qui précèdent le procès. Elle peut intervenir à divers moments, par exemple avant même que des accusations soient portées, lorsque entrent en jeu les pouvoirs discrétionnaires de la police ; elle peut aussi intervenir plus tard, juste avant la détermination de la peine, au moment où s'exercent les pouvoirs du poursuivant et du juge. On ne trouve ni au Code ni ailleurs de disposition concernant la déjudiciarisation avant le dépôt d'accusations, ni concernant les programmes de réconciliation victime-délinquant. À l'opposé, la déjudiciarisation postérieure au dépôt d'accusations est reconnue, aux termes de la *Loi sur les jeunes contrevenants*, précitée, note 49, comme « mesure de rechange ».

175. La réparation joue un rôle important dans la résolution des conflits chez les autochtones. Voir M. JACKSON, *op. cit.*, note 28. Elle est étroitement liée à la notion de réconciliation victime-délinquant et se présente sous diverses formes : la restitution des biens volés, les excuses, le paiement volontaire, les services à la victime ou à la collectivité. Voir CRD, *Le dédommagement et l'indemnisation*, Document de travail n° 5, Ottawa, Information Canada, 1974. Des modifications apportées récemment au *Code criminel* ont élargi la portée des dispositions concernant la réparation, en grande partie dans l'esprit des recommandations formulées dans CRD, *Principes directeurs : sentences et mesures non sentencielles dans le processus pénal*, Rapport n° 2, Ottawa, Information Canada, 1976.

la paix dans la collectivité grâce à la réconciliation des intéressés. On en trouve dans diverses régions du Canada, à l'exception de Terre-Neuve, de l'Île-du-Prince-Édouard, de la Nouvelle-Écosse, du Nouveau-Brunswick et de l'Alberta[176].

RECOMMANDATION

13. (4) Les programmes de réconciliation victime-délinquant devraient être étendus et faire l'objet d'analyses plus approfondies que cela n'a été le cas jusqu'à présent. Les gouvernements fédéral et provinciaux devraient fournir l'appui financier nécessaire pour que les programmes de la collectivité deviennent plus accessibles et mieux exploités.

Des ressources supplémentaires doivent être mises à la disposition des collectivités pour garantir l'efficacité de ces programmes.

RECOMMANDATION

13. (5) Le *Code criminel* devrait contenir un mécanisme analogue à celui de la *Loi sur les jeunes contrevenants* relativement aux « mesures de rechange », pour ce qui concerne le règlement et la déjudiciarisation des affaires mettant en cause des délinquants autochtones d'âge adulte.

À notre avis, du reste, ces mesures de rechange devraient pouvoir s'appliquer dans toutes les affaires pénales.

Ces mesures sont en meilleure harmonie avec la philosophie des autochtones au sujet de l'administration de la justice pénale. Elles correspondent à leurs valeurs et peuvent même constituer un excellent moyen pour eux d'avoir plus de prise sur le système de justice pénale. Suivant une étude que nous avons commandée, l'incarcération des délinquants autochtones ferait plus de tort que de bien : le contact de la vie carcérale [TRADUCTION] « peut faire d'eux, à leur sortie de prison, une plus grande menace pour l'ordre établi dans leur collectivité que lorsqu'ils ont quitté celle-ci[177]. » Réhabilitation et réconciliation sont des notions primordiales chez les autochtones.

(2) L'amende

De façon générale, l'amende ne donne de résultats que lorsque le délinquant participe pleinement à l'économie fondée sur l'échange monétaire, hypothèse qui ne s'applique pas dans le cas des autochtones ayant des démêlés avec la justice pénale. Les amendes suscitent très peu de respect dans les collectivités autochtones et leur effet dissuasif est

---

176. COMMISSION CANADIENNE SUR LA DÉTERMINATION DE LA PEINE, *Réformer la sentence : une approche canadienne*, Ottawa, Approvisionnements et Services Canada, 1987, p. 386.

177. IBA, *op. cit.*, note 24, p. 25.

inexistant puisqu'il est bien connu que les délinquants sont incapables de les payer. Une forte proportion des autochtones qui peuplent les prisons sont détenus tout simplement parce qu'ils n'ont pas les moyens d'acquitter les amendes qui leur ont été infligées. Par conséquent, la condamnation à une amende ne sert souvent qu'à différer l'emprisonnement. Trois éléments de solution peuvent atténuer ce problème : les programmes de travaux compensatoires, le système de « jours/amendes » et la réforme des règles concernant l'emprisonnement pour défaut de payer une amende.

a) Les programmes de travaux compensatoires

Cette solution vient d'être incorporée au *Code criminel*[178]. Elle permet au délinquant d'éviter l'emprisonnement pour non-paiement d'une amende en accomplissant, dans le cadre d'un programme établi à cette fin, des travaux communautaires qui lui sont crédités suivant un taux horaire donné. Malheureusement, ces programmes ne sont ni universellement accessibles ni de qualité égale[179]. Dans certaines régions, par exemple, les femmes autochtones peuvent difficilement s'en prévaloir, en raison de problèmes de transport et de l'insuffisance des services de garderie dans leur collectivité[180]. Mais un autre problème se pose :

[TRADUCTION]
Les programmes de travaux compensatoires posent parfois un dilemme pour les administrateurs des collectivités autochtones, car ils ne sont pas intégrés à des projets authentiques débouchant sur un sentiment d'épanouissement et de réalisation de soi. La mise sur pied d'un programme n'a rien de facile, et il faut faire preuve d'ingéniosité pour qu'il porte fruit en milieu autochtone. Dans les collectivités où les ressources sont habituellement limitées sur le plan administratif, il n'est pas toujours prioritaire d'éparpiller les efforts de la sorte[181].

RECOMMANDATION

13. (6) Des programmes de travaux compensatoires devraient être institués dans les collectivités qui le désirent. Des ressources financières suffisantes devraient être mises à la disposition des collectivités afin de leur permettre de réaliser des projets qui favoriseront l'épanouissement et la réalisation de soi. Des mesures spéciales devraient être prises afin de rendre ces programmes accessibles aux femmes autochtones.

---

178. Voir l'art. 718.1.

179. Voir *Justice on Trial*, *op. cit.*, note 14, pp. 6-40 et 6-41 pour une description de certaines lacunes caractéristiques de ces programmes dans les collectivités autochtones albertaines.

180. *Id.*, p. 6-41.

181. IBA, *op. cit.*, note 24, p. 49.

b)   Le système des jours/amendes

Dans le document de travail que nous avons publié en 1974 sous le titre *L'amende*[182], nous examinions le système suédois de « jours/amendes » suivant lequel le montant d'une amende est calculé en fonction du revenu annuel brut du délinquant. La Commission canadienne sur la détermination de la peine a laissé entendre récemment qu'il fallait étudier plus à fond l'opportunité d'instaurer un système de jours/amendes au Canada, en raison de nos méthodes différentes d'imposition et de déclaration du revenu[183]. La Commission concluait, et nous sommes d'accord avec elle, qu'il fallait inciter les provinces à mettre sur pied des projets-pilotes sur le recours au système des jours/amendes. À notre avis, les collectivités autochtones devraient compter parmi les premières à bénéficier de ces projets.

RECOMMANDATION

13. (7) Les provinces devraient être encouragées à mettre sur pied des projets-pilotes sur le recours au système des jours/amendes ; les collectivités autochtones devraient compter parmi les premières à bénéficier de ces projets.

c)   L'incarcération pour défaut de payer une amende

Les études sur la détermination des sentences ont fortement critiqué l'imposition d'une peine d'emprisonnement « quasi automatique » pour défaut de payer l'amende. Les statistiques sont là pour prouver que c'est faire preuve de discrimination envers les contrevenants aux ressources limitées que d'emprisonner, sans tenir compte de leurs moyens de payer, les personnes qui n'ont pas payé leur amende. L'une des conséquences les plus visibles de cette discrimination est le nombre démesuré des autochtones dans les établissements provinciaux par rapport à leur population[184].

On a proposé divers moyens d'éviter l'incarcération pour défaut de payer une amende, moyens qui ont tous en commun certaines caractéristiques[185].

---

182. CRD, *L'amende*, Document de travail n° 6, Ottawa, Information Canada, 1974.

183. Voir COMMISSION CANADIENNE SUR LA DÉTERMINATION DE LA PEINE, *op. cit.*, note 176, pp. 416-417.

184. *Id.*, p. 419.

185. Nous en avons proposé un dans notre document de travail n° 5, *op. cit.*, note 175. On en trouve un autre dans la *Loi modifiant le Code criminel* . . ., projet de loi C-19 (1re lecture), 2e session, 32e législature (Can.), et la COMMISSION CANADIENNE SUR LA DÉTERMINATION DE LA PEINE, *op. cit.*, note 176, a présenté une recommandation à cet égard dans son rapport.

RECOMMANDATION

13. (8) Le non-paiement d'une amende devrait entraîner l'emprisonnement seulement si la personne refuse ou néglige sciemment de payer l'amende, et non lorsqu'elle est incapable de le faire. Le délinquant ne devrait être emprisonné qu'après que les solutions de rechange suivantes ont été envisagées :

a) **la tenue d'une audience permettant au délinquant d'expliquer pourquoi il n'a pas payé l'amende ;**

b) **la saisie-arrêt du salaire et d'autres sommes d'argent ;**

c) **la saisie des biens du délinquant ;**

d) **des travaux communautaires correspondant à l'amende ;**

e) **le recours à d'autres sanctions dont dispose la collectivité[186].**

(3) L'ordonnance de service communautaire

Tout comme les programmes de travaux compensatoires, l'ordonnance de service communautaire est un mécanisme prometteur. Mais lorsqu'il est mal structuré, il peut devenir un fardeau pour la collectivité et manquer à sa promesse[187].

Habituellement, l'ordonnance de service communautaire oblige le délinquant à travailler un certain nombre d'heures pour la collectivité sans être rémunéré[188]. Elle peut contribuer à réconcilier le délinquant et la collectivité par la réparation du préjudice causé et par le résultat favorable qui découle des mesures adoptées pour sanctionner le comportement délictueux[189]. L'expérience générale (par opposition à l'expérience particulière chez les autochtones) en ce qui concerne les ordonnances de service communautaire s'est révélée prometteuse[190].

---

186. Il faudrait également envisager l'abolition de l'incarcération pour défaut de payer une amende. Il existe des moyens plus créatifs d'assurer le paiement d'une dette. Cette proposition est conforme à l'approche adoptée par la Commission de réforme du droit dans un document de travail à paraître sous le titre *Les frais en matière pénale.*

187. Voir *Justice on Trial, op. cit.,* note 14, pp. 6-40 à 6-42.

188. L'ordonnance peut être délivrée en vertu de l'alinéa 737(2)*h*) du *Code criminel,* qui permet au tribunal de joindre des « conditions raisonnables » à une ordonnance de probation. Apparemment, le Nouveau-Brunswick est le seul endroit au Canada où l'ordonnance de service communautaire ne soit jamais utilisée. Voir *Des responsabilités à assumer, op. cit.,* note 171, p. 86.

189. Voir CRD, Rapport n° 2, *op. cit.,* note 175, p. 23.

190. *Des responsabilités à assumer, op. cit.,* note 171, pp. 86-87.

À l'issue d'une étude réalisée au Manitoba sur les programmes de travaux compensatoires et les ordonnances de service communautaire, on a conclu que ces mesures [TRADUCTION] « semblent très bien servir la collectivité des Indiens inscrits, des Métis et des Indiens non inscrits. Le nombre d'autochtones ayant recours à ces mesures est élevé, leur taux de réussite est supérieur à la moyenne, et le nombre d'incarcérations pour défaut est sensiblement le même, toutes proportions gardées, que chez les non-autochtones[191]. » Par contre, d'après une autre étude portant sur deux programmes expressément conçus pour les autochtones de London et de Kenora en Ontario, les ordonnances de service communautaire ont donné des résultats mitigés[192]. Il est clair qu'on ne peut pas tirer de conclusions définitives de l'expérience jusqu'à ce jour. Pour que ces programmes de type communautaire portent fruit, il faudra consacrer des ressources nettement plus considérables à leur conception et à leur mise en œuvre. De même, la rareté des ressources sur le plan administratif peut faire en sorte qu'un programme théoriquement avantageux finisse par nuire à la collectivité qui l'administre. À l'instar des autres solutions de rechange, le système d'ordonnance de service communautaire doit jouir de l'appui de la collectivité.

RECOMMANDATION

13. (9) Des programmes d'ordonnance de service communautaire devraient être mis sur pied dans les collectivités qui le désirent. Des ressources adéquates devraient être affectées à ces programmes, afin de définir quels types de travaux communautaires pourraient être réalisés et de déterminer les ressources dont la collectivité a besoin pour assurer la réussite de ces programmes. Il conviendrait de mettre beaucoup plus de soin à la conception des programmes, et la loi ou le règlement d'habilitation devrait clairement en énoncer les buts. Il faudrait faire en sorte que les juges, les procureurs du ministère public et les avocats de la défense soient bien informés de l'existence des programmes et de leurs objectifs[193]. Bien qu'il faille en encourager l'utilisation, le *Code criminel* devrait préciser qu'aucune ordonnance de service communautaire ne peut être émise à moins que le tribunal n'ait obtenu l'assurance, de la part de la collectivité, qu'il existe des possibilités de service bénévole et que la collectivité est disposée à accueillir le délinquant.

B.   La probation

La probation consiste essentiellement dans la surveillance qui s'exerce sur les condamnés à qui on permet de rester en liberté ou qu'on réintègre dans leur collectivité après qu'ils ont purgé une partie de leur peine de prison. Il s'agit aussi d'un mécanisme qui permet d'offrir aux condamnés un traitement ou d'autres moyens d'assistance.

---

191. L. J. BARKWELL et autres, *loc. cit.*, note 18, 138.

192. Margaret JACKSON et John EKSTEDT, *Programmes de mesures de remplacement de l'incarcération ou de solutions de rechange : quelles sont les options ?*, rapport de recherche de la Commission canadienne sur la détermination de la peine, Ottawa, ministère de la Justice, 1988, p. 26 ; les auteurs précisent qu'il ne se manifeste aucun indicateur de réussite ou d'échec.

193. M. JACKSON et J. EKSTEDT, *id.*, p. 25, révèlent que certains juges ont mal compris la nature de l'ordonnance de service communautaire, minant du même coup sa valeur et son utilité.

Les conditions habituellement énoncées dans les ordonnances de probation ne conviennent pas toujours aux autochtones. L'obligation de se présenter régulièrement à un agent de probation peut créer des difficultés lorsque le délinquant habite une collectivité isolée. Nombre de programmes de traitement n'ont pas été conçus à l'intention des autochtones. Certaines ordonnances de non-fréquentation sont difficiles à faire respecter dans les petites collectivités et correspondent, à toutes fins utiles, à l'exil.

La prise en charge de la probation à l'échelle locale serait une amélioration majeure[194]. La difficulté consiste toutefois à obtenir un appui suffisamment important de la part de la collectivité. Il n'en reste pas moins que si des membres choisis de la collectivité recevaient une formation d'agent de probation, les difficultés seraient bien moindres. Même là où on ne dispose pas d'agent de probation qualifié, de nombreuses tâches pourraient être accomplies par des membres influents de la collectivité, sous la direction d'un agent de probation établi ailleurs[195]. En outre, la surveillance des activités du délinquant devrait être comprise de manière à tirer le meilleur parti possible de l'aptitude de ce dernier à mener une vie productive. Les délinquants qui vivent de la chasse, par exemple, pourraient être surveillés par un accompagnateur choisi localement, à moins que l'on ne décide tout simplement de différer l'obligation de se présenter à un agent de probation.

RECOMMANDATION

13. (10) Des services de probation adaptés aux besoins des délinquants autochtones devraient être offerts dans un large éventail de collectivités autochtones. Il y aurait lieu de faire davantage appel aux ressources de la collectivité et d'assurer une formation d'agent de probation à des personnes issues du milieu.

Chaque fois qu'ils envisagent une ordonnance de probation, les juges qui prononcent la sentence se plaignent de l'absence d'installations adéquates ou de programmes de traitement, ou encore de l'impossibilité d'intégrer les délinquants dans les programmes existants. Des ressources supplémentaires sont nécessaires pour assurer des installations adéquates, un personnel qualifié et un ensemble de programmes de traitement efficaces. Le tribunal qui prononce la sentence ne sera en mesure de décider d'une solution opportune que si de telles ressources sont disponibles.

---

194. Il faudrait ouvrir des établissements correctionnels spécialisés et adapter les programmes en fonction des besoins des délinquants autochtones. Il faut également s'attaquer à un certain nombre de problèmes comme l'emplacement des établissements de probation et la formation du personnel des établissements correctionnels, des services de probation, de libération conditionnelle et de réinsertion, et des services aux ex-détenus. Il y a un certain nombre de leçons qu'on peut tirer dans ce domaine. Signalons en particulier l'entente de la baie James intervenue en 1975, mais qui n'a pas été mise en œuvre, et la critique qu'en fait M. JACKSON, *loc. cit.*, note 18, 257-260.

195. Voir *Justice on Trial*, *op. cit.*, note 14, pp. 6-42 et 6-43. En Ontario, le ministère des Services correctionnels embauche des adjoints aux agents de probation qui habitent dans les collectivités autochtones. Ils jouent le rôle d'amis et de conseillers auprès des personnes en probation ou en liberté conditionnelle. Voir Stan JOLLY, C. PETERS et S. SPIEGEL, *Progress Report on Government Action Taken Since the 1975 Federal-Provincial Conference on Native Peoples and the Criminal Justice System*, rapport préparé pour le Ontario Native Council on Justice, Toronto, le Conseil, 1979.

On entend souvent dire que les délinquants autochtones ne sont habituellement pas considérés par les juges comme de bons candidats à la probation[196]. Les raisons en sont complexes. Cependant, le facteur culturel est important. Les juges doivent comprendre que [TRADUCTION] « nos techniques de réinsertion, de " guérison ", peuvent être non seulement tout à fait différentes, mais aussi paraître incongrues au regard des traditions[197]. »

RECOMMANDATION

13. (11) Les critères d'admissibilité à la probation devraient être formulés de manière à tenir compte des différences culturelles et à combler les besoins des délinquants et des collectivités autochtones. De plus, les rapports de probation devraient mettre davantage l'accent sur des facteurs comme les capacités professionnelles du délinquant, ses aptitudes à trouver un emploi et sa volonté de suivre un programme de traitement ou de formation. Il faudrait également attacher une importance plus grande à la volonté de la collectivité de participer à la probation et à la surveillance du délinquant.

C. Ajustements structurels et réforme du processus

(1) La nécessité d'une nouvelle structure de détermination de la peine

Les règles actuelles du droit canadien en matière de détermination de la peine sont archaïques et inadéquates. Le *Code criminel* manque de cohérence en cette matière et offre une orientation négligeable aux juges chargés de déterminer la peine. Ces lacunes entraînent des disparités importantes au chapitre des peines. À notre avis, le régime actuel ne respecte pas, sous plusieurs rapports importants, les garanties d'égalité et de justice fondamentales énoncées par la Charte. En vue de remédier à ces défauts, nous avons recommandé ailleurs la refonte des pratiques actuelles en matière de détermination de la peine, l'établissement de peines repères, l'abolition de la libération conditionnelle et la création d'une commission permanente sur la détermination de la peine[198]. En outre, les recommandations faites ailleurs dans le présent rapport au sujet des structures du système de

---

196. Voir les sources citées dans Susan V. ZIMMERMAN, *The Revolving Door of Despair: Native Involvement in the Criminal Justice System* (document préparé pour la Commission de réforme du droit du Canada, 1991), pp. 46-49 [non publié]. Cette position est remise en question par C. P. LaPRAIRIE, *loc. cit.*, note 168, 433.

197. R. Ross, *op. cit.*, note 21, p. 10.

198. Voir, par ex., CRD, Rapport n° 2, *op. cit.*, note 175. Le rapport de 1987 de la COMMISSION CANADIENNE SUR LA DÉTERMINATION DE LA PEINE, *op. cit.*, note 176, et le rapport de 1988 intitulé *Des responsabilités à assumer*, *op. cit.*, note 171, préconisaient aussi la création d'une commission permanente sur la détermination de la peine.

justice pénale, comme celles où il est question de la création d'un Institut de justice autochtone, de la participation accrue des aînés et des travailleurs sociaux auprès des tribunaux, ainsi que de l'établissement de mécanismes de liaison officielle avec les collectivités, offrent des possibilités avantageuses aux autochtones dans le processus de détermination de la peine.

(2) Racisme, discrimination et détermination de la peine

Les personnes que nous avons consultées se sont dites très préoccupées par la question du racisme. Il existe des indices anecdotiques de racisme, mais on en tient rarement compte, car il est difficile d'en faire la preuve conformément aux critères des sciences sociales[199]. Le racisme déclaré se prouve difficilement, en partie parce que les coupables sont assez habiles pour masquer leurs penchants. S'agissant de racisme déclaré et de discrimination systémique, [TRADUCTION] « l'absence de fondements empiriques solides nous empêche de bien savoir s'il existe ou non un parti pris dans les condamnations et les peines infligées aux accusés autochtones[200]. »

RECOMMANDATION

13. (12) Des recherches devraient être effectuées afin de déterminer si les autochtones se voient imposer des peines plus sévères que les autres Canadiens et, dans l'affirmative, quelles sont les causes de cette disparité.

Même s'il nous répugne de penser que des peines plus sévères puissent être imposées en raison de la race ou de la culture, nous n'en concluons pas pour autant qu'il faille toujours faire abstraction des facteurs raciaux ou culturels dans le prononcé d'une sentence. La Commission canadienne sur la détermination de la peine proposait, dans *Réformer la sentence*, des lignes de conduite à l'échelle nationale en matière de détermination de la peine, dont il ne faudrait s'écarter que si des circonstances aggravantes ou atténuantes prévues par le régime légal entraient en jeu[201]. Les circonstances atténuantes, comme la réparation ou l'indemnisation éventuelle par le délinquant, sont envisagées dans la recommandation de la Commission sur la détermination de la peine. Dans cette optique, et compte tenu de la pratique actuelle en matière de détermination de la peine, la race ou la culture du délinquant devraient également contribuer, avec d'autres facteurs, à atténuer la peine.

RECOMMANDATION

13. (13) Une liste de facteurs qui, conjugués à d'autres circonstances, viendraient atténuer la peine lorsque le délinquant est un autochtone devrait être dressée. Par exemple, la peine devrait être moins sévère si le délinquant autochtone a fait ou fera l'objet de sanctions traditionnelles infligées par la collectivité.

---

199. Voir C. P. LaPrairie, *loc. cit.*, note 168, 436.
200. *Id.*, 432, citant Clark.
201. *Op. cit.*, note 176, p. 320 et suiv.

Ces circonstances atténuantes pourraient être combinées avec d'autres facteurs généralement reconnus, comme la preuve que le délinquant reconnaît sa responsabilité envers
la victime et la collectivité. Cette proposition est conforme au principe voulant que
l'incarcération soit une mesure de dernier recours et à la nécessité de favoriser une
individualisation adéquate de la peine.

(3) La négociation du plaidoyer

La négociation du plaidoyer consiste dans la recherche d'une entente suivant laquelle
le prévenu plaide coupable, à condition que le ministère public retire certaines accusations ou recommande une peine atténuée. Les personnes que nous avons consultées nous
ont laissé entendre — et les sondages le confirment — que les autochtones ont souvent
le sentiment qu'un plaidoyer est négocié sans qu'ils aient eu conscience de participer au
processus[202]. À l'évidence, cet état de choses est inacceptable.

On connaît peu les effets des facteurs raciaux et culturels sur la négociation du
plaidoyer, et les études ne s'accordent pas sur la mesure dans laquelle les autochtones
en souffrent[203]. Une étude révèle que les autochtones comprennent extrêmement mal le
processus, souvent parce que personne, y compris l'avocat de la défense, ne le leur a
expliqué[204]. Une plus grande transparence du processus et une définition plus claire des
rôles joués par tous et chacun — avocat de la défense, procureur du ministère public et
juge — contribueraient grandement à corriger la situation.

Dans notre document de travail n° 60, *Les discussions et ententes sur le plaidoyer*[205],
nous avons soutenu que le système de justice pénale se prête à un processus ouvert et
responsable de discussions et d'ententes sur le plaidoyer. Nous avons proposé la mise au
point d'un processus s'articulant autour de dispositions législatives et de lignes de con-
duites publiées. Dans le cadre de ce régime, les détails des négociations seraient commu-
niqués au tribunal, et on prendrait le temps de s'assurer que l'accusé, la victime et le public
ont bien saisi la nature exacte de l'opération. La mise en place d'un régime de ce type
ferait beaucoup pour que le délinquant autochtone soit convenablement informé de la nature
du processus.

RECOMMANDATION

**13. (14) Comme nous l'avons recommandé antérieurement, un processus bien
structuré, ouvert et responsable de discussions et d'ententes sur le plaidoyer devrait
être mis en place.**

---

202. Voir B. Morse et L. Lock, *op. cit.*, note 89.

203. Comparer John Hagan, « Parameters of Criminal Prosecution: An Application of Path Analysis to a Problem
of Criminal Justice » (1974), 65 *J. Crim. L. & Criminology* 536, 542, et Derek F. Wynne et Timothy F.
Hartnagel, « Race and Plea Negotiation: An Analysis of Some Canadian Data » (1975), 1:2 *Cahiers
canadiens de sociologie* 147, 149.

204. B. Morse et L. Lock, *op. cit.*, note 89, p. 40.

205. CRD, *Les discussions et ententes sur le plaidoyer*, Document de travail n° 60, Ottawa, la Commission, 1989.

(4) Les rapports préalables à la sentence

Le paragraphe 735(1) du *Code criminel* fait état en termes très laconiques du pouvoir qu'a le juge qui prononce la sentence d'exiger un rapport préalable à la sentence. Ces rapports sont souvent très utiles mais le mécanisme devrait être amélioré.

RECOMMANDATION

13. (15) Les dispositions du *Code criminel* relatives aux rapports préalables à la sentence devraient être beaucoup plus détaillées qu'elles ne le sont à l'heure actuelle. À tout le moins, le contenu des rapports et les circonstances qui en commanderaient l'établissement devraient faire l'objet de dispositions législatives claires.

Un rapport préalable à la sentence contient habituellement des renseignements sur l'âge du délinquant, son emploi, sa situation de famille, ses antécédents, ses études et sa situation financière. Ce sont là des catégories de renseignements utiles qui devraient être énumérées dans la disposition législative décrivant le contenu des rapports. Cela dit, le chômage chronique dans les collectivités autochtones, l'éclatement de la famille, l'insuffisance de l'enseignement et la pauvreté généralisée du milieu sont autant de facteurs qui empêchent de s'en remettre à un rapport où l'on ne trouverait que les renseignements qui y figurent actuellement.

RECOMMANDATION

13. (16) Le *Code criminel* devrait préciser que les rapports préalables à la sentence doivent faire état de la condition particulière des délinquants autochtones et en tenir compte.

Il faudrait également tenir compte des vues de la collectivité concernant l'éventuelle réinsertion du délinquant et signaler toute mesure de réinsertion entreprise ou prévue par le délinquant conjointement avec la collectivité. Enfin, il faudrait envisager l'opportunité d'accorder un traitement particulier au délinquant ou de l'inscrire dans un programme spécial. Il est possible que ces mesures soient déjà pratique courante dans certaines régions du pays. Cependant, dans un souci d'uniformité et pour dissiper toute ambiguïté, nous proposons que la législation soit modifiée afin de donner un caractère officiel et durable à la réforme. En outre, vu le contenu délicat de ces rapports, nous considérons comme primordiale l'exigence formulée ci-dessous :

RECOMMANDATION

13. (17) Seules les personnes bien au fait des conditions de vie des autochtones et de leurs coutumes, de leur culture et de leurs valeurs devraient être autorisées à dresser des rapports préalables à la sentence.

Ajoutons que la jurisprudence fait état de difficultés lorsqu'un tribunal ordonne l'incarcération en l'absence d'un rapport préalable à la sentence[206].

RECOMMANDATION

13. (18) Lorsque l'incarcération d'un délinquant est envisagée pour la première fois (et n'est pas requise par la loi), le tribunal devrait être expressément tenu d'ordonner l'établissement d'un rapport préalable à la sentence. La loi devrait en outre préciser que, chaque fois que l'incarcération est envisagée, le juge devrait songer à ordonner l'établissement d'un rapport.

L'établissement d'un rapport préalable à la sentence ne devrait pas être conditionné par la demande du délinquant. Nous croyons aussi que l'assistance d'un avocat avant la rédaction du rapport peut revêtir une importance vitale.

RECOMMANDATION

13. (19) Lorsque l'établissement d'un rapport préalable à la sentence est ordonné, le tribunal devrait s'assurer que le délinquant non représenté est informé des avantages que peuvent lui rapporter les services d'un avocat.

Le juge n'a pas à remplir cette tâche en personne. Il devrait plutôt faire appel aux ressources de la collectivité, peut-être par l'entremise des travailleurs sociaux autochtones auprès du tribunal.

(5) L'interdiction de porter une arme

Nombreux sont les autochtones qui dépendent, pour leur subsistance, de la chasse, de la pêche et du trappage. En règle générale, les traités ont préservé à perpétuité les droits de chasse et de pêche des autochtones, et [TRADUCTION] « l'exercice des droits de chasse et de pêche est un élément essentiel de la culture des autochtones, au même titre que toutes les autres caractéristiques qui leur sont propres[207]. » Certains conflits tirent leur origine des exigences inhérentes à ce mode de vie. Ainsi, la possession d'une arme revêt une importance particulière chez les autochtones.

L'article 100 du *Code criminel* interdit à la personne convaincue de certains types de crimes de posséder une arme à feu pendant une période déterminée. L'application prétendument égale de cette disposition peut être source d'iniquité. Une interdiction de port d'arme aura un impact beaucoup plus profond sur un autochtone qui gagne sa vie en chassant

---

206. Voir, par ex., *R.* c. *Young* (1982), 39 Nfld. & P.E.I.R. 76 (C.S. Î.-P.-É.).

207. IBA, *op. cit.*, note 24, pp. 42-43.

et en pêchant, comme les traités le lui permettent, et qui n'a pas d'autre profession. Deux cours d'appel n'en ont pas moins conclu qu'une interdiction de port d'arme ne constitue pas une entorse aux dispositions de la Charte[208] . À l'opposé, on a jugé dans l'affaire *R. c. Chief* que, [TRADUCTION] « dans le cas d'un trappeur du Yukon, [...] [une interdiction de port d'arme] correspond à toutes fins utiles à une interdiction de travailler dans son seul champ d'activité[209] » et contrevient aux dispositions de l'article 12 de la Charte. En conséquence, la cour a accordé au délinquant une « exemption constitutionnelle » de l'interdiction absolue en lui permettant de porter une arme quand il chassait[210]. Nous souscrivons à cette position.

RECOMMANDATION

13. (20) Le paragraphe 100(1) du *Code criminel* devrait être modifié de manière à prévoir une exemption limitée de l'interdiction impérative de posséder une arme lorsque le juge est convaincu que l'interdiction serait oppressive et injuste, et que le fait de permettre au délinquant de porter une arme pour gagner sa vie ne menacerait en rien la sécurité du public.

VII. Les mesures correctionnelles

Au cours des dernières années, le Service correctionnel du Canada et la Commission nationale des libérations conditionnelles ont déployé des efforts louables pour répondre aux préoccupations et aux besoins des délinquants autochtones ; cependant, le processus en est à ses débuts, et il reste beaucoup à faire. En général, les autochtones sont incarcérés dans des pénitenciers situés très loin de chez eux, dans un tout autre univers culturel. Et jusqu'à maintenant, les programmes et services offerts dans ces établissements faisaient bien peu de cas de la culture des détenus autochtones et, en particulier, de leurs besoins spirituels. Très peu d'autochtones travaillent au sein du système correctionnel. Les fraternités et sororités autochtones ont accompli un travail important, mais elles souffrent d'un manque de ressources et de reconnaissance. De plus, les délinquants autochtones doivent satisfaire à des critères de libération conditionnelle et de libération anticipée qui, à certains égards, paraissent culturellement inopportuns[211]. Enfin, de nombreux rapports ont commenté l'insuffisance des services offerts aux ex-détenus autochtones, que ce soit dans leur collectivité ou ailleurs[212].

---

208. Voir *R. c. Tobac* (1985), 60 A.R. 253 (C.A. T.N.-O.) ; *R. c. Weyallon* (1985), 60 A.R. 79 (C.A. T.N.-O.) ; *R. c. Kelly* (1990), 80 C.R. (3e) 185 (C.A. Ont.). Dans la dernière affaire, le trappage est abordé, même s'il ne s'agit pas en soi d'une « affaire de trappeur ».

209. Précité, note 159, 270-271.

210. Voir *R. c. McGillivary*, précité, note 159, où la Cour en vient à la même conclusion.

211. La COMMISSION NATIONALE DES LIBÉRATIONS CONDITIONNELLES dans son *Rapport final du Groupe d'étude sur les autochtones au sein du régime correctionnel fédéral*, Ottawa, Approvisionnements et Services Canada, 1988, p. 38, formulait la recommandation suivante : « Il faudrait évaluer l'applicabilité aux détenus autochtones des instruments, critères et méthodes d'évaluation actuels. »

212. Voir, par ex., le Rapport de la commission d'enquête sur l'affaire Marshall, *op. cit.*, note 14, p. 181 ; *Justice on Trial*, *op. cit.*, note 14, pp. 6-18 à 6-21 ; COMMISSION NATIONALE DES LIBÉRATIONS CONDITION-NELLES, *op. cit.*, note 211, pp. 73-74.

A.   La spiritualité et les aînés

L'importance de la spiritualité et des aînés dans la réinsertion des délinquants autochtones est généralement reconnue, du moins en théorie. En pratique, toutefois, les aînés semblent jouir de moins de liberté et de confiance que d'autres chefs spirituels : leurs cérémonies et leurs activités sont supervisées. Même les aînés connus des autorités pénitentiaires et considérés comme ne présentant aucune menace réelle doivent se soumettre à la fouille de leur trousse médicinale lorsqu'ils entrent dans l'établissement[213]. De plus, la glycérie est souvent assimilée à un stupéfiant dans l'esprit des agents correctionnels, tandis que la purification par l'étuve est jugée suspecte[214].

RECOMMANDATION

14. (1) Il y aurait lieu, dans un texte de loi, de conférer à la spiritualité autochtone la même reconnaissance qu'aux autres religions, et les aînés devraient avoir le même statut et jouir de la même liberté de manœuvre que les aumôniers des pénitenciers[215].

À l'occasion, cela pourrait vouloir dire qu'on libère un prisonnier pendant une journée pour lui permettre d'assister, sous la garde des membres de sa collectivité, à des cérémonies tenues à l'extérieur de la prison.

B.   Élaboration et mise en œuvre des programmes

Jusqu'à tout récemment, les programmes et services offerts dans les établissements correctionnels fédéraux et provinciaux proposaient en général aux délinquants autochtones très peu d'éléments en rapport avec leur culture et leurs besoins. Le coût — déjà élevé — que représente la détention pour la société est d'autant plus lourd que les programmes et services offerts ne comportent pas d'avantage perceptible pour les détenus.

RECOMMANDATION

14. (2) Une étude de tous les programmes devrait être entreprise, en collaboration avec les autochtones (les personnes comme les organismes), dans le but de mettre au point des programmes et services adaptés à la culture des détenus autochtones. Les organismes d'entraide autochtones et les groupes de soutien aux détenus devraient participer systématiquement à la mise en œuvre des programmes et services, et devraient disposer d'un financement suffisant à cette fin.

---

213. *Justice on Trial, op. cit.*, note 14, p. 6-27.

214. M. JACKSON, *loc. cit.*, note 18, 289. Voir aussi *Questions correctionnelles concernant les autochtones, op. cit.*, note 166, p. 38 : « puisque des plaintes continuent d'être formulées au sujet de la reconnaissance de la spiritualité autochtone en tant que religion et des particularités de l'observance des rites autochtones, certains seraient en faveur des garanties spéciales. »

215. On trouvera une recommandation au même effet dans *Questions correctionnelles concernant les autochtones, op. cit.*, note 166, pp. 38-39.

C. La libération conditionnelle

Les délinquants autochtones sont moins susceptibles que les autres d'être remis en liberté sous condition : en 1987, par exemple, seulement 9,5 % d'entre eux ont bénéficié d'une libération conditionnelle, comparativement à 24 % des autres détenus[216]. Les délinquants autochtones libérés sous condition sont par ailleurs plus susceptibles de se retrouver en prison[217], et on soupçonne qu'ils renoncent à leur droit de demander une libération conditionnelle plus fréquemment que les autres détenus[218].

On a proposé plusieurs explications à ces phénomènes. Il est possible que les délinquants autochtones comprennent mal le système et n'affirment pas tous leurs droits[219]. Très peu d'agents de gestion des cas sont autochtones d'origine ou ont reçu une formation leur permettant de reconnaître les besoins des autochtones ; ils pourraient donc se méprendre sur l'admissibilité d'un détenu autochtone à la libération conditionnelle[220]. Par ailleurs, certains critères de libération conditionnelle défavorisent les délinquants autochtones[221], qui peuvent donc rester en détention parce qu'on aura mal analysé leur comportement

---

216. COMMISSION NATIONALE DES LIBÉRATIONS CONDITIONNELLES, *op. cit.*, note 211, tableau 7, p. 30.

217. Une étude réalisée en 1986 a montré que les autochtones détenus dans les pénitenciers obtenaient les pires résultats au chapitre de la supervision des libérations : leur taux de réussite n'était que de 55,9 %, alors qu'il atteignait 66,2 % chez les Blancs, et 74,2 % chez les détenus d'autres origines raciales. Voir William G. HARMAN et Robert G. HANN, *Release Risk Assessment: An Historical Descriptive Analysis*, Rapport n° 1986-32, Ottawa, Solliciteur général Canada, 1986, pp. 2-9 et 4-4.

218. COMMISSION NATIONALE DES LIBÉRATIONS CONDITIONNELLES, *op. cit.*, note 211, p. 29.

219. *Des responsabilités à assumer*, *op. cit.*, note 171, p. 240.

220. Voir COMMISSION NATIONALE DES LIBÉRATIONS CONDITIONNELLES, *Pre- and Post-Release Decision Policies*, Ottawa, la Commission, 1989, Annexe A : le système de notation de la prévision générale de la récidive en vigueur n'est pas appliqué aux délinquants autochtones, parce qu'on a manqué de données sur les autochtones au moment de mettre le système au point. Aucune mesure de rechange propre aux autochtones n'a été adoptée. Voir, toutefois, Robert G. HANN et William G. HARMAN, *Release Risk Prediction: Testing the Nuffield Scoring System for Native and Female Inmates*, Rapport n° 1989-4, Ottawa, Solliciteur général Canada, 1989, p. 6 : les auteurs soutiennent que, à l'exception d'une catégorie, [TRADUCTION] « le système de notation Nuffield semble départager les détenus à faible risque et les détenus à risque élevé, aussi bien chez les autochtones que chez les autres détenus », et qu'en [TRADUCTION] « fondant les décisions de libérer sous condition les autochtones en fonction de la notation Nuffield, on aurait fait passer de 12 % à 41 % le taux de libération conditionnelle des autochtones » (*id.*, p. 9).

221. Par ex., le critère des perspectives d'emploi joue contre les autochtones. Voir à ce sujet le rapport de la commission d'enquête sur l'affaire Marshall, *op. cit.*, note 18, p. 44. Nos consultants soulignent que l'interdiction de fréquenter une personne ayant des antécédents criminels suscite des difficultés, étant donné le pourcentage élevé d'autochtones qui possèdent un casier judiciaire. Voir aussi *Des responsabilités à assumer*, *op. cit.*, note 171, p. 241.

ou mal apprécié le risque qu'ils représentent pour la société[222]. On a également laissé entendre que les conditions de libération sont appliquées avec plus de rigueur chez les autochtones, et que le soutien qui leur est offert à la libération est insuffisant[223].

Nous avons formulé, ailleurs dans le présent rapport, diverses recommandations en vue d'une sensibilisation accrue aux différences culturelles, du recrutement d'un plus grand nombre d'autochtones au sein du système de justice pénale, de rapports plus soutenus avec les collectivités autochtones et de consultations sur les critères de libération et les plans de sortie : ces recommandations ont une pertinence particulière dans le contexte de la libération conditionnelle. En outre, il faudrait prendre des mesures pour éviter que les autochtones renoncent, sous la pression subtile des agents de gestion des cas, à leur droit de demander une libération conditionnelle ou une audience en révision[224].

RECOMMANDATION

14. (3) La Commission nationale des libérations conditionnelles et le Service correctionnel du Canada devraient établir une politique et des directives nationales en matière de renonciation au droit à la demande, à une audience et à la révision de la libération conditionnelle, et le personnel des services correctionnels devrait être formé en conséquence. L'information sur cette politique et ces directives nationales devrait être communiquée aux détenus[225].

D.   Les services aux ex-détenus

La récidive constitue un autre aspect des rapports entre les autochtones et le système de justice pénale. La réinsertion est le moyen le plus sûr d'éviter la récidive, mais elle repose sur l'existence de services et de programmes adéquats pour les ex-détenus. Plus précisément, il faut des maisons de transition, des programmes de traitement des toxicomanes, des programmes de formation professionnelle et des programmes d'apprentissage de l'autonomie fonctionnelle adaptés aux besoins particuliers des autochtones. Les principaux programmes et établissements existants ne sont conçus ni par ni pour les autochtones : le moyen le plus efficace de répondre aux besoins des délinquants autochtones est d'intéresser les collectivités et les organismes d'entraide autochtones aux services aux ex-détenus.

---

222. Voir CANADA, CHAMBRE DES COMMUNES, *Procès-verbaux et témoignages du Comité permanent de la Justice et du Solliciteur général*, fascicule n° 58, pp. 57:10-57:11 (18 décembre 1990), dans le mémoire de l'Indigenous Bar Association présenté au Comité.

223. COMMISSION NATIONALE DES LIBÉRATIONS CONDITIONNELLES, *op. cit.*, note 211, pp. 32-33.

224. *Id.*, p. 51.

225. Voir *id.*, rec. 17, pour des propositions au même effet.

Les collectivités ont un rôle à jouer dans la formulation et la prestation des services dont peuvent avoir besoin les ex-détenus qui rentrent chez eux[226]. L'autochtone qui prend le chemin d'un centre urbain a besoin de retrouver une structure sociale semblable à celle de son milieu ; c'est là le rôle des centres d'accueil autochtones, des organismes communautaires métis et des groupes de femmes autochtones. Si tel est leur choix, ces organismes pourraient fournir les structures et le leadership que les conseils de bande assurent dans les réserves et les collectivités éloignées[227]. À l'heure actuelle, le budget de ces organismes est en général très maigre, et les besoins sont trop importants pour qu'ils puissent assumer la surveillance des délinquants libérés sous condition. Pourtant, si le Service correctionnel du Canada leur fournissait l'aide financière et la formation voulues, ils pourraient mettre sur pied des programmes tout à fait convenables.

RECOMMANDATION

14. (4) Les organismes communautaires autochtones devraient recevoir une aide financière leur permettant de concevoir et d'assurer des services aux ex-détenus autochtones. En particulier, la création d'établissements d'accueil pour les délinquants autochtones devrait être encouragée là où les maisons de transition ne sont ni accessibles ni économiquement viables[228].

E.   Les établissements locaux et régionaux

La famille, la collectivité, la culture et la spiritualité sont des éléments importants dans le processus de réinsertion de tout délinquant. Cependant, contrairement à la plupart des autres détenus, les autochtones sont incarcérés dans un milieu culturel qui leur est tout à fait étranger. Il est donc important, pour leur réinsertion, que les autochtones soient incarcérés le plus près possible de chez eux, et qu'ils puissent compter sur la présence de leur famille et des aînés, et sur le soutien de la collectivité.

---

226. Voir aussi notre analyse sous la rubrique IV, « Mieux intégrer les collectivités dans le système judiciaire », *supra*, au ch. V, p. 36. Certaines collectivités, nous dit-on, ont mis en commun leurs ressources : les maisons de transition, refuges et autres peuvent être subventionnés par cinq ou six collectivités, chaque établissement étant situé dans une collectivité distincte. Bien entendu, ce ne sont pas toutes les collectivités qui voudront participer aux services aux ex-détenus, et ces programmes ne pourront être instaurés que là où ils bénéficient de l'appui local.

227. Ainsi, le Grierson Centre à Edmonton, administré par les Native Counselling Services of Alberta depuis l'automne 1989, a été salué comme un « modèle de collaboration » entre les gouvernements fédéral et provincial, et un organisme d'entraide autochtone. Voir les observations de Carola CUNNINGHAM, dans *Sharing Our Future: A Conference of Aboriginal Leaders and Correctional Service Managers*, congrès tenu à Kananaskis (Alb.), du 11 au 13 février 1991, Ottawa, Service correctionnel du Canada, 1991. Voir aussi le passage sur les Native Counselling Services of Alberta dans *Questions correctionnelles concernant les autochtones*, *op. cit.*, note 166, pp. 30-31.

228. Signalons, par ex., la recommandation concernant l'utilisation de maisons privées, où les personnes libérées sous condition seraient surveillées indirectement, dans COMMISSION NATIONALE DES LIBÉRATIONS CONDITIONNELLES, *op. cit.*, note 211, rec. 37, p. 75.

Les agents de gestion des cas tiennent effectivement compte du lieu d'origine des délinquants, et les ententes de transfèrement leur permettent souvent d'être incarcérés le plus près possible de chez eux. Cependant, le transfèrement n'est pas toujours possible pour les autochtones du Nord à cause du manque d'espace ; pour leur part, les délinquantes autochtones ressortissant aux autorités fédérales sont souvent incarcérées loin de chez elles, car il n'existe qu'un pénitencier fédéral pour les femmes[229].

RECOMMANDATION

14. (5) Des établissements correctionnels locaux de dimensions réduites devraient être créés et placés sous la responsabilité des collectivités autochtones[230].

Dans certaines localités, nous dit-on, on a créé des programmes en vertu desquels on envoie les délinquants autochtones faire du trappage au lieu de les emprisonner. Comme nous l'avons mentionné sous la rubrique « La détermination de la peine », nous favorisons ce type de solutions de rechange.

À la prison des femmes de Kingston, seul pénitencier féminin relevant des autorités fédérales à l'heure actuelle, de 20 % à 30 % des détenues sont des autochtones. Ces dernières années, quatre d'entre elles se sont suicidées au pénitencier, et une cinquième a fait de même peu après sa libération. Parce que les conditions dans cet établissement ont des effets particulièrement affligeants sur les femmes autochtones, au moins un juge s'est dit d'avis que l'incarcération d'une femme autochtone à Kingston constituait une peine cruelle et inusitée au sens de la Charte[231].

Le Groupe de travail sur les femmes purgeant une peine fédérale recommandait récemment qu'un pavillon de ressourcement pour autochtones (*healing lodge*) compte parmi les cinq pénitenciers régionaux qui doivent succéder à la prison des femmes. Le succès de ce projet dépend de la mesure dans laquelle les femmes autochtones participeront effectivement à sa conception et à sa gestion.

---

229. Suivant une politique gouvernementale récente on s'apprêterait à créer cinq prisons régionales pour femmes. Voilà qui améliorera dans une certaine mesure les conditions pénibles auxquelles font face les délinquantes autochtones ressortissant aux autorités fédérales.

230. Voir *Justice on Trial*, *op. cit.*, note 14, p. 6-28, et le Rapport Osnaburgh/Windigo, *op. cit.*, note 43, p. 65. Signalons aussi la remarque formulée dans *Questions correctionnelles concernant les autochtones*, *op. cit.*, note 166, p. 30 : « Il faudra donc vraisemblablement que la législation soit assez souple pour tenir compte de l'immense diversité des arrangements [. . .] Pour tenter d'élaborer un système qui soit fondé sur leur culture, il est possible que les groupes autochtones proposent des services correctionnels très différents de ceux qui existent. »

231. *R. c. Daniels*, [1990] 4 C.N.L.R. 51 (B.R. Sask.) ; décision infirmée en appel pour des motifs de compétence, 6 juin 1991.

RECOMMANDATION

14. (6) Le Service correctionnel du Canada devrait mettre sur pied le pavillon de ressourcement pour autochtones conformément à la recommandation du Groupe de travail sur les femmes purgeant une peine fédérale. Les peuples autochtones devraient être consultés et exercer un pouvoir réel sur ce projet[232].

---

232. Les problèmes propres aux femmes autochtones, notamment sur le plan correctionnel, figurent parmi les sujets particulièrement importants auxquels nous comptons consacrer des recherches plus poussées.

CHAPITRE SEPT

Assurer la mise en œuvre de la réforme

Points saillants

*Nous recommandons la création de l'*Institut de justice autochtone *dont le vaste mandat embrasserait toute question touchant la situation des autochtones au sein du système de justice pénale. L'Institut serait chargé de recueillir des données, d'élaborer des programmes à l'intérieur du système judiciaire ou des solutions de rechange à l'appareil existant, de prêter assistance aux collectivités autochtones dans l'établissement des programmes et de formuler des orientations relativement aux questions que pose la justice pénale pour les autochtones. Le personnel, la gestion et l'activité de l'Institut de justice autochtone seraient du ressort des autochtones dans toute la mesure du possible.*

Le lecteur averti aura constaté que, pour une bonne part, nos recommandations n'ont rien de neuf et s'apparentent à celles formulées ailleurs depuis des années. On peut lire ce qui suit dans un rapport que nous avons commandé :

[TRADUCTION]
À l'issue de la Conférence nationale sur les autochtones tenue en 1975 à Edmonton, on a formulé un certain nombre de recommandations facilement réalisables. On y proposait que les tribunaux siègent dans les collectivités autochtones, que des mesures soient prises pour sensibiliser davantage les juges à ces collectivités, et que les juges et juges de paix résidents soient recrutés à l'intérieur des collectivités. Seize ans plus tard, en 1991, le groupe d'étude albertain chargé d'analyser l'impact du système judiciaire sur les Indiens et les Métis de cette province a jugé nécessaire de formuler essentiellement les mêmes recommandations[233].

Une chose est claire : la grande difficulté en ce qui concerne les problèmes que pose la justice pénale pour les autochtones n'est pas de trouver les solutions, mais bien de les appliquer. Voilà pourquoi nous estimons nécessaire de formuler des recommandations particulières à cet égard.

---

233. IBA, *op. cit.*, note 24, p. 12.

I. Déterminer le coût de la réforme

De toute évidence, la question financière est importante. On pourrait croire que la mise en œuvre de nos recommandations coûtera cher. Il est indéniable qu'il faudra engager des ressources supplémentaires, mais nos recommandations ne sont pas toutes onéreuses. Certaines se traduiront même par une baisse de coûts, car bon nombre de nos suggestions amélioreront ou simplifieront les procédures. Une partie très importante de nos recommandations seront sans effet sur les coûts, n'entraînant ni dépense ni économie. D'autres recommandations sont réalisables sans qu'on augmente pour autant les budgets actuels de façon notable. (Parfois, on atteindra l'objectif en réaffectant prudemment les crédits budgétaires existants.) Néanmoins, beaucoup de nos recommandations s'accompagneront d'une hausse des coûts. Le financement des systèmes de justice autochtones, en particulier, exigera des ressources supplémentaires.

À l'heure actuelle, les programmes de justice autochtones sont financés de diverses sources. Les ministères fédéraux — Affaires indiennes et du Nord, Justice, Solliciteur général, Secrétariat d'État — contribuent tous, à l'instar de bien des ministères provinciaux et d'autres organismes comme les barreaux et les universités. Nous proposons que les ressources consacrées à l'heure actuelle aux affaires autochtones en matière de justice (y compris les ressources provenant des provinces) soient définies et évaluées avec précision. Il faudrait fixer les priorités en matière de dépenses, en consultation avec les peuples autochtones, pour décider de la meilleure façon de déployer les ressources et supprimer le double emploi[234]. Le processus devrait englober non seulement les programmes propres aux autochtones, mais aussi les dépenses qui concernent en grande partie les autochtones, comme le financement des établissements correctionnels et des services policiers. Il faudrait entreprendre dès maintenant des études de faisabilité globales concernant toutes les recommandations du présent rapport impliquant l'affectation de ressources.

On a passé sous silence pendant trop longtemps les inégalités historiques dont les autochtones ont eu à souffrir sur le plan judiciaire. Si les réformes nécessaires ont tardé, nous ne pouvons plus invoquer le manque de ressources pour justifier notre inaction[235].

---

234. Ce travail a été amorcé par le groupe de travail Nielsen en 1985. Voir GROUPE DE TRAVAIL CHARGÉ DE L'EXAMEN DES PROGRAMMES, *Programmes destinés aux autochtones : rapport du groupe d'étude au Groupe de travail chargé de l'examen des programmes*, Ottawa, le Groupe de travail, 1985 (président : Eric Nielsen). L'étude portait, entre autres, sur le double emploi et la fragmentation dans les ministères et organismes fédéraux. On a également étudié les programmes à l'échelle provinciale.

235. Le Premier ministre canadien a fait part des décisions de son gouvernement d'augmenter les crédits budgétaires affectés aux affaires autochtones en soulignant que : « nous avons pris ces décisions parce que ce sont les bonnes. » Le Très Honorable Brian Mulroney, Allocution, Congrès des premières nations, Victoria (C.-B.), 23 avril 1991, p. 7.

RECOMMANDATION

15. (1) Les ressources consacrées à l'heure actuelle aux affaires autochtones en matière de justice (y compris les ressources provenant des provinces) devraient être définies et évaluées avec précision. Les priorités en matière de dépenses devraient être établies en consultation avec les peuples autochtones, pour décider de la meilleure façon de déployer les ressources et supprimer le double emploi. Des études de faisabilité globales devraient être entreprises immédiatement concernant toutes les recommandations du présent rapport impliquant l'affectation de ressources.

En outre, même s'il est nécessaire d'affecter des sommes dès à présent, une perspective à court terme n'est pas à conseiller. Il est possible que les systèmes de justice autochtones coûtent cher à courte échéance, mais l'investissement rapportera à long terme[236]. Les économies découleront en partie de la réduction des ressources que le reste de l'appareil judiciaire — le système correctionnel en particulier — devra consacrer aux autochtones. Mais, chose plus importante encore, le fait de rendre aux collectivités le pouvoir de veiller à l'ordre social peut contribuer à renverser le processus de colonisation qui est à l'origine des problèmes que l'appareil judiciaire pose pour les autochtones. Cette responsabilisation devrait déboucher sur une criminalité moindre et sur un recours moins grand à la justice, blanche ou autochtone.

Outre la question du financement, d'autres mesures sont nécessaires à la réalisation des réformes.

II. La création de l'Institut de justice autochtone

Nous suggérons la création d'un institut de justice autochtone, qui serait chargé expressément d'apporter des solutions aux questions que soulève la justice pénale pour les autochtones et de superviser la mise en œuvre des présentes recommandations. L'Institut pourrait remplir plusieurs fonctions très utiles[237].

---

236. Une demande de financement adressée par les Gitksan et Wet'suwet'en aux fins de recherche, de conception et de réalisation d'un projet de règlement des conflits fait valoir que [TRADUCTION] « les problèmes que la justice des Blancs pose aux autochtones ont été recensés en long et en large par un grand nombre d'enquêtes menées partout au Canada ; chacune d'elles a coûté certainement plus cher que la réalisation de ce projet » (M. JACKSON, *op. cit.*, note 28, pp. 94-95).

237. En particulier, la création de l'Institut aurait pour effet d'associer plus étroitement et plus activement les peuples autochtones au processus de réforme, mesure dont on nous a, à juste titre, signalé l'importance. Voir IBA, *op. cit.*, note 24, pp. 52, 58-59.

D'abord, l'Institut pourrait orienter les recherches empiriques à entreprendre dans l'avenir. Même si d'importantes recherches ont été effectuées sur diverses questions concernant la justice pour les autochtones, nos connaissances restent très incomplètes. Par exemple, nous ne savons pas avec certitude si les préjugés raciaux jouent un rôle dans la détermination des peines infligées aux délinquants autochtones[238]. D'aucuns remettent même en question l'hypothèse qui, à bien des yeux, sous-tend la réalisation d'études comme celle-ci — l'hypothèse de la surreprésentation des autochtones dans les prisons.

La surreprésentation est un aspect important des problèmes que pose la justice pour les autochtones[239], et des renseignements plus complets sur certaines questions seraient les bienvenus. Ainsi, la forte population d'autochtones dans les pénitenciers s'explique-t-elle par un revenu plus faible et par une moyenne d'âge moins élevée[240] ? Les autochtones seraient-ils toujours surreprésentés dans les établissements provinciaux si on retranchait toutes les personnes incarcérées pour défaut de payer une amende ? Les réponses à ces questions ne feront pas disparaître le problème — qu'un autochtone âgé de 16 ans soit sûr à 70 % de se retrouver en prison[241] constitue un problème bien réel, quelle qu'en soit la cause —, mais elles peuvent contribuer à en cerner les causes. Des chiffres montrant s'il existe ou non des différences dans la proportion d'autochtones mis en accusation, plaidant coupable, condamnés ou incarcérés pourraient nous indiquer si les solutions doivent porter sur l'ensemble du processus ou sur certains aspects seulement[242].

---

238. C. P. LaPrairie, *loc. cit.*, note 168.

239. Même s'il n'était pas question de surreprésentation, il faudrait néanmoins aborder une foule d'autres problèmes auxquels font face les autochtones — traduction, compréhension du processus pénal, obtention des services d'un avocat, conditions de mise en liberté provisoire et conditions de probation.

240. Certaines données laissent croire qu'en fait, les détenus autochtones sont plus âgés en moyenne. Voir Alberta, Board of Review on the Administration of Justice in the Provincial Courts of Alberta, *Native People in the Administration of Justice in the Provincial Courts of Alberta*, Rapport n° 4, Edmonton, the Board, 1978 (président : W. J. C. Kirby). Ce résultat donne à penser que la moyenne d'âge moins élevée de la population autochtone n'explique pas la forte proportion de délinquants autochtones.

241. John Hylton, « Locking Up Indians in Saskatchewan », qu'on aborde dans M. Jackson, *loc. cit.*, note 18, 216.

242. Certaines données existent à ce sujet : voir, par ex., C. P. LaPrairie, *loc. cit.*, note 168, et les sources qui y sont citées ; Nouvelle-Écosse, Royal Commission on the Donald Marshall, Jr., Prosecution, *Discrimination against Blacks in Nova Scotia*, par Wilson Head et Don Clairmont, vol. 4, Halifax, la Commission, 1989 (président : T. A. Hickman) ; J. Hagan, *loc. cit.*, note 203, mais il en faudrait davantage. Les pratiques en matière de collecte des données varient considérablement d'une région à l'autre du pays : certains territoires disposent de données très limitées sur les facteurs raciaux ou sont incapables de les relier à d'autres données comme le type d'infraction. Précisons que le Centre canadien de la statistique juridique a décidé de ne pas réunir de données sur les facteurs ethniques : d'aucuns craignent qu'on utilise ces données pour faire valoir que certaines races sont davantage portées vers les comportements criminels. L'absence de données fait qu'il est difficile de savoir si les personnes appartenant à telle ou telle race sont traitées injustement : comment peut-on prétendre, en effet, que *trop* de Noirs sont traduits en justice si on ne sait pas *combien* sont effectivement accusés ?

Mais au-delà de la simple collecte de données, l'Institut de justice autochtone aurait pour mission de contribuer à l'élaboration de politiques. Il pourrait étudier les grandes questions de principe en matière de détermination de la peine, établir des lignes de conduite à ce sujet ou encore proposer des modifications ou des solutions de rechange au système actuel. Il pourrait même remettre en question l'hypothèse voulant que les critères de détermination de la peine doivent s'appliquer à l'ensemble d'une province, et formuler des lignes de conduite sur l'interaction des différences culturelles et locales et des principes généraux de détermination de la peine. L'Institut pourrait, jusqu'à un certain point, faire office de commission autochtone sur la détermination de la peine.

L'Institut devrait également participer de près à l'application des recommandations du présent rapport ou de celles qui pourraient être formulées à l'issue d'autres projets portant sur la justice pénale et les autochtones. L'Institut pourrait commander ou entreprendre lui-même des recherches sur le droit coutumier, participer à la formation des juges de paix autochtones, contribuer à la mise sur pied de programmes de sensibilisation aux différences culturelles et de formation des interprètes judiciaires. Il pourrait fournir des conseils sur la tenue des séances des tribunaux dans les collectivités autochtones, et élaborer des critères adaptés à la situation particulière des autochtones en matière de mise en liberté provisoire et de libération conditionnelle.

L'Institut pourrait, en outre, porter un jugement sur les programmes existants en matière de déjudiciarisation, de travaux compensatoires et de service communautaire, créer des programmes de son cru et conseiller les collectivités désireuses d'instaurer de tels programmes. Il pourrait aider à la présentation des demandes de subvention, à moins qu'on ne lui confie tout simplement la responsabilité de pourvoir lui-même au financement des programmes. Cette solution pourrait faciliter la mise en œuvre des programmes et les rendre plus efficaces : il pourrait en effet être plus économique d'organiser les services et les ressources sur une grande échelle. Cela dit, comme cette mesure est susceptible de soulever d'autres problèmes, nous préférons ne pas faire de recommandation à ce sujet pour l'instant.

RECOMMANDATIONS

15. (2) Il y aurait lieu de créer l'Institut de justice autochtone, dont le vaste mandat embrasserait toute question touchant la situation des autochtones au sein du système de justice pénale. L'Institut aurait notamment les responsabilités suivantes :

a) **mener des recherches empiriques ;**

b) **réunir des données ;**

c) **élaborer des programmes à l'intérieur du système de justice pénale actuel ou des solutions de rechange à l'appareil existant, et porter un jugement sur la valeur de ces programmes ;**

d) **prêter assistance aux collectivités autochtones dans l'établissement de programmes ;**

e) **formuler des orientations relativement aux questions que pose la justice pénale pour les autochtones.**

(3) L'Institut de justice autochtone devrait jouer un rôle capital dans la conception, la mise en œuvre et la supervision des projets touchant la justice pénale, et découlant des propositions formulées dans le présent rapport et par diverses commissions d'enquête. Le personnel, la gestion et l'activité de l'Institut de justice autochtone seraient du ressort des autochtones dans toute la mesure du possible.

CHAPITRE HUIT

Conclusion

I.   Un plan d'action pour l'avenir

Étant donné les contraintes qui se sont imposées à l'élaboration du présent rapport, il y a évidemment de nombreux aspects qu'il nous a été impossible d'aborder ou à l'égard desquels nous n'avons pu entrer dans les détails. Il convient donc d'énumérer certains thèmes sur lesquels il sera nécessaire de poursuivre les travaux.

Nous avons décidé de reporter à plus tard l'étude de deux questions, à savoir le procès par jury et le harcèlement policier. Nous les examinerons dans le second volet du mandat que nous a confié la ministre de la Justice, où nous traiterons des questions que soulève la justice pour les minorités religieuses et multiculturelles. La raison en est qu'à notre avis, les intérêts des peuples autochtones au regard de ces deux questions sont essentiellement semblables à ceux des minorités ethniques et religieuses.

L'un des buts du procès devant jury est de permettre à l'accusé d'être jugé par ses pairs[243]. Or, cet objectif suppose que les jurés partagent certaines caractéristiques avec l'accusé. Si les jurés n'ont rien en commun avec l'accusé sur le plan culturel et sur le plan des expériences, il se pourrait bien que les avantages du procès devant jury soient réduits à néant. Toutefois, la question se complique du fait que le jury est censé représenter la collectivité. Quels intérêts faut-il privilégier et comment réconcilier les intérêts divergents ?

La police a parfois été accusée d'abuser de ses vastes pouvoirs discrétionnaires pour harceler les autochtones. Ainsi, tout récemment, les contrôles routiers systématiques auxquels s'est livrée la Sûreté du Québec à Kahnawake, au nom de l'application du code de la route, n'ont fait qu'accentuer la tension au lendemain des événements d'Oka[244]. En temps opportun, nous comptons examiner à fond diverses méthodes pour répondre à ces griefs — par exemple, la procédure de plainte contre la police, les poursuites en justice et la législation sur les droits de la personne —, mais nous ne sommes pas encore en mesure de formuler de recommandation précise à ce sujet.

---

243. D'après une étude datant de 1989, il n'y aurait pas une seule cause où un autochtone aurait agi comme juré en Nouvelle-Écosse. Voir le rapport de la commission d'enquête sur l'affaire Marshall, *op. cit.*, note 18, p. 48.

244. Voir « Armed Mohawks, Police Clash Violently », *The [Toronto] Globe and Mail*, 9 janvier 1991, A1-A2 ; « Issue of Policing at Centre of Storm », « Police Patrols Increased on Reserve » et « Oka Lesson Ignored, Natives Say », *The [Toronto] Globe and Mail*, 10 janvier 1991, A5.

Comme le montre le présent rapport, il reste beaucoup à faire pour régler les difficultés auxquelles font face les autochtones, et il faudrait s'y mettre dans le cadre de la mise en œuvre des recommandations formulées ici. Parmi les tâches qui nous attendent, mentionnons la nécessité d'entreprendre des recherches sur le droit coutumier, de revoir les critères d'admissibilité à l'aide juridique et d'élaborer des règles particulières pour les interrogatoires policiers. Suivant notre recommandation, l'Institut de justice autochtone devrait commander des études empiriques sur un certain nombre de sujets, telle la disparité des peines.

Nous avons par ailleurs proposé l'établissement de règles spéciales à l'intention des délinquants autochtones dans certains contextes. Le détail de ces règles spécifiques, tout comme les solutions à d'autres questions plus fondamentales, restent donc à arrêter. Ces règles doivent-elles être enchâssées dans la loi ou prendre la forme de lignes de conduite ? S'appliqueront-elles à tous les autochtones ? À qui incombera la responsabilité de les invoquer ? Quelles conséquences entraînera le défaut de les observer ? Voilà autant de questions qui exigent un examen distinct et approfondi.

Mais il y a d'autres domaines où il faudra poursuivre les recherches. La situation des femmes autochtones en est un de toute première importance. Les autochtones en général sont incarcérés dans une proportion qui dépasse de loin leur pourcentage par rapport à la population totale, et cette disproportion est encore plus marquée chez les femmes[245]. De plus, rappelons que les délinquantes autochtones sont plus susceptibles d'être incarcérées loin de chez elles. D'autres problèmes de nature correctionnelle se présentent : les normes applicables au classement sécuritaire des délinquantes ou à l'étude des demandes de transfèrement, par exemple, défavorisent-elles intrinsèquement les femmes autochtones ? On peut citer aussi plusieurs affaires notoires où le système n'a pas su rendre justice aux femmes autochtones victimes de crimes[246]. Il importe donc d'examiner spécifiquement la situation dans laquelle se trouvent les femmes autochtones au sein du système de justice pénale. Pour des raisons analogues, nous devons également accorder une attention particulière à la délinquance chez les jeunes autochtones.

La suffisance et la qualité des services juridiques que reçoivent les autochtones suscitent souvent l'inquiétude. Appartient-il au fédéral de fixer des normes minimales pour l'ensemble du pays en finançant l'aide juridique (seuls certains avocats y sont inscrits), ou de quelque autre façon ? Cette question devrait être approfondie.

Nous avons proposé que les collectivités prennent en charge les services policiers. Certaines questions se posent à ce sujet. Ainsi, à qui, à l'intérieur d'une collectivité, les corps policiers devront-ils rendre compte ? Leur responsabilité s'arrêterait-elle aux autorités locales ? Conviendrait-il d'établir une autorité supérieure afin d'empêcher l'utilisation des corps policiers à des fins politiques ?

---

245. D'après le CENTRE CANADIEN DE LA STATISTIQUE JURIDIQUE, « Les contrevenantes adultes dans les systèmes correctionnels provinciaux et territoriaux, 1989-1990 » (1991), 11:6 *Juristat* 1, 5, 29,1 % des femmes admises dans des établissements provinciaux et territoriaux étaient autochtones, contre 16,9 % du côté des détenus de sexe masculin. « Ces proportions sont demeurées stables depuis 1986-1987. »

246. Le meurtre de Helen Betty Osborne est l'exemple le plus connu.

On nous a également laissé entendre que certains mécanismes devraient être mis au point pour permettre aux collectivités d'avoir leur mot à dire sur la nomination des juges qui y travailleraient. Nous convenons que l'idée mérite réflexion, mais nous tenons à en étudier toutes les répercussions avant de formuler une recommandation. Dans la même veine, des recommandations concernant le processus de nomination des juges pourraient également être opportunes, mais nous croyons que des travaux supplémentaires s'imposent à ce sujet.

Le nombre de délinquantes autochtones qui se suicident en prison est troublant, tout comme le taux de suicide très élevé observé pour l'ensemble des autochtones[247]. Il faudrait donc étudier le taux de suicide chez les autochtones et ses rapports avec l'emprisonnement et le système de justice pénale.

Voilà quelques-uns des domaines où il importe de pousser les recherches. Une partie des travaux pourrait être entreprise par l'Institut de justice autochtone ; comme nous l'avons déjà signalé, nous souhaitons en assumer une partie nous-mêmes. Cependant, ce programme de recherche et d'étude ne devrait pas servir de prétexte à différer la mise en œuvre immédiate d'autres réformes opportunes. Certaines de nos recommandations sont suffisamment détaillées, tandis que d'autres devront être précisées et complétées à la faveur de négociations ou de l'expérience. Quoi qu'il en soit, même si des études plus poussées sont toujours justifiables, il est nécessaire — et possible — de passer à l'action dès maintenant.

II.   Quelques observations finales

Le système que bon nombre d'autochtones souhaitent remplacer ou transformer radicalement est admiré dans le monde entier en raison de son caractère humanitaire et de son respect pour la dignité humaine. Toutefois, nous en avons largement fait état, l'expérience des autochtones a été tout autre.

L'histoire nous apprend que les autochtones du Canada ont subi des torts considérables, au point où leur mode de vie traditionnel s'en est trouvé bouleversé, quand il n'est pas disparu tout à fait, ce qui a amené certains à conclure que [TRADUCTION] « les autochtones ne retrouveront jamais complètement le mode de vie qui prévalait avant l'arrivée des Européens[248]. » La valeur de ce pronostic a peu d'importance, à vrai dire, du moins au regard des aspirations et du combat politique des autochtones. Ces derniers n'ont jamais cessé d'affirmer leur volonté d'instaurer un système de justice qui intègre leurs valeurs, coutumes, traditions et croyances propres, tout en leur permettant d'adapter ces particularités aux réalités de la vie moderne. S'ils préfèrent cette vision au système de justice pénale actuel, c'est qu'ils ont des arguments solides et bien étayés. Ils ne pourront jamais respecter un système qui leur a été imposé.

---

247. En 1986, on comptait 34 suicides chez les Indiens inscrits et 54 chez les Inuit, alors qu'on en relevait seulement 15 par 100 000 habitants dans l'ensemble du pays. Voir COMITÉ PERMANENT DES AFFAIRES AUTOCHTONES, *Questions en suspens : programme d'action pour tous les Canadiens dans les années 1990*, Deuxième rapport, Ottawa, le Comité, 1990, Annexe C.

248. Rapport Osnaburgh/Windigo, *op. cit.*, note 43, p. 37.

Aujourd'hui, les Canadiens comprennent mieux la réalité des autochtones et en sont venus à reconnaître la légitimité de leurs revendications historiques[249]. Les Canadiens sont maintenant disposés à réparer les injustices commises dans le passé[250].

Il est urgent de réformer le système. Les travaux que nous avons menés au cours des vingt dernières années en droit pénal substantiel et processuel en témoignent abondamment. Les nombreuses modifications que nous proposons sont nécessaires, à notre avis, pour corriger efficacement la situation. Nous croyons que nos recommandations peuvent favoriser le pluralisme juridique que souhaitent les autochtones, et que nos institutions constitutionnelles sont en mesure de satisfaire.

Nous acceptons la nécessité de remanier à fond le système de justice pénale pour que les autochtones soient traités avec équité et respect. Dans ce contexte, l'égalité d'accès à la justice est synonyme d'égalité d'accès à un système qui répond aux besoins et aspirations de cette partie de la population. Comme nous l'avons maintes fois souligné tout au long du présent rapport, il n'est pas indispensable que ce système soit uniforme, ni qu'il s'écarte beaucoup de sa forme actuelle. Ce qui compte, c'est qu'il ait été pensé et façonné par les autochtones, à l'image des besoins qui leur sont propres.

249. Voir *Le Forum des citoyens sur l'avenir du Canada : Rapport à la population et au gouvernement du Canada*, Ottawa, Approvisionnements et Services Canada, 1991, pp. 84-136.

250. *Id.*, pp. 135-136.

Sommaire des recommandations

Les notions d'égalité d'accès à la justice, de traitement équitable et de respect

1. Le système de justice pénale doit fournir à tous le même niveau minimal de services, et doit traiter les autochtones avec équité et respect. Pour cela, il faudrait reconnaître et respecter les spécificités culturelles des peuples autochtones et, là où cela est indiqué, les intégrer au système de justice pénale.

Des systèmes de justice autochtones

2. Les collectivités autochtones que les représentants légitimes des autochtones auront désignées comme disposées et aptes à établir un système de justice qui leur est propre devraient être investies du pouvoir de le faire. Les gouvernements fédéral et provinciaux devraient engager des négociations pour transférer ce pouvoir aux collectivités autochtones visées.

Le recrutement et la formation à l'intérieur du système de justice pénale

3. (1) Des programmes devraient être élaborés afin d'augmenter la participation des autochtones dans tous les aspects du système de justice pénale, notamment à titre d'agents de police, d'avocats, de juges, d'agents de probation et d'agents des services correctionnels. Plus précisément, les mesures suivantes devraient être prises :

a) **les corps policiers et les services correctionnels devraient recruter des autochtones, au besoin dans le cadre d'un programme d'action positive, et une politique d'action positive devrait être élaborée à l'égard de la formation et des décisions touchant l'avancement ;**

b) **les programmes de recrutement visant à attirer davantage d'autochtones dans les facultés de droit devraient bénéficier d'un appui financier plus important qu'à l'heure actuelle ;**

c) **des juges autochtones devraient être nommés à tous les niveaux de juridiction, en consultation avec les collectivités autochtones sur le choix des candidats.**

(2) Les programmes concernant les travailleurs sociaux autochtones auprès des tribunaux devraient être étendus, et les fonctions de ceux-ci devraient comprendre la tâche d'être en contact avec les prévenus autochtones à toutes les étapes des enquêtes et des procédures, notamment lorsqu'il est impossible d'avoir accès aux services d'un avocat dans l'immédiat et de façon suivie.

(3) Les programmes de sensibilisation aux différences culturelles devraient être améliorés et étendus à tous ceux qui jouent un rôle dans le système de justice pénale, notamment les policiers, les avocats, les juges, les agents de probation et les agents des services correctionnels. Cette formation devrait être obligatoire et permanente pour les personnes obligées, de par leurs fonctions, d'entrer souvent en contact avec des autochtones. Les groupes locaux d'autochtones devraient participer de près à la conception des programmes et à leur mise en œuvre.

(4) Les programmes des facultés de droit devraient comprendre des cours sur la culture autochtone.

(5) Les services d'aide juridique devraient permettre à des avocats de se spécialiser dans la représentation des autochtones.

Surmonter les barrières linguistiques et culturelles

4. (1) Le droit des autochtones de s'exprimer dans leur propre langue dans toute procédure judiciaire devrait être reconnu par la loi. Les services d'interprètes qualifiés devraient être offerts aux frais de l'État à tout autochtone qui en a besoin dans le cadre d'une procédure judiciaire.

(2) La loi devrait prévoir que des services d'interprétation doivent être mis à la disposition de tout suspect qui a besoin d'assistance au cours des étapes préalables au procès d'une enquête menée par la police, y compris l'interrogatoire.

(3) Le *Code criminel* et la *Loi sur la preuve au Canada* devraient préciser que l'État prend à sa charge le coût des services d'interprétation fournis à un accusé, à quelque étape du processus pénal.

(4) Des avis rédigés dans les langues couramment utilisées dans la collectivité et expliquant le droit à l'assistance d'un interprète garanti par l'article 14 de la Charte devraient être affichés en des endroits bien en vue dans chaque palais de justice ou, de préférence, à l'extérieur de chaque salle d'audience. Ces avis devraient préciser :

a) les conditions d'admissibilité aux services d'un interprète ;

b) le fait que l'accusé ou le témoin maîtrisant assez bien l'anglais ou le français peut néanmoins avoir droit aux services d'un interprète ;

c) le fait que l'accusé ou le témoin ne sera pas tenu de défrayer les services d'interprétation ordonnés par le tribunal.

(5) L'avocat de service devrait avoir pour instruction de prêter une attention particulière aux compétences linguistiques de tout accusé autochtone.

(6) À moins que l'avocat ne lui ait fait savoir que la chose est inutile, le juge devrait s'assurer, dès la première comparution, que l'accusé ou le témoin autochtone parle et comprend la langue dans laquelle se déroulera la procédure.

(7) La possibilité de fournir des services d'interprétation simultanée aux autochtones qui assistent aux procès se déroulant dans une réserve ou à proximité devrait être examinée du point de vue de l'opportunité, de la faisabilité et du coût.

(8) Un système devrait être établi afin de former des interprètes professionnels qualifiés et indépendants pour les causes criminelles. En règle générale, seuls ces interprètes seraient habilités à servir dans les causes criminelles.

Mieux intégrer les collectivités dans le système judiciaire

5. (1) Les « conciliateurs » (*peacemakers*) devraient se voir conférer un rôle officiel de médiation des conflits à l'intérieur du système de justice.

(2) Des mécanismes de liaison permanente devraient être établis entre les poursuivants locaux, d'une part, et les collectivités et dirigeants autochtones, d'autre part.

(3) Les représentants de la collectivité à laquelle appartient le prévenu devraient être autorisés à déposer, au cours de l'enquête sur cautionnement, au sujet des solutions de rechange à l'incarcération en attendant le procès.

(4) La loi devrait permettre expressément à des assesseurs non juristes (des aînés ou d'autres membres respectés de la collectivité) de siéger avec le juge et de donner leur avis sur la peine à imposer.

(5) Un processus permanent de consultation devrait être établi entre les personnes et organismes qui fournissent des services aux autochtones, les fonctionnaires du Service correctionnel du Canada et la Commission nationale des libérations conditionnelles.

(6) Les collectivités autochtones devraient participer à l'établissement de plans de sortie pour les délinquants autochtones et à la surveillance de ceux-ci dans la collectivité après leur libération.

Appliquer le droit coutumier et ses pratiques

6. Le gouvernement fédéral devrait subventionner la recherche en matière de droit coutumier autochtone.

Les droits issus de traités devant la juridiction criminelle

7. Les gouvernements devraient adopter des politiques officielles claires concernant les méthodes à privilégier pour définir les droits ancestraux et les droits issus de traités. Ces politiques devraient encourager le dialogue avec les collectivités autochtones, en vue de cerner les points de désaccord et d'en arriver à la conclusion d'ententes négociées avec les parties concernées. Lorsque l'intervention des tribunaux est nécessaire, le jugement déclaratoire ou le renvoi constitutionnel devrait être préféré à un procès pénal ; toutefois, si des poursuites sont entamées, la multiplication des procédures devrait être vigoureusement découragée au profit d'une seule procédure type.

La police

8. (1) La police devrait être plus présente dans les collectivités qu'elle sert et leur rendre compte de façon plus rigoureuse.

(2) Il y aurait lieu de donner, dans toute la mesure du possible, une certaine permanence à la présence de la police dans les collectivités autochtones qui désirent continuer à bénéficier d'un service de police externe.

(3) Les gouvernements fédéral et provinciaux devraient favoriser la création de corps policiers autochtones autonomes dans les collectivités qui le désirent. Il n'y aurait pas lieu d'exiger pour ces corps policiers ni une structure ni un rôle uniques. L'autonomie implique qu'il faut laisser à la collectivité le pouvoir de décider de la structure qu'elle lui donnera.

(4) Le financement d'un corps policier autonome ne devrait pas se limiter aux programmes en tous points semblables à ceux des organismes existants.

(5) Les policiers devraient conserver le pouvoir discrétionnaire de porter des accusations quand bon leur semble, mais ils devraient systématiquement demander conseil aux procureurs du ministère public, notamment quant à l'opportunité de porter ou non des accusations.

(6) Les policiers devraient prendre tout le soin voulu, lorsqu'ils remettent un avis de comparution à un autochtone, pour s'assurer que cette personne comprend bien la gravité du défaut de comparaître devant le tribunal et pour lui indiquer la date de sa comparution. En particulier, l'agent devrait demander à la personne si un motif quelconque l'empêche de se présenter et, le cas échéant, faire preuve de souplesse concernant la date de comparution. Il convient toutefois de préciser qu'aucun accusé ne devrait être détenu inutilement aux seules fins de l'application de la présente recommandation.

(7) Les corps policiers devraient être encouragés à employer des formulaires traduits dans la langue de la collectivité lorsque la chose est possible et que la nature et l'étendue des contacts policiers avec la collectivité le justifient.

Les poursuivants

9. (1) Toutes les poursuites pénales publiques devraient être exercées par un avocat qui relève du procureur général et sous la surveillance de celui-ci.

(2) Personne d'autre qu'un avocat relevant du procureur général et sous la responsabilité de celui-ci ne devrait être autorisé à poursuivre des infractions en matière de chasse, de trappage et de pêche.

(3) Il y aurait lieu de faire savoir clairement aux poursuivants, par le biais des directives et de la formation qu'ils reçoivent, qu'ils doivent exercer leurs pouvoirs discrétionnaires indépendamment de l'influence ou des pressions exercées par la police, et que les conseils qu'ils donnent aux policiers doivent demeurer objectifs et impartiaux.

(4) Une politique clairement énoncée devrait être publiée et mise en œuvre concernant les facteurs d'intérêt public dont il devrait ou non être tenu compte dans la décision d'engager ou d'interrompre des poursuites.

(5) Le *Code criminel* devrait être modifié de manière à imposer l'obligation de communiquer intégralement et en temps voulu la preuve de la poursuite dans toutes les poursuites.

(6) Les procureurs généraux, aux paliers fédéral et provincial, devraient adopter une ligne de conduite faisant aux procureurs du ministère public l'obligation de filtrer les accusations dès que possible après qu'elles ont été portées.

Les avocats de la défense

10. (1) Les barreaux et les organismes d'aide juridique provinciaux devraient mettre à la disposition des autochtones du matériel éducatif sur le droit, notamment sur les modalités d'obtention des services de l'aide juridique. Au besoin, on devrait faire appel à la technologie vidéo ou faire en sorte que le matériel soit produit en langues autochtones.

(2) Les critères d'admissibilité à l'aide juridique devraient être revus de façon qu'ils n'aient aucun effet inéquitable sur les autochtones. Les gouvernements concernés devraient s'assurer que les fonds nécessaires sont disponibles pour financer les services juridiques dont tout autochtone peut avoir besoin.

(3) Des règles d'interrogation particulières devraient être formulées pour la réception des déclarations des autochtones, notamment en ce qui a trait à la présence d'un avocat ou d'une autre personne au cours de l'interrogatoire.

Les tribunaux

11. (1) Les salles d'audience qui sont utilisées pour les collectivités autochtones devraient être aménagées de manière à respecter la culture et les traditions des autochtones.

(2) La législation fédérale devrait reconnaître aux juges de paix nommés par le fédéral toutes les compétences que confèrent aux juges de paix le *Code criminel* et la *Loi sur les Indiens*. Le fédéral devrait utiliser davantage son pouvoir de nomination pour nommer un plus grand nombre de juges de paix autochtones.

(3) Le droit des autochtones de prêter serment selon leurs rites traditionnels lorsqu'ils témoignent devant un tribunal devrait être reconnu.

(4) Dans le cas d'accusés autochtones, les dates de comparution devraient être fixées de façon à éviter, dans la mesure du possible, les saisons de chasse et de trappage. La politique d'établissement du calendrier judiciaire devrait être mise au point par les juges en chef des tribunaux concernés, en collaboration avec les représentants de la collectivité.

(5) La loi devrait permettre que les comparutions se fassent par des moyens électroniques.

(6) L'accusé qui est relâché par un tribunal loin de l'endroit où il a été arrêté devrait, à la discrétion du tribunal, être retourné chez lui ou dans un lieu raisonnable qu'il aura lui-même désigné. Le *Code criminel* devrait obliger le juge à se renseigner à ce sujet. Les frais de transport devraient être à la charge de l'État.

(7) Le Code devrait prévoir qu'une personne libérée inconditionnellement (c'est-à-dire sans que des accusations aient été portées) est en droit d'être transportée à l'endroit où elle a été arrêtée ou dans tout autre lieu raisonnable qu'elle aura désigné.

(8) Lorsqu'un tribunal ne tient pas ses audiences dans une collectivité autochtone ou à proximité de celle-ci, l'accusé et les témoins assignés à comparaître devraient bénéficier d'un service de transport entre leur domicile et l'endroit où se tiennent les audiences, ou encore être remboursés de leurs frais de déplacement.

(9) Dans la mesure du possible et lorsque la collectivité le souhaite, les audiences des tribunaux devraient se dérouler dans la collectivité autochtone où a été commise l'infraction, ou à proximité.

(10) Puisque les tribunaux itinérants qui se déplacent en avion ne fournissent pas aux collectivités éloignées des services juridiques équivalents à ceux disponibles ailleurs, il faudrait donc, dans la mesure du possible, les éliminer progressivement. Là où on les maintiendra, il faudrait prendre les mesures nécessaires pour offrir les garanties suivantes :

a) les services d'un avocat de la défense sont proposés à l'accusé à une date suffisamment antérieure à l'audition de l'affaire ;

b) les procureurs du ministère public consultent les collectivités touchées avec suffisamment d'avance pour veiller à ce que l'intérêt public soit protégé ;

c) on affecte des ressources suffisantes, notamment par le biais de nominations judiciaires additionnelles s'il y a lieu, de manière à ne pas précipiter les audiences et à pouvoir les tenir dans un délai raisonnable à compter de la perpétration de l'infraction.

La mise en liberté provisoire

12. (1) Le visa permettant à l'agent de la paix de relâcher un prévenu après lui avoir remis un avis de comparution devrait pouvoir être apposé sur un mandat d'arrestation à l'égard de n'importe quel crime. Le juge devrait être expressément requis par la loi de considérer l'opportunité d'apposer un visa sur tout mandat d'arrestation qu'il délivre.

(2) Tout agent de la paix devrait avoir le pouvoir discrétionnaire de libérer une personne qu'il a arrêtée, quel que soit le crime qui lui est reproché, après lui avoir remis un avis de comparution de portée plus étendue qui pourrait renfermer des conditions que le fonctionnaire responsable est seul, à l'heure actuelle, à pouvoir imposer. L'agent devrait être tenu de libérer la personne à moins qu'il n'existe des motifs précis de détention.

(3) Les dispositions relatives à la mise en liberté provisoire devraient faire au juge de paix appelé à apprécier le caractère raisonnable d'une condition de mise en liberté l'obligation expresse de considérer les facteurs suivants :

a) la profession du prévenu, son lieu de résidence et ses origines culturelles ;

b) l'emplacement géographique et l'importance de la collectivité à laquelle appartient le prévenu ;

c) les exigences particulières liées aux aspirations traditionnelles des autochtones.

(4) L'interdiction de consommer de l'alcool ne devrait être imposée comme condition que si l'alcool a joué un rôle dans l'infraction reprochée au prévenu.

(5) La violation des conditions non financières de la mise en liberté ne devrait pas engager la responsabilité pénale.

(6) Les dispositions relatives à la mise en liberté provisoire devraient être modifiées de manière à préciser que le juge doit tenir compte des facteurs suivants au moment d'apprécier l'admissibilité d'une personne à titre de caution :

a) les ressources financières de la personne ou celles qu'on peut raisonnablement lui attribuer ;

b) sa réputation et la nature de toute condamnation antérieure ;

c) ses liens (de parenté, de voisinage ou autres) avec le prévenu ;

d) tout autre facteur pertinent.

(7) Le juge de paix ne devrait être autorisé à exiger que la caution dépose une somme d'argent ou une autre garantie que s'il est convaincu que la situation exceptionnelle de la caution (le fait de résider dans un autre ressort, par exemple) exige une telle ordonnance.

(8) La caution devrait avoir l'obligation de prendre tous les moyens raisonnables pour que le prévenu se présente devant le tribunal. En revanche, elle ne devrait pas encourir l'exécution du cautionnement parce que le prévenu n'a pas rempli les autres conditions de sa mise en liberté.

(9) Lorsqu'un juge de paix ordonne à un prévenu de fournir caution et que cette condition n'est pas remplie dans les vingt-quatre heures, l'opportunité de cette condition devrait être reconsidérée.

(10) La possibilité d'exiger un dépôt en argent comptant du prévenu devrait être abolie ou assujettie à des restrictions plus importantes ; par exemple, le dépôt en argent comptant pourrait être exigé seulement si le juge de paix a des motifs raisonnables de croire que cela est nécessaire pour empêcher le prévenu de fuir le pays.

La détermination de la peine

13. (1) Les solutions de rechange à l'incarcération devraient être utilisées dans toute la mesure du possible. Les dispositions du *Code criminel* qui prévoient ces solutions de rechange devraient préciser qu'elles doivent être considérées en priorité au moment de la détermination de la peine. Le juge qui condamne un autochtone à l'emprisonnement pour une infraction se prêtant à l'une ou l'autre de ces solutions devrait être tenu de préciser les raisons pour lesquelles il a opté pour l'incarcération.

(2) Les programmes offrant des solutions de rechange à l'incarcération devraient, dans toute la mesure du possible, comporter un caractère universel. À cette fin, des ressources humaines et financières suffisantes devraient être réunies, et des études complètes de faisabilité devraient être entreprises dès maintenant.

(3) Les recherches devraient s'accompagner d'un suivi des programmes et d'analyses de politiques qui permettront d'ajuster le tir à la faveur de l'expérience.

(4) Les programmes de réconciliation victime-délinquant devraient être étendus et faire l'objet d'analyses plus approfondies que cela n'a été le cas jusqu'à présent. Les gouvernements fédéral et provinciaux devraient fournir l'appui financier nécessaire pour que les programmes de la collectivité deviennent plus accessibles et mieux exploités.

(5) Le *Code criminel* devrait contenir un mécanisme analogue à celui de la *Loi sur les jeunes contrevenants* relativement aux « mesures de rechange », pour ce qui concerne le règlement et la déjudiciarisation des affaires mettant en cause des délinquants autochtones d'âge adulte.

(6) Des programmes de travaux compensatoires devraient être institués dans les collectivités qui le désirent. Des ressources financières suffisantes devraient être mises à la disposition des collectivités afin de leur permettre de réaliser des projets qui favoriseront l'épanouissement et la réalisation de soi. Des mesures spéciales devraient être prises afin de rendre ces programmes accessibles aux femmes autochtones.

(7) Les provinces devraient être encouragées à mettre sur pied des projets-pilotes sur le recours au système des jours/amendes ; les collectivités autochtones devraient compter parmi les premières à bénéficier de ces projets.

(8) Le non-paiement d'une amende devrait entraîner l'emprisonnement seulement si la personne refuse ou néglige sciemment de payer l'amende, et non lorsqu'elle est incapable de le faire. Le délinquant ne devrait être emprisonné qu'après que les solutions de rechange suivantes ont été envisagées :

a) la tenue d'une audience permettant au délinquant d'expliquer pourquoi il n'a pas payé l'amende ;

b) la saisie-arrêt du salaire et d'autres sommes d'argent ;

c) la saisie des biens du délinquant ;

d) des travaux communautaires correspondant à l'amende ;

e) le recours à d'autres sanctions dont dispose la collectivité.

(9) Des programmes d'ordonnance de service communautaire devraient être mis sur pied dans les collectivités qui le désirent. Des ressources adéquates devraient être affectées à ces programmes, afin de définir quels types de travaux communautaires pourraient être réalisés et de déterminer les ressources dont la collectivité a besoin pour assurer la réussite de ces programmes. Il conviendrait de mettre beaucoup plus de soin à la conception des programmes, et la loi ou le règlement d'habilitation devrait clairement en énoncer les buts. Il faudrait faire en sorte que les juges, les procureurs du ministère public et les avocats de la défense soient bien informés de l'existence des programmes et de leurs objectifs. Bien qu'il faille en encourager l'utilisation, le *Code criminel* devrait préciser qu'aucune ordonnance de service communautaire ne peut être émise à moins que le tribunal n'ait obtenu l'assurance, de la part de la collectivité, qu'il existe des possibilités de service bénévole et que la collectivité est disposée à accueillir le délinquant.

(10) Des services de probation adaptés aux besoins des délinquants autochtones devraient être offerts dans un large éventail de collectivités autochtones. Il y aurait lieu de faire davantage appel aux ressources de la collectivité et d'assurer une formation d'agent de probation à des personnes issues du milieu.

(11) Les critères d'admissibilité à la probation devraient être formulés de manière à tenir compte des différences culturelles et à combler les besoins des délinquants et des collectivités autochtones. De plus, les rapports de probation devraient mettre davantage l'accent sur des facteurs comme les capacités professionnelles du délinquant, ses aptitudes à trouver un emploi et sa volonté de suivre un programme de traitement ou de formation. Il faudrait également attacher une importance plus grande à la volonté de la collectivité de participer à la probation et à la surveillance du délinquant.

(12) Des recherches devraient être effectuées afin de déterminer si les autochtones se voient imposer des peines plus sévères que les autres Canadiens et, dans l'affirmative, quelles sont les causes de cette disparité.

(13) Une liste de facteurs qui, conjugués à d'autres circonstances, viendraient atténuer la peine lorsque le délinquant est un autochtone devrait être dressée. Par exemple, la peine devrait être moins sévère si le délinquant autochtone a fait ou fera l'objet de sanctions traditionnelles infligées par la collectivité.

(14) Comme nous l'avons recommandé antérieurement, un processus bien structuré, ouvert et responsable de discussions et d'ententes sur le plaidoyer devrait être mis en place.

(15) Les dispositions du *Code criminel* relatives aux rapports préalables à la sentence devraient être beaucoup plus détaillées qu'elles ne le sont à l'heure actuelle. À tout le moins, le contenu des rapports et les circonstances qui en commanderaient l'établissement devraient faire l'objet de dispositions législatives claires.

(16) Le *Code criminel* devrait préciser que les rapports préalables à la sentence doivent faire état de la condition particulière des délinquants autochtones et en tenir compte.

(17) Seules les personnes bien au fait des conditions de vie des autochtones et de leurs coutumes, de leur culture et de leurs valeurs devraient être autorisées à dresser des rapports préalables à la sentence.

(18) Lorsque l'incarcération d'un délinquant est envisagée pour la première fois (et n'est pas requise par la loi), le tribunal devrait être expressément tenu d'ordonner l'établissement d'un rapport préalable à la sentence. La loi devrait en outre préciser que, chaque fois que l'incarcération est envisagée, le juge devrait songer à ordonner l'établissement d'un rapport.

(19) Lorsque l'établissement d'un rapport préalable à la sentence est ordonné, le tribunal devrait s'assurer que le délinquant non représenté est informé des avantages que peuvent lui rapporter les services d'un avocat.

(20) Le paragraphe 100(1) du *Code criminel* devrait être modifié de manière à prévoir une exemption limitée de l'interdiction impérative de posséder une arme lorsque le juge est convaincu que l'interdiction serait oppressive et injuste, et que le fait de permettre au délinquant de porter une arme pour gagner sa vie ne menacerait en rien la sécurité du public.

Les mesures correctionnelles

14. (1) Il y aurait lieu, dans un texte de loi, de conférer à la spiritualité autochtone la même reconnaissance qu'aux autres religions, et les aînés devraient avoir le même statut et jouir de la même liberté de manœuvre que les aumôniers des pénitenciers.

(2) Une étude de tous les programmes devrait être entreprise, en collaboration avec les autochtones (les personnes comme les organismes), dans le but de mettre au point des programmes et services adaptés à la culture des détenus autochtones. Les organismes d'entraide autochtones et les groupes de soutien aux détenus devraient participer systématiquement à la mise en œuvre des programmes et services, et devraient disposer d'un financement suffisant à cette fin.

(3) La Commission nationale des libérations conditionnelles et le Service correctionnel du Canada devraient établir une politique et des directives nationales en matière de renonciation au droit à la demande, à une audience et à la révision de la libération conditionnelle, et le personnel des services correctionnels devrait être formé en conséquence. L'information sur cette politique et ces directives nationales devrait être communiquée aux détenus.

(4) Les organismes communautaires autochtones devraient recevoir une aide financière leur permettant de concevoir et d'assurer des services aux ex-détenus autochtones. En particulier, la création d'établissements d'accueil pour les délinquants autochtones devrait être encouragée là où les maisons de transition ne sont ni accessibles ni économiquement viables.

(5) Des établissements correctionnels locaux de dimensions réduites devraient être créés et placés sous la responsabilité des collectivités autochtones.

(6) Le Service correctionnel du Canada devrait mettre sur pied le pavillon de ressourcement pour autochtones conformément à la recommandation du Groupe de travail sur les femmes purgeant une peine fédérale. Les peuples autochtones devraient être consultés et exercer un pouvoir réel sur ce projet.

Assurer la mise en œuvre de la réforme

15. (1) Les ressources consacrées à l'heure actuelle aux affaires autochtones en matière de justice (y compris les ressources provenant des provinces) devraient être définies et évaluées avec précision. Les priorités en matière de dépenses devraient être établies en consultation avec les peuples autochtones, pour décider de la meilleure façon de déployer les ressources et supprimer le double emploi. Des études de faisabilité globales devraient être entreprises immédiatement concernant toutes les recommandations du présent rapport impliquant l'affectation de ressources.

(2) Il y aurait lieu de créer l'Institut de justice autochtone, dont le vaste mandat embrasserait toute question touchant la situation des autochtones au sein du système de justice pénale. L'Institut aurait notamment les responsabilités suivantes :

a) mener des recherches empiriques ;

b) réunir des données ;

c) élaborer des programmes à l'intérieur du système de justice pénale actuel ou des solutions de rechange à l'appareil existant, et porter un jugement sur la valeur de ces programmes ;

d) prêter assistance aux collectivités autochtones dans l'établissement de programmes ;

e) formuler des orientations relativement aux questions que pose la justice pénale pour les autochtones.

(3) L'Institut de justice autochtone devrait jouer un rôle capital dans la conception, la mise en œuvre et la supervision des projets touchant la justice pénale, et découlant des propositions formulées dans le présent rapport et par diverses commissions d'enquête. Le personnel, la gestion et l'activité de l'Institut de justice autochtone seraient du ressort des autochtones dans toute la mesure du possible.

ANNEXE A

Documents inédits préparés pour la Commission de réforme du droit dans le cadre du présent renvoi

DOOB, Anthony N. et Philip C. STENNING, *Report to the Law Reform Commission of Canada on the Aboriginal Reference from the Minister of Justice, Canada*, 1991.

INDIGENOUS BAR ASSOCIATION, *The Criminal Code and Aboriginal People*, 1991.

JACKSON, Michael, *In Search of the Pathways to Justice: Alternative Dispute Resolution in Aboriginal Communities*, 1991.

KAISER, H. Archibald, *The Criminal Code of Canada: A Review Based on the Minister's Reference*, 1991.

MONTURE, Patricia A. et Mary Ellen TURPEL (dir.), *Aboriginal Peoples and Canadian Criminal Law: Rethinking Justice*, 1991.

ZIMMERMAN, Susan V., *The Revolving Door of Despair: Native Involvement in the Criminal Justice System**, 1991.

Les cinq derniers titres seront publiés séparément.

---

* Cette étude a été élaborée conjointement avec le Aboriginal Justice Inquiry du Manitoba et est tirée en partie d'un document de soutien préparé par Kenneth Chasse.

ANNEXE B

Consultations

La Commission a rencontré les personnes suivantes les 18 et 19 mars 1991 à Edmonton :

M. Daniel Bellgarde
Premier vice-chef
Federation of Saskatchewan Indian Nations

Mme Marion Buller
Avocate
Membre, Indigenous Bar Association

M. Dennis Callihoo
Avocat

M. Larry Chartrand
Président
Indigenous Bar Association,
   comité sur la justice

M. le professeur Paul L.A.H. Chartrand
Département des études autochtones
Université du Manitoba

M. le professeur Michael Jackson
Faculté de droit
Université de la Colombie-Britannique

Mme Deborah Jacobs
Directrice adjointe de l'éducation
Squamish Nation

M. le professeur H. Archibald Kaiser
Dalhousie Law School

Mme Joan Lavalée
Aînée

M. Leonard (Tony) Mandamin
Avocat

M. Ovide Mercredi
Avocat
Vice-chef
Assemblée des premières nations

Mme la professeure Patricia A. Monture
Dalhousie Law School

Mme Eileen Powless
Avocate
Indian Association of Alberta

Mme Carol Roberts
Avocate-conseil
Ministère de la Justice
   (Territoires du Nord-Ouest)

M. le professeur Philip C. Stenning
Centre de criminologie
Université de Toronto
Ancien membre de la Commission
   d'enquête sur l'affaire Marshall

Mme Fran Sugar
Groupe de travail sur les femmes purgeant
   une peine fédérale

M. Allan Torbitt
Coordonnateur politique
Assembly of Manitoba Chiefs

Mme Rosemary Trehearne
Gestionnaire des programmes de justice
Council for Yukon Indians

La Commission a tenu une consultation à Toronto les 25 et 26 mars 1991. Ont pris part aux délibérations :

M. Jerome Berthellete
Directeur général
Association nationale des centres d'amitié

M. Ian Cowie
Avocat
Conseiller

Sergent Bob Crawford
Police de Toronto

M. Chester Cunningham
Directeur général
Native Counselling Services of Alberta

M. Ab Currie
Ministère de la Justice

M. le professeur Anthony N. Doob
Centre de criminologie
Université de Toronto
Ancien membre de la Commission
    canadienne sur la détermination
    de la peine
Conseiller, Nishnawbe-Aski Legal
    Services Corporation

Grand chef Phil Fontaine
Association of Manitoba Chiefs

M. John Giokas
Ministère de la Justice

M. Roger Jones
Avocat
Ancien président
Indigenous Bar Association

Mme Rosemarie Kuptana
Ancienne vice-présidente
Conférence circumpolaire inuit

M. Harry Laforme
Commissaire
Commission sur les Indiens de l'Ontario

M. Ovide Mercredi
Avocat
Vice-chef
Assemblée des premières nations

Chef Henry Mianscum
Bande Mistissini (Cri)

Mme la professeure Patricia A. Monture
Dalhousie Law School

Grand chef Mike Mitchell
Conseil Mohawk
Territoire d'Akwesasne

Mme Carole V. Montagnes
Directrice générale
Ontario Native Council on Justice

M. le professeur Graydon Nicholas
Directeur, études autochtones
Université St-Thomas
Ancien président
Union of New Brunswick Indians

M. Moses Okimaw
Avocat
Association of Manitoba Chiefs

Chef Violet Pachanos
Bande Chisasibi (Cri)

M. Gordon Peters
Chef régional de l'Ontario
Chefs de l'Ontario

Ms. Viola Robinson
Présidente
Conseil national des autochtones
    du Canada

Chef Tom Sampson
Président
First Nations of the South Island Tribal
  Council
Colombie-Britannique

M. Art Solomon
Aîné

M. Lewis Staats
Membre
Six Nations Police Commission

M. le professeur Philip C. Stenning
Centre de criminologie
Université de Toronto
Ancien membre de la Commission
  d'enquête sur l'affaire Marshall

M. Paul Williams
Avocat exerçant exclusivement en droit des
  autochtones
Iroquois Confederacy

Chef Bill Wilson
Avocat
First Nations Congress

À la demande du Ralliement national des Métis, la Commission a organisé une consultation auprès du groupe à Winnipeg le 30 avril 1991. Ont participé aux discussions :

Mme Cynthia Bertolin
Avocate

M. David Chartrand
Manitoba Métis Federation

M. le professeur Paul L.A.H. Chartrand
Département des études autochtones
Université du Manitoba

M. Norman Evans
Avocat

M. David Gray
Avocat-conseil
Manitoba Métis Federation

M. Ron Rivard
Directeur général
Ralliement national des Métis

M. Edward Swain
Manitoba Métis Federation

Les 25, 26 et 30 juillet 1991, la Commission a rencontré à Ottawa un groupe de critiques qui nous ont fait part de leurs commentaires sur une ébauche du présent rapport. Ont participé à cette rencontre :

M. le professeur Jean-Paul Brodeur
Centre international de criminologie comparée
Université de Montréal

Mme Marion Buller
Avocate
Membre, Indigenous Bar Association

M. le professeur Paul L.A.H. Chartrand
Département des études autochtones
Université du Manitoba

M. le professeur Michael Jackson
Faculté de droit
Université de la Colombie-Britannique

M. Roger Jones
Avocat
Ancien président
Indigenous Bar Association

Mme Rosemary Trehearne
Gestionnaire des programmes de justice
Council for Yukon Indians

M. Paul Williams
Avocat exerçant exclusivement en droit des autochtones
Iroquois Confederacy

DATE DUE